# Pluralistic Approaches
# to
# Art Criticism

# Pluralistic Approaches to Art Criticism

*Edited by*
*Doug Blandy*
*and*
*Kristin G. Congdon*

Bowling Green State University Popular Press
Bowling Green, Ohio 43403

To Dennis Bye
because he so loves books

and

To Bernadine Stetzel
because her art makes for such good stories

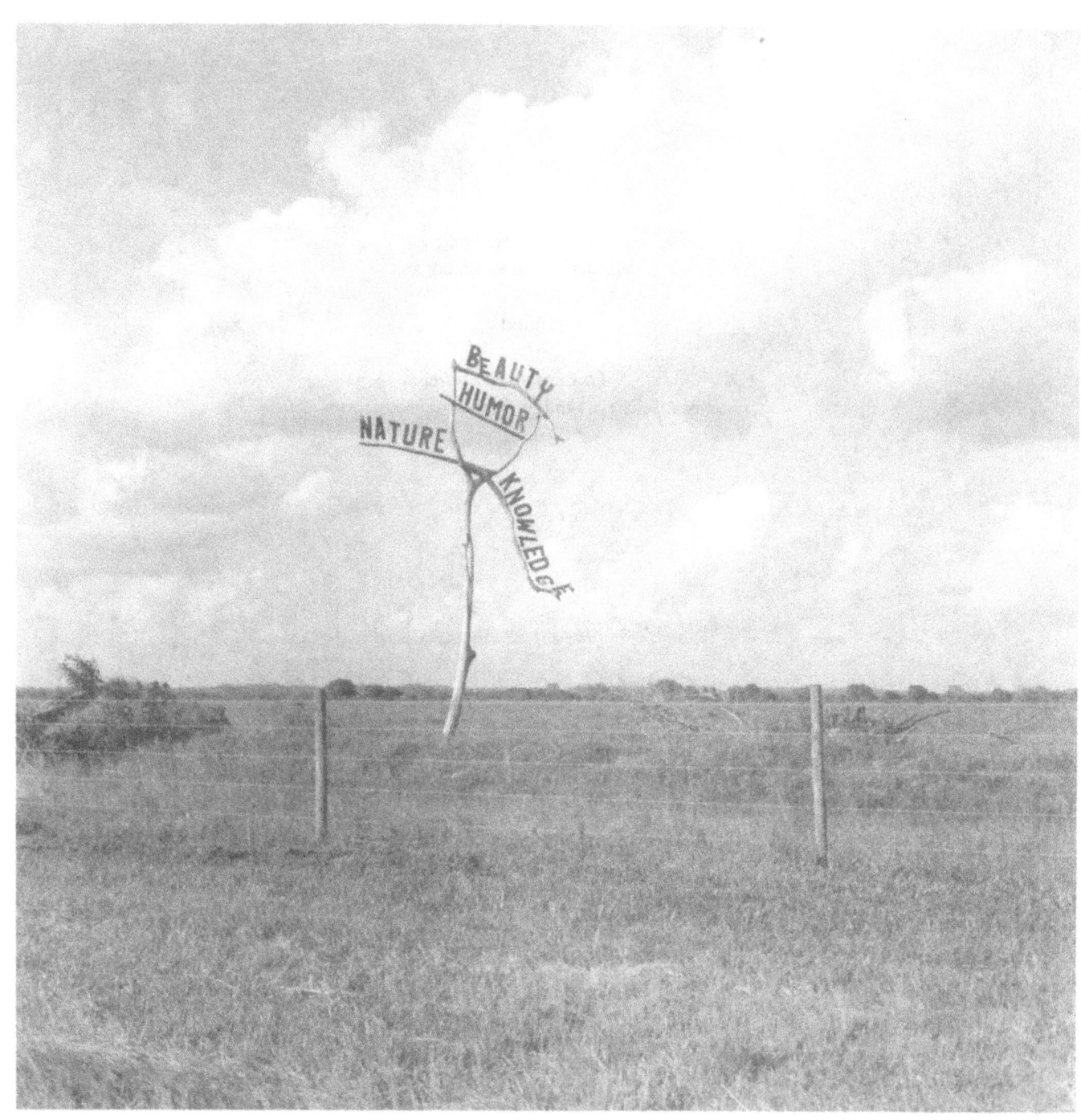

"VS27 South of Venus," 1989. Photography by Eric Breintenbach

# Contents

# Acknowledgements

We wish to thank all of the many artists who work diligently to expose racism, sexism, classism and ageism and who help us see life from varying perspectives. We have learned from you. We wish to thank the theorists who have shown us the connections that need to be made between art and ecosystems, politics, economics and cultures. We move in your footsteps. We also wish to thank our contributors who have believed in us, worked with us and encouraged us. We are indebted to you for your participation.

There are others, of course: we appreciate the support of our institutions, the University of Oregon and the University of Central Florida, which offered support and resources. The generous help of many others bears acknowledging: our assistant, Barbara Benson, for typing and correspondence; University of Central Florida work study students, Rhonda Gay and Deborah Pengatore, who photocopied, compiled and sorted; and Susan Mielke and Lisa DeLeón at the University of Oregon for word processing manuscripts. We also wish to thank our students at the University of Oregon and the University of Central Florida for their discussions with us about many of the ideas presented in this book. The support of this project by Pat Browne, editor and business manager of the Popular Press at Bowling Green State University, has been greatly appreciated.

And we thank our family members who once again acknowledged and supported our work and ideas as primary concerns. To David Congdon and Linda, Brendan and Lydia Blandy, we again gratefully appreciate your indulgence, your criticism and your encouragement.

# Introduction

It is no great secret to anyone who is involved with the collection, study or education of the visual arts that art criticism as practiced by the "professional critic" continues to take an increasingly important role in influencing people's perceptions of art.[1] Professional critics are included among those "tastemakers" with professional or commercial interests who are advocating on behalf of contemporary art. Their advocacy is meant to involve a global audience (Glueck, 1987). Critical publications like *Art in America*, *Art News* and *Art Forum International* include reviews and articles on international exhibits. *Art Forum International* recognizes its world-wide coverage in the magazine's title. *Art in America* includes representatives from London, Rome and Germany among the contributing editors.

Art criticism at its best is "a creative act of the mind" (Clements, 1979, 76). Edmund Feldman (1982) describes art criticism as "the sharing of discoveries about art, in some cases, about life, where art has its beginnings" (457). Perhaps all those who engage in the act of art criticism will agree that its purpose should be to enrich and expand on our experiences with art (Perkins, 1977) as it also assists us in making judgments about our experiences with human-made objects (Berry, 1987). It is through the critical act that we can make judgments about aesthetic value. However, art criticism is not meant to be an end in itself. Jacques Barzun (1987) warns us that it is not the purpose of art criticism to be so complete that we have no interest in seeing the work of art about which the language speaks. Criticism must not make us forget that it is important to learn not only *about* art but to first and foremost learn *from* art (Berry, 1987). Art criticism is intended to encourage new ways of seeing, to give us new perspectives on possibilities and suggest new directions for imagining and constructing reality.

Criticism that subscribes to these aims will ultimately respond to quality in art as well as to its potential for meeting the basic needs of "human and natural communities."[2] We concur with Berry's belief that the world and its myriad biological and geological systems must be viewed ecologically. The needs and actions of one system or community will have ramifications for all communities. To not be cognizant of the ramifications of our judgments and creative processes is to encourage ecological imbalance. The critical act including the criticism of art should work to insure that we recognize the needs of all communities as we do our own. Consequently art critics must approach their work with the understanding that criticism and what it attends to is part of a larger system and that their judgments will have far reaching ramifications.

When most of us visualize people who call themselves art critics, we see lofty university-trained writers and speakers who live in large metropolitan areas, publish in the major art journals and lecture in the auditoriums of our universities and museums. They speak from their academic training, and they frequent galleries and artists' lofts. We may imagine that they "do lunch" with well-known or hopefully-soon-to-be-famous artists. Their coffee tables are full of glossy art magazines and art books, and their evenings are filled with art exhibition openings. For many, the critical methods of these learned individuals are deemed as the models for all of us, and in general, the art works they most often attend to are seen as the art works that should employ the attention of everyone (Smith, 1985). Many of these so-called great works of art will be sought after by persons and institutions of wealth and do perhaps have the potential to enhance and enrich the lives of—shall we cautiously say—all people.

However, we need to recognize that there exists a certain amount of power in having one's perspective on art and criticism modeled by the masses through art education programs and having one's artistic choices emulated. Although there has been great discussion on the existence or nonexistence of a universal aesthetic response, Milton C. Albrecht (1968) suggests that it is our way of perceiving art that has become universal, and its exclusive imposition is dangerous: "Art has become 'universal' with a meaning that is being projected around the world from the fine arts tradition of Western Europe and the United States. This process represents not a military or political invasion of the world, but an artistic one" (393). Karen Hamblen (1984) called the language used in this so-called established Art World as the "Culture of Aesthetic Discourse," and she suggests that the exclusive use of this criticism mode for the public at large may be "alien to their everyday experiences in art" (29). In order to make art appreciation more democratic and responsive to varying populations, many scholars who see their task as the teaching of art criticism to the general public now feel that the aesthetic experiences, art worlds and expressive language inherent in a variety of populations should be recognized, encouraged and expanded (Lanier, 1968; Schellin, 1973; Blandy & Congdon, 1987).

Duerr (1985), using a metaphor derived from Wittgenstein, can be helpful here. He sees the various forms of life and lifestyle as fibers in a cord. They intertwine but are not connected by a single thread. There is no basic fibre in this cord just as we believe there is no one basic form of art criticism. Criticism may take many forms which overlap and intertwine but no singular form can be seen as being the connection between all forms.

Art criticism derived from one tradition will not meet the needs of all communities. Criticism as it is practiced by academically trained specialists in the arts has taken precedence over other critical traditions. Literature from the field of art education is rich in the number of critical models prescribed for use by students; however, the majority of these prescriptions come from academic specialists in art, history, philosophy and anthropology. It is important to acknowledge that these models are largely derived from modern European criticism which was a rebellious response to absolutist monarchical politics in the seventeenth and eighteenth centuries (Eagleton, 1984). What we now see occurring is that a once liberating model for discourse is increasingly absolutist in the precedence it is taking over other critical methods.

The reader might protest that there is a difference between professional critics and lay critics and that we should not model our criticism activities on those who are not scholarly in this pursuit. The former group, writes Feldman (1973), has a structure for their talk whereas the lay person does not. However, it can also be argued that this structure is a "specialized professional language" that is only understood by a few and which disregards the richness in approach and language structure of other groups of people. We do acknowledge that there are lazy "lay" critics who haphazardly make judgments about art. However, we believe there is a need to acknowledge, develop and expand on varying modes of art criticism and that many verifiable intelligent approaches to art do exist within our diverse populations. These structures are often accepted within groups, and certain people (with and without university art training) are acknowledged (in perhaps different ways) as those individuals most capable of wisely engaging in art criticism, and it is these people who communicate most clearly to those who share, to some degree, in their particular world view. There are recognizable patterns of aesthetic choice that are repeated throughout cultures. These choices are made for reasons.

Many of those reasons are explained by the functions of the artistic expressions which are dependent on individual and cultural world views. Art functions differently for different individuals and groups of people as does the language used to discuss it. These functions play a large role in how one critiques an art work. For the established Art World, although their critics would like to consider ranking and valuation of least importance, this goal "absorbs most of the energy of the contemporary art world and has most influence on the destinies of artists, the aspirations of art students, perhaps the teaching of art, and the complex business of exhibiting and selling art" (Feldman, 1967, 447). In somewhat the same vein, though using different language, the subway graffiti artists say that "getting fame" is the stated goal of their activity (Cooper & Chalfant, 1984, 28). Albrecht (1968) describes art's function:

Directly or indirectly, art may bolster the morale of groups and help create a sense of unity, of social solidarity; as used by dissident groups it may create awareness of social issues and provide rallying cries for action and for social change. In our society, it may thus be used to criticize as well as to support the social order while performing essentially the same function: that of heightening awareness of the context in which it appears and constituting an object from symbolizing essential values of the context. (390)

It is these contexts that can be better explored through the use of criticism modes that help to reflect those aspects of the art most relevant to a specific group and that group's needs.

Those of us who educate others about art and who employ art criticism methodologies are aware of specific approaches which emphasize focal points that should be noted in a work of art. (In the field of art education examples can be found in Lanier, 1968; McFee and Degge, 1977; and Feldman, 1967.) Karen Hamblen (1986) has worked with students and museum patrons of all ages and varying cultural groups, engaging them in art criticism, and feels very strongly that many formats for this process need to be acknowledged, developed and utilized which will present diverse perspectives. If "the critic is properly a servant, of the public and the artist, both" (Barzun, 1987, 28), then he or she should choose varying ways of serving that public in order to best communicate and make the unseeable visible in a language that is understood by the public. As critics are also models and teachers for those who are learning to engage themselves in criticism, they should look to express themselves in varying ways. The public should also demand that critics from differing lifestyles and world views be heard and valued. Alice Walker (1983) writes: "The absence of models, in literature as in life, to say nothing of painting, is an occupational hazard for the artist, simply because models in art, in behavior, in growth of spirit and intellect—even if rejected— enrich and enlarge one's view of existence" (4-5).

Ultimately we must acknowledge that people's world views are so diverse that one or even a few models of criticism could not possibly respond to all aesthetic experiences or expressions. What Feyerabend (cited in Duerr, 1985) stated about Carlos Castaneda's experience has application here. He argues that the criteria Don Juan would apply to Castaneda's experience as opposed to the criteria that Castaneda or we would apply are so different that there is "no objective possibility to make a choice among them, unless we would find a superworld that would include experiences of both kinds" (100).

John Berger (1972) has shown us that the passing of time, the application of new values and the juxtaposition of images can change how we view art. Linguists are making it clear how language functions to formulate our thoughts and images in certain ways. Language carries with it the power of possibilities and the language we choose to use to unveil hidden art meanings varies (and it should) from one culture to another (Congdon, 1986). If a critic chooses to exclusively remove a work of art from its own language, that critic has moved it from its context and its history. Sociologists (Fitzgerald, 1986: Bellah et al., 1985) are repeatedly warning us that America is becoming more and more of a country which neglects its context, its history, its traditions and its sense of collective purpose and connections. A disregard for those who have gone before us and who live beside us in different ways helps to fuel the fire of a directionless population which lacks the ability to learn from available wisdom. When art critics attempt to root all art work—or worse, just a select group of art works—in one basic criticism format (most often that which focuses on formalism), not only do they neglect to utilize other inspiring routes for understanding, they participate in cultural invasion and political suppression. Berger (1972) tells us that when people are prevented from participating in their history, the past becomes mystified and a privileged minority invents it for us, and this history is then used to justify the role of the ruling class. Thus the process of art criticism is political. It is also economical and cultural. In order to prevent oppression by those in power, art criticism should be reflective of many traditions, world views and values. It should inspire us, teach us, enlighten us. We need to be concerned with the pluralistic nature of art criticism as it involves itself in social justice. Those who promote only the established Art World methodologies oppress others but also oppress themselves with their myopia.

This book consists of a collection of original essays about the qualitative expansion of criticism and art experiences, the uncovering of oppressive historical understandings, the empowerment of artistic groups who are often not heard, and a move toward individual and group participation in the consequences realized by the act of art criticism. The underlying beliefs of this anthology are that all people can and sometimes do involve themselves in art criticism or aesthetic discourse. To intelligently and appropriately engage in this activity will enhance one's understanding of art, life experiences and the well-being of communities. This anthology derives its purpose through an effort to enrich artistic knowledge and to encourage and uncover greater participation in the sharing of these experiences.

The contributors to this volume may acknowledge the existence of a universal aesthetic, but it is the cultural or situational perspective for the choice of objects for contemplation and the format for the criticism that is emphasized. To be critical is to be political. The focus here is to acknowledge Wendell Berry's (1987) belief that criticism is an act which considers art in its recognition of the needs of human and natural communities. In this political context the critical methodology employed should be acknowledged by the community as the most appropriate methodology for use in the community. No singular methodology derived from any one tradition can work in all situations or cultures. The contributors to this anthology are not primarily interested in creating new methodologies as much as they are in recognizing and appropriately applying the many critical approaches that currently exist.

This anthology is divided into three parts. In the first part, "Changes and Extensions in Critical Approaches," authors cite specific contexts in which universal critical criteria are being challenged in favor of site specific methodologies. In the second part, "Valuing Diverse Critical Expressions," contributors persuasively argue, through example, for the legitimization of currently unrecognized forms of art criticism and expanding audiences in respectful ways. In the third part, "Criticism that Asserts Life, History and Human Rights," authors cite specific examples of how criticism can be used as a method for advocating social change.

Our purpose for compiling these essays and presenting them in the way that we have is to propose that art criticism can be an act in which critical theory and methodology are used to recognize and respond to art as it meets the needs of a community. It assumes that theory and methodology will be congruent with a community's aesthetic values and world views and that criticism will be communicated in a way that is in keeping with and expressive of structures of discourse as they exist within a community. One may also introduce new criticism structures but only after existing structures have been recognized and validated.

In advocating for a community-based art criticism we are indebted to Terry Eagleton (1983) and his efforts to convince literary theorists and critics that to be critical is to work for social transformation towards human emancipation. Recognizing, encouraging and developing existing criticism structures in and between myriad cultures acknowledges that the right and power to be critical exists within the community. We are not opposed to the transplantation of one community's critical model to another, but we insist that this transplantation be initiated in the form of a proposition and not an imposition. Like Eagleton, we see this approach to the study and practice of art criticism as one in which the boundaries that have been constructed to define categories such as fine art, popular art, folk art, etc. diminish in importance as a community's goals for social transformation increase in importance. Criticism studied and practiced in this way recognizes the cultural, political, sociological, ecological and economical aspects of art and communicates that recognition to others. Not only will this approach give us a greater range of art works from which to learn, but the process of participating in and recognizing varying art criticism models will extend the creative possibilities of our minds. Works from all cultures will be appreciable in terms of their ability to contribute to the individual and community.

Doug Blandy
Kristin G. Congdon

# Notes

[1]In this anthology the term "art" is used cautiously and in a way which acknowledges that many cultures have not constructed a category of things that they call "art." We will use the word "art" to refer to those human-made objects meant to, among other purposes, encourage an aesthetic response and/or are revered or esteemed as special in a culture.

[2]Berry (1987) suggests that community is a concept which can be applied not only to the ways in which people organize themselves but also to the ways in which other life forms such as wolves, dolphins or honey bees may be organized. In doing this, he articulates a view of the world in which people are integral and common to the ecosystem, are not inherently superior to that system and are responsible to that system.

# Works Cited

Albrecht, M.C. Art as an Institution. *American Sociologist Review, 33*, (1968): 383-397.

Barzun, J. A little matter of sense. *The New York Times Book Review*, (June 21, 1987): 1, 27-29.

Bellah, R.H., Madsen, R., Sullivan, W.M., Swidler, A., & Tipton, S.M. *Habits of the Heart: Individualism and Commitment in American Life.* Berkeley: U of

California P. (1983).

Berry, W. *Home economics.* San Francisco: North Point P. (1987).

Berger, J. *Ways of seeing.* London: British Broadcasting Corporation and Penguin Books Ltd. (1972).

Blandy, D. and Congdon, K.G. (Eds.), *Art in a democracy.* New York: Columbia Teachers College P. (1987).

Clements, R.D. The inductive method of teaching visual art criticism. *Journal of Aesthetic Education, 13* (3), (1979): 67-78.

Congdon, K.G. The meaning and use of folk speech in art criticism. *Studies in Art Education, 27* (3), (1986): 140-148.

Cooper, M. & Chalfant, H. *Subway art.* New York: Holt, Rinehart and Winston. (1984).

Duerr, H.P. *Dreamtime: Concerning the boundary between wilderness and civilization.* (F. Goodman, Trans.). Oxford: Basil Blackwell (original work published in 1978). (1985).

Eagleton, T. *Literary theory: An introduction.* Minneapolis: U of Minnesota P. (1983).

Eagleton, T. *The function of criticism: From "The Spectator" to post-structuralism.* London: Verso. (1984).

Feldman, E.B. *Varieties of visual experience.* (Second Edition), New York: Harry N. Abrams, Inc. (1982).

Feldman, E.B. The teacher as model critic. *Journal of Aesthetic Education, 7* (1), (1973): 50-57.

Feldman, E. *Art as image and idea,* Englewood Cliffs, NJ: Prentice Hall. (1967).

Fitzgerald, F. *Cities on a hill: A journey through contemporary American cultures.* New York: Simon and Schuster. (1986).

Glueck, G. Tastemakers. *The New York Times Magazine.* (August 30, 1987): 72, 113.

Hamblen, K.A. The Feldman approach: A catalyst for examining issues in art criticism instruction. *The Bulletin of the Caucus on Social Theory and Art Education, 6.* (1986): 79-86.

Hamblen, K.A. The culture of aesthetic discourse (CAD): Origins, contradictions, and implications. *The Bulletin of the Caucus on Social Theory and Art Education, 4.* (1984): 22-34.

Lanier, V. Talking about art: An experimental course in high school art appreciation. *Studies in Art Education, 9* (3). (Spring 1968): 32-44.

McFee, J.K. & Degge, R.M. *Art culture and environment.* Dubuque, IA: Kendall/Hunt. (1977).

Perkins, D. Talk about art. In S.E. Madeja (Ed.), *Arts and aesthetics: An agenda for the future.* St. Louis, MO: Central Mid-Western Regional Education Laboratory. (1977): 279-304.

Schellin, P. Is it Wilshire Boulevard which is ugly or is it we? *Art Education, 26* (9), (1973): 6-9.

Smith, R.A. A right to the best: Or, once more, elitism versus populism in art education. *Studies in Art Education, 26* (3), (1985): 169-175.

Walker, A. *In search of our mother's gardens.* New York: Harcourt Brace Jovanovich. (1983).

# Part I
# Changes and Extensions
# in Critical Approaches

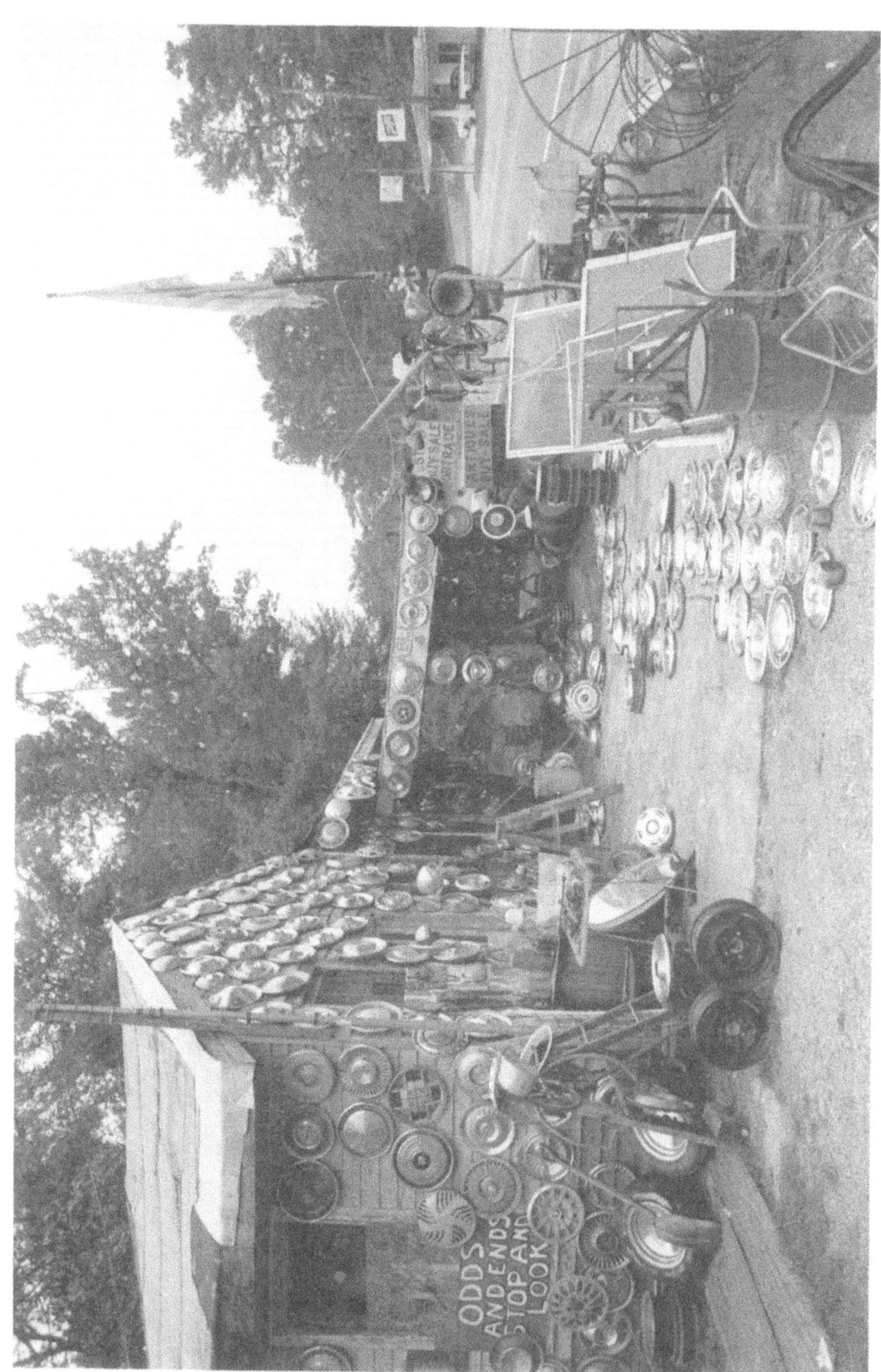

"Roadside Business Along Hwy. 441, North Georgia, 1987". Photograph by Peter Schreyer.

# Beyond Universalism in Art Criticism

## Karen A. Hamblen

Until fairly recently, studies of artistic meaning have tended to focus on the characteristics of the object of art or, perhaps, the psychology and career of the artist. There has been a lesser concern with the characteristics of the appreciators of art and their statements of response. This focus is subtly changing with post-modern interest in the contexts of human actions and the variable meanings given to phenomena. In art, this change is reflected in developmental studies of aesthetic response, in field research on the types of actions and statements that "surround" the physical entity of the art object, and in proposals that art instruction include art criticism. It would appear that the semiotic triad of object-actor-meaning is beginning to take shape, and in this paper, the focus will be on how that could be manifested in the implementation of art criticism instruction.

Art criticism has been defined as more or less organized talk about art (Feldman, 1973). Unlike aesthetics, in which the focus is on the nature of art and an examination of why we respond to art as we do, art criticism is talk about art that examines a specific object's meaning and value (Sharer, 1986). Such talk can spontaneously occur, or it can be part of a particularized pedagogical practice. The former will be referred to as vernacular art criticism and the latter as academic art criticism.

Our long history of focusing primarily on the object of art in regard to its stylistic characteristics, formal qualities, and aesthetic values can serve us well as we embark on the study and implementation of art criticism in educational settings. It is hoped that an awareness of this history could spare art criticism study some of the more blatant oversights that have occurred in the search for concrete physical characteristics of the art object that might have universal implications. Basing artistic judgments of value on formal aesthetic qualities and on the extent to which the object can be classified as "fine art" are but two areas in which much art study has obscured variable meanings and values of art. These have also obscured the differential class-based manner in which artistic designations are made and in which aesthetic knowledge is distributed in Western societies (Bersson, 1987).

If the shortcomings of the past are not heeded, art criticism could easily succumb to claims of universalism and to a lack of attention to vernacular forms of art criticism. History could repeat itself. For example, it has often been believed that art objects possess immutable characteristics that communicate across time and space. Likewise, art criticism could become a more-or-less specific procedure of analysis by which it is believed a pansocial meaning and evaluation of art can be achieved. This danger is especially acute at this time when major educators and scholars are claiming that there is a common fund of knowledge that needs to be learned if we are to be culturally literate (Hirsch, 1987), that there is a common culture in the United States, that there should be a common language, and that we should all have access to our [sic] common aesthetic heritage (Bennett, 1987/1988). Moreover, major philanthropic and professional institutions of art are proposing that art study and monetary support be focused on artistic exemplars that have been so designated by experts in the mainstream art world (Bersson, 1987; Getty Trust, 1985).

The purpose of this paper is to examine claims for universalism in art and in art criticism, how art criticism could be organized and studied to avoid such claims, and how talk about art can be studied and engaged in for purposes of critical consciousness. It will be proposed that the character of art criticism, both how it naturally occurs and how it is academically constructed, is reflective of social and aesthetic value orientations—much as the art object itself has been found to be a clue to the values of the society in which it is produced, used, and appreciated.

Although the art object is certainly the impetus for art criticism, the focus here is on the character of art criticism as an entity in its own right and on art criticism study as having implications for critical consciousness. The belief that the art object possesses characteristics and meanings separate from its sociocultural context, and separate from how it has been interpreted in various times and spaces, has resulted in assumptions of universalism that have served to legitimate certain types of art and to denigrate other types. Emphasis on the singularity of the art object and its perceptual qualities has also resulted in an isolated, bracketed response to art as an aesthetic goal and talk about the formal qualities of art as an art criticism standard. To examine the sources and character of universalism in art and to explore alternatives for art criticism, the following will be discussed: 1) art criticism as a process of selection and valuation, 2) fallacies and consequences of assumptions of universalism, 3) the educational implications of vernacular and academic modes of art critical discussion, 4) the distribution of aesthetic discourse, and 5) art criticism for critical consciousness.

### Art Criticism Origins

Although talk about the merits of art and of specific objects has a lengthy history in academic and literary settings and an even longer history as informal discussions among the makers and appreciators of art, both aesthetics and art criticism as specific formalized areas of study are relatively recent activities in most Western cultures. In the eighteenth century, Baumgarten coined the term "aesthetics" and associated its philosophical origins and psychological perception with the nature of beauty (Osborne, 1970, 1972). Art criticism has a less precise academic genesis, with much art critical discussion falling under the general category of art appreciation. Formalized analyses of specific works of art became particularly important during the last century. Academy-supported works which often dealt with mythic subject matter and esoteric story lines required explanation. As dissident groups of artists in Europe broke with Academy traditions, their works also required interpretation and evaluation for a confused, if not embittered, public:

He who depends, as his grandfather might have done, on the normal processes of his social environment to introduce him to the paintings and sculptures that form part of his culture will end with neither art nor knowledge.

This is another way of saying that art has become part of "language"; it is a writing of sorts; and there is a growing difficulty in detaching the work from meanings of a literary and theoretical order. (Rosenberg, 1966, 198)

The point needs to be made that art criticism does not need to be a conscious analytical probing of meaning and the formulation of a concise evaluation. It can be a verbalization of meanings and valuations that are already possessed. Meaning may or may not change during the interactive process of making meaning public and sharing it with others. An analytical probing of meaning and value is most characteristic of formalized academic art criticism and of art criticism dealing with unfamiliar art forms. Not surprisingly, art criticism as a formalized activity and as an art career option owes much to the inception of abstract and non-objective art in the twentieth century, to our access to a wealth of cross-cultural and historic arts, and to the rapid proliferation of art styles

during this century. Art critics in vernacular and academic settings arbitrate meaning, significance, and value. With familiar art forms, art critics stabilize meaning or provide new insights. With the unfamiliar, they explain and evaluate.

Art criticism in America's schools has traditionally been more a form of generalized art appreciation or even art historical study than of art criticism per se. Visual qualities, the biography of the artist, stylistic designation, media considerations, and so on have been discussed or even presented by the teacher as information for students to learn. Such was the case with the Picture Study Movement which began around the turn of the twentieth century with postcard-size reproductions of works of art (Logan, 1955). We can still see vestiges of this approach in teachers' discussions of art reproductions and in the obligatory critique that follows the conclusion of a studio production lesson. Art criticism as a distinct area of study was specifically discussed in the 1960s (Mattil, 1966), but it was not until 1985 that there was a widespread concern with how such instruction could be organized (Getty Trust, 1985).

### Characteristics of Art Criticism Instruction

As a result of the previous inattention to art criticism, relatively little research and theory development has been done on academic options for instruction, let alone the role vernacular art criticism could have in school settings or upon the art commentary that appears on the pages of newspapers and magazines. The result of this lack of research and theory development has been that a few academic art criticism formats have been presented in the literature as correct approaches. Feldman's (1981) "critical performance" consisting of the categories of description, analysis, interpretation, and evaluation and Broudy's (1972) "aesthetic scanning" consisting of the discussion categories of sensory, formal, expressive, and technical qualities have received primary attention and instructional implementation. Aesthetic scanning, in particular, has been discussed as an art critical approach that should be an integral part of art instruction inasmuch as it is believed to be an approach that can be replicated in any setting. It is, in other words, believed to be context free. Any object can, in effect, be aesthetically scanned for the above-mentioned qualities.

Although Feldman's approach can be readily adapted to an exploration of an object's sociocultural meanings and functions (Hamblen, 1986), both Feldman's and Broudy's methods have been primarily focused toward an analysis of the perceptual, ostensibly intrinsic, qualities of the art work. It is assumed that an analysis and interpretation of art's formal qualities (i.e., qualities of line, shape, color, etc., and their relationships) are universally applicable. Art criticism is given a formalistic interpretation in curriculum guidelines, scholarly research journals, and magazines for the practicing art teacher and general classroom teacher.

A survey of art criticism discussions in art and art education literature has revealed a range of academic procedures or formats for organizing talk about art (Hamblen, 1985). These formats were found to vary in the particular discussion categories delineated and in the extent to which they allow for student-initiated responses. As such, these academic modes of art criticism represent options that need to be made available to teachers so that a broader focus can be allowed in such instruction. However, even though these identified formats do provide a broadening of focus and options beyond the current fare of Feldman's and Broudy's approaches, they still represent a limiting perspective. Most have in common a focus on intrinsic [read formalistic] qualities of the object, and many were designed to parallel closely the steps of some human process or activity believed to be universally experienced. For example, a format discussed by Mittler (1976) consists of discussion categories assumed to parallel the stages of recognition and interpretation involved in visual perception. Critical thinking, artistic expression, cognitive development, and scientific investigation are some of the other behaviors that art criticism formats are believed to parallel (Hamblen, 1985).

Art criticism format selection is not just a curriculum choice predicated on certain beliefs about education. When a particular art criticism approach is linked to a universal behavior, it takes on the validity of that behavior and its assumed universal presence. There is a certain correctness or even absolutism that surrounds the art criticism enterprise, and a missionary zeal for a particular approach can easily develop.

In addition to linking the format to a major human process or activity and to a focus on what is considered intrinsic to the physical object, most formats also have the stated purpose of weaning the individual away from the language and associational meanings of his/her everyday life. As such, art criticism format selection takes on pansocial significance and is supposedly applicable to all populations and situations. These latter characteristics are also prerequisites for aesthetic experiences as defined in this century. Art criticism, therefore, has often assumed a correctness and a universalism based on at least three linkages to properties of the object or to behaviors of humans that are assumed to be universally accessible, i.e., the aesthetic experience, formal qualities of the object, and pansocial human activities.

*Assumptions of Universalism*
That perception and experience of formal qualities of art are a necessary good is found to be engrained in modern aesthetic theory and in theories of aesthetic perception. Although Immanuel Kant realized that all people will not judge an art work similarly, nonetheless he believed that they ought to do so. Kant's optimism in a convergence of judgment was dependent upon viewers' abilities to rise above the exigencies of time and place. In the 1700s, Shaftesbury introduced the artistic idea of "disinterestedness" wherein the viewer does not desire the object in a physical or possessive sense, and Schopenhauer, in the following century, shifted the emphasis from the art object to the contemplative state in which the qualities of the object are experienced (Dickie, 1971; Osborne, 1970, 1972). It was, however, Kant in his 1790 publication of *Critique of Judgement* who formulated a theory of aesthetic response, interpretation, and judgment that serves as the cornerstone of modern aesthetic theory and formalism. According to Kant, all people would judge art in a similar manner if they would experience the art object in-and-of itself, isolated from all personal, associational, and extrinsic purposes. To accomplish this, the object must be viewed free of interest and even without an interest in the very existence of the object. Form is essentially an internal-mental construct of the experience; it is within the experience of the viewer. However, the aesthetic judgment is neither personal nor relative. This supra-state of sensory awareness is accomplished by the object being experienced as a thing-in-and-of-itself, isolated from utility; the viewer is required to rise above the exigencies of time, place, and personal idiosyncrasies. Therefore, when a judgment is made, the viewer, in Kant's infamous phrase, "judges not merely for himself, but for all men" (52).

In 1913 Bullough (1913/1935) introduced the idea of psychic distancing which is instigated by "putting the phenomenon...out of gear with our practical, actual self...by looking at it 'objectively' " (317). The experience may personally engage the viewer, but it is not a particularized personal experience. Although a strict formalist such as Clive Bell (1913/1958) would abide no contamination of the pure perceptual response to form, other aestheticians would admit within the aesthetic brackets what is considered part of the art context, such as relationships to other art works and the biography of the artist (Dickie 1971; Kaelin 1972; Rosenberg, 1966). Linking art criticism to the twentieth-century character of aesthetic experiencing has meant that statements about an object must be referential to the object itself. Some art educators suggest that when students engage in art criticism, they must remain focused on what can be grounded in the object itself (Feinstein, 1983). This emanates from the modern idea that "a work of art...does not point beyond itself to something else"

(Langer, 1971, 91).

Philosophically, and even anthropologically, the aesthetic experience requires a bracketing out of personal and cultural baggage. How the bracketed experience comes to have any meaning in a mental state of *tabula rasa* is, however, a matter of psychological theorizing. In the aesthetically isolated state, the viewer has no choice but to judge on the basis of a universal apprehension since only universal cognitive structures are operative. In a judgment of beauty, universal individualism is operative, and there is a so-called fit between artistic form and cognitive structure. The form is judged as beautiful or pleasant when it is congruent with such mental structures, and the aesthetic is subjective only in the sense that it is internally experienced. In such cases, the art response would seem to be free from tradition or, for that matter, from special learning or privilege. It would appear that a democratic condition of equal access to aesthetic qualities would be operative. This, however, assumes that bracketing itself is a natural process, perhaps attained through maturity. The lack of recognizable subject matter, such as in much modern fine art, would even seem to facilitate bracketing—i.e., providing the means of reaching a universal state. However, the confusion modern abstract art has engendered among the general population would suggest that aesthetic qualities, as defined in modern aesthetic theory, are far from being equally accessible or merely a matter of attaining some sort of aesthetic maturity.

The analogy of a painting to a window with a view of a garden is often used to illustrate the difference between what is intrinsic and extrinsic to art as well as how art is to be viewed in the twentieth century compared to past viewing expectations. Prior to this century, the viewer would look through the window (painting) to the garden beyond, recognizing types of vegetation, cloud formations, people in the garden, and so on. Utilitarian functions, personal associations, and cultural values from one's life and memories were allowed in the view into the garden. In contrast, in the twentieth century the viewer is to eschew all personal and cultural associations and look only at the flat surface of the window pane itself on which are seen the garden's abstracted colors, textures, and shapes. According to Clive Bell (1913/1958),

the representative element in a work of art may or may not be harmful, but it is always irrelevant. For to appreciate a work of art, we must bring with us nothing from life, no knowledge of its affairs and ideas, no familiarity with its emotions. (27)

According to formalist theory, artists, albeit subconsciously, in all times and places have been concerned with arrangements of the formal elements of design. This is what is believed to be intrinsic to art throughout time and space irrespective of style, function, or cultural meaning:

One should remember that a painting—before being a warhorse, a nude woman or some anecdote—is essentially a flat surface covered with colors arranged in a certain order. (Maurice Denis, *Theories 1890-1910*. Paris. 1912, 1. qtd. in Jaffe, 1965, 139)

When the viewer of art is bracketed from the personal and the cultural, there is a free play of cognitive powers, and such free play is the same for all minds. The physical aspects of art are an analogue of mental and perceptual structuring. In this sense, Gestalt principles of visual organization afforded aestheticians a rational explanation of judgments of pleasure, beauty, order, and general fitness of form (Segy, 1967).

It is beyond the scope of this paper to describe the tremendous influence the formalist aesthetic has had on art production, response, and interpretation, e.g., the proliferation of abstract and nonobjective art, the subject of art being the material means of art, the creation of art-for-art's sake, the artist's artist, and so on. There is, of course, also the influence art critics have had on artists' creation of art and the prescriptive and defining function art criticism has played.

Vasily Kandinsky (1912/1947) believed that the causes of democracy would be served by abstract or nonobjective art in that no prior knowledge would be required for understanding or appreciation. Modern abstract art may have in part arisen as a reaction against the literary excesses of Academy art which often required a classical education for interpretation and appreciation. Kandinsky thought that abstract art could foster a universal spiritual awakening. The democratic ideals of abstraction were, however, circumvented by their own cultural embeddedness. The more abstract art became, the more it became dependent on art critical explanations, to the point where even the explanations themselves sometimes required explanation (T. Wolfe, 1975).

Art in the past centuries has gone though a series of separations and specializations, i.e., the separation of craft from art, of artisan from artist, and the spiritual object from the secular. Fine art became defined as that which rises above the exigencies of ordinary life and, through aesthetic bracketing, supposedly can be experienced irrespective of one's personal, social, and educational background.

It is not serendipitous that the abstract formulations of Kandinsky and the Russian constructivists; the Gestalt psychology of Koehler, Koffka and Wertheimer; and modern aesthetic theory as delineated in the formalism of Fry and Bell coincided in the early part of this century (Bloomer & Moore, 1977; Segy, 1967). Abstraction, Gestalt principles of perception, and formalism gave credence to a pan-aestheticism that informed the methods of study and analysis in art theory, art instruction, art history, and art criticism during much of the twentieth century. The power of formalism is that it seems to be applicable to all types of art and all types of people:

In the visual arts, I believe certain formal categories are universally attended to. These include, at the very least, symmetry, proportion and balance, surface finish, and where pertinent, structural soundness. Cultures may differ widely in terms of what exactly is valued in these categories, but the categories themselves are attended to by artist and audience alike. Each culture recognizes canons in these areas, and their violation stems from either lack of skill or deliberate intent to jar the average viewer. (Silver, 1979, 290-291)

Waddington (1969), however, believed that a perceptual response to pure sensate data requires more sophistication than does functional perception. Moreover, the visual immediacy of the aesthetic experience has been found to be highly dependent upon cultural expectations that such and such objects might afford aesthetic contemplation based on learned perceptual conventions (Q. Bell, 1974; Gombrich, 1969).

With art criticism associated with aesthetic experience, with it focused toward the analysis of formal qualities within the self-contained world of art, and with an eschewing of all personal and cultural associations as a requirement, it is not surprising that academic art criticism requires instruction and a fair amount of practice. Recent studies of the developmental character of verbal responses to art suggest that the ability to deal with the intrinsic qualities of art is not merely a matter of maturation (D. Wolfe, 1988). An ability to "overcome" personal preferences and associational interpretations in order to deal with art formalistically is highly dependent on educational training. This suggests that the perception of abstract elements of design are a particular, culturally based outcome that may have little to do with a universal way of perceiving and evaluating and more to do with cultural values and training. Even Kant knew that all people would not judge in a similar manner. He, however, attributed differences in judgment to sensibility, not to cultural values.

*Valuation, Selection, and Emphasis*

Specific academic art criticism formats are often discussed as having universal application due to their similarities to constructs explanatory of valued human activities, to their focus on the art object per se, to the minimizing of subjective responses, and to their association with the aesthetic experience. These similarities need to be understood as being culturally biased and biased in support of the values of particular segments of society. They have little relationship to how talk about art naturally occurs, and they have obscured the rich options for art criticism that could

exist. At this time, art criticism, as evidenced in art education, is characterized by very little research on alternative methods, and, as a result, a few formalistic approaches predominate. Not surprisingly, even less research has been done on vernacular art criticism—either to study it in its natural settings or to bring it into educational settings (Congdon, 1986).

According to Weitz (1962), there is no one all-inclusive theory that can explain art in its many manifestations; rather, any given theory of art tends to highlight some aspects of art while it obscures others. The formulation or the selection of a theory is contingent upon human meaning and intent. In other words, it is not just the art object per se that gives us information about social and aesthetic meaning but also the entire configuration of functions, meanings, and evaluations that serve to define the art object. The ascendancy of particular theories of art can be related to social values and aesthetic priorities at given times and places (Hamblen, 1988). In much the same way, the particular forms that art criticism assumes represent selected, humanly authored traditions of talk about art that are predicated on personal and social value orientations. The fact that developmental stages of aesthetic response do not naturally, as a matter of maturation, result in the designed end goals of nonsubjective formalistic interpretations suggests that a selection process of social evaluation is operative in the use of formalistic art criticism.

Formalist theory, as applied to art criticism, is just one approach. There are other art theories that have application to art criticism: imitationalist theories of art, expressive theories, instrumental theories, and so on (Abrams, 1953). Any one of these theories or variations within them can be selected as an approach that might be given social validation and, eventually, educational implementation. For example, the end goal of art criticism could be that of understanding and evaluating art on the basis of social utility as, perhaps, some variation on Marxist instrumental aesthetics. Within a given community, such talk about art would be focused toward this goal with the result that one might ascertain stages of development for social-aesthetic understanding. In other words, developmental patterns, and certainly their endpoints, are culturally variable. There may well be developmental patterns for imitationalist, formalist, expressive, and instrumental theories of art and for art criticism. These four theories, although not exclusive of other theoretical possibilities, focus on aspects which all art objects possess to some extent, and to that extent these aspects are universal. It is, however, in a cultural context that particular aspects are given social artworld validity and become the way in which art talk is framed and becomes taken-for-granted. In a given sociocultural context, art talk may take on a correctness that, from an ethnocentric perspective, has an assumed universalism. When researchers begin to listen to vernacular art criticism, it becomes apparent that there are many naturalistically occurring approaches to art criticism. Likewise, specific art criticism approaches, much like art theories, can be consciously selected to highlight particular aspects, meanings, and functions of art. There is a need to bring to consciousness that both vernacular and academic art criticism are part of systems of choice and selection that shape aesthetic reality.

We are continually finding that many of the developmental structures that we assumed were universally applicable have actually been formulated from highly culturally biased phenomena and data. Although there may be a certain cross-cultural similarity among various developmental stages in early childhood, levels of development at adolescence—or when children enter the socializing world of formal schooling—often veer in a variety of directions due to personality differences, socioeconomic background, gender, religious affiliations, and so on. For example, Gilligan (1982) found that females in Western cultures tend to have different moral and cognitive developmental patterns than those outlined by Kohlberg and Piaget. The tragedy, of course, is that only certain developmental patterns and their end points may be given legitimacy in a given culture with the result that alternatives are ignored or are labelled as deviant, retarded, or just plainly wrong.

### The Distribution of Aesthetic Discourse

At this crucial juncture in the history of art criticism and its possible widespread instructional implementation, it is essential that the differential distribution of aesthetic discourse be examined. Both the social assumptions underlying talk about art and how access is limited to legitimated types of talk can be easily obscured inasmuch as the formalistic, self-referent, and art-specific nature of much art criticism parallels many of the characteristics of western modernity. Formalist art criticism *seems* correct in the academic world. It has acquired a taken-for-granted "fit" to much fine art partly because it has a compatibility with the characteristics of knowledge in general that are socially legitimated. And, of course, it possesses many similarities with how other subject areas are taught in our nation's schools. As such, formalistic art criticism partakes of larger societal legitimations regarding abstract knowledge, a reliance on expert pronouncements of meaning, a decontextualization of experience, self-referent specialization, and a hierarchy of legitimated knowledge and professions.

In past centuries, power and capital resided in the possession of tangible goods (Gouldner, 1979). In the twentieth century of information societies, capital has increasingly been concentrated in particular types of knowledge and the ability to manipulate abstract language systems. The cash culture and its cash languages are characterized by self-referent codes of meaning that are acquired through highly specialized education that is exclusionary, if not totally inaccessible, to those who are not or cannot be part of this culture. Membership in the cash culture allows access not only to monetary advantages but also access to the very way this dominant culture is managed, distributed, and defined. Gouldner (1979) has called this new class of knowledge brokers the culture of critical discourse (CCD). It is manifested in the official fine art world as the culture of aesthetic discourse (CAD) (Hamblen, 1984). In the culture of aesthetic discourse, what is known *about* art is a form of capital that can be bartered for incomes, prestige, and access to social groups wherein talk about art is a prerequisite. The CAD is characterized by formalistic, self-referent talk about art requiring highly specialized and particularized knowledge about primarily Western fine art forms. The CAD has among its assumptions the view that art is a specialized area of study engaged in by individuals knowledgeable about fine art traditions, that there are recognized artistic exemplars, that art is ultimately about art, and that expert judgments should prevail.

Art criticism instruction that would introduce students to these assumptions and to the culture of aesthetic discourse would supposedly be democratic in its intent to allow students to become part of the aesthetic cash culture—as well as experience the very best the artworld has to offer—assuming that there is primarily one legitimated artworld and that there is a consensus on this matter. This is the rationale used by those who call for art education as an institution that acts as an open elite organization (Smith, 1987). The conundrum presented by open elite education and, more specifically, by the ostensible democracy of the CAD is that the human authorship and the selectivity of this tradition is obscured, and it denigrates by omission other traditions—in much the same way that a democratic farce is perpetuated by dictators who allow for free elections with only one candidate listed on the ballot. Access to just one artistic tradition that is presented as inevitable, ahistorical, and "the best" usurps the educational goals of choice, participation, and broad human and aesthetic understandings.

The culture of aesthetic discourse is alien to the everyday experience of art. It is "impersonal, theoretical, and autonomous" (Hamblen, 1984, 31). The CAD is integral to the artworld of the gallery dealer, museum director, historian, and academic. The democratic paradox is that while art is often considered inaccessible to those without such language skills, accessibility imposes a class structure: "The New Class silently inaugurates a new hierarchy of the knowing, the knowledgeable, the reflexive and insightful. Those who talk well, it is held, excel over those who talk poorly or not at all" (Gouldner, 1979, 85); "aesthetic knowledge is democratized at the expense of a loss of warmth, imagination, and spontaneity of subcultural art experiences" (Hamblen, 1984, 31). When singular perspectives on art are considered correct, albeit based on an open elite, entry into the CAD "distances persons from local cultures, so that they feel an alienation from all particularistic, history-bound places and from ordinary, everyday life" (Gouldner, 1979, 59).

Linkages to aesthetic experience, to pansocial human activities, and to the physical integrity of the art object tend to obscure formalistic art criticism's origins and the fact that any one art criticism approach represents a particular choice among many possibilities. An attempt needs to be made to give equal representation and access to as many aesthetic viewpoints as are feasible. This does not mean that current art criticism formats are not valuable. Formalist approaches can provide a valuable tool for analysis. In particular, formal analysis can initially be a highly valuable approach for dealing with abstract art and with exotic art. Formal analysis, however, should not be an end goal in and of itself nor should this type of art criticism—nor any other type—take on an exclusionary correctness that excludes other modes of talking about art. Formal analysis of modern fine art, for example, has resulted in an almost complete ignoring of how this art is very much about modern society and that abstract art of all types has content and meaning beyond its formal relationships (Hamblen, 1983).

The democratic fallacy of an open elite is that equal access means access to a singular, preselected view of reality. It is exclusionary and is based on a reliance of experts' opinions which have developed within the self-contained assumptions that have given legitimacy to the open elite institutions themselves. This incestuous relationship of self-referent legitimation of aesthetic knowledge needs to be examined if aesthetic democracy is to prevail and if the chosenness of current approaches is to be revealed. Rather than supporting a range of ways of understanding and appreciating art, certain artworlds are being given legitimacy, and art criticism knowledge is distributed along social class lines. The official world of art, as defined by the cultural elite, is part of the larger knowledge industry on which our information society depends.

## Prescriptions for the Future

Since art criticism is not yet entrenched as an instructional practice with engrained expectations, it is possible that at this nascent stage the opportunity exists to begin such instruction with an inclusive base. I am suggesting that future planning for art criticism instruction attend to three aspects. First, a variety of academic art criticism formats need to be developed and instructionally implemented according to the needs, abilities, and interests of teachers and students. At this point, very little research has been done as to how individual differences influence what can be learned in regard to art criticism. Studio instruction has a long history of sensitivity to how students relate to particular types of studio activities and content—on the basis of age, gender, socioeconomic background, developmental level, cultural values, aesthetic experiences, and cognitive style. The role individual differences play in art criticism instruction should stimulate the use of different types of approaches. Also, art criticism formats should be developed that allow for the exploration of different meanings of art as well as be directed toward a variety of art forms, i.e., fine art, popular arts, folk art, commercial art. Increasing the sophistication and elaboration of imitationalist, formalist, expressive, and instrumental meanings would be possible through the use of variable academic art criticism formats.

Second, vernacular, naturally occurring art criticism needs to be allowed expression within the classroom setting. Also, vernacular art criticism needs to be studied in its natural settings as valid ways of understanding and appreciating art. Just as a variety of artistic types should be created and studied, so also a range of types of art criticism should be engaged in and studied. Undoubtedly, a study of vernacular art criticism would generate new ways of considering art criticism and the formulation of new academic approaches.

Third, the act of art criticism itself, its origins and the use of particular approaches, needs to be examined for its taken-for-granted assumptions and for its ability to illuminate some aspects of art and to obscure others. Talk about art represents socially and personally embedded choices; talk about art can also be a way to examine the basis for those choices. I have elsewhere proposed that students, for example, not only need to know how to read and study their textbooks; they also need the ability to examine the choices made by the authors of their texts (Hamblen, 1988). Likewise, for art criticism instruction, students should be given the opportunity to ask what has been included, what has been excluded and why, what is the result of such inclusions and exclusions, who has made such choices, who benefits, and who does not benefit. A curriculum choice is a sociopolitical decision inasmuch as it allows for some views of reality and it disallows for others. Art criticism, no less than other aspects of art instruction, presents occasions for elaborated artistic understandings as well as a critical consciousness of the origins, range, and possible consequences of instructional choices.

# Works Cited

Abrams, M.D. *The mirror and the lamp.* Oxford: Oxford U P, (1953).

Bell, C. *Art.* New York: Capricorn. (Original work published 1913). (1958).

Bell, Q. Art and the elite. *Critical Inquiry, 1*(1) (1974): 33-46.

Bennett, W.J. Why the arts are essential. *Educational Leadership, 45*(4), (1987/1988): 4-5.

Bersson, R. Why art education is neither socially relevant nor culturally democratic: A contextual analysis. In D. Blandy and K. Congdon (Eds.), *Art in a democracy.* 78-90. New York: Teachers C P, (1987).

Bloomer, K.C., & Moore, C.W. *Body, memory and architecture.* New Haven: Yale U P, (1977).

Broudy, H.S. *Enlightened cherishing: An essay on esthetic education.* Urbana: U of Illinois P, (1972).

Bullough, R. "Psychical distance" as a factor in art and an esthetic principle. In M.M. Rader (Ed.), *A modern book of esthetics: An anthology.* New York: Henry Holt. (Original work published 1913). (1935).

Congdon, K. The meaning and use of folk art speech in art criticism. *Studies in Art Education, 27*(3) (1986): 140-148.

Dickie, G. *Aesthetics: An introduction.* New York: Bobbs-Merrill. (1971).

Feinstein, H. The therapeutic trap in metaphoric interpretation. *Art Education, 36*(4) (1983): 30-33.

Feldman, E. The teacher as model critic. *Journal of Aesthetic Education, 7*(1), (1973): 50-57.

Feldman, E. *Varieties of visual experience.* Englewood Cliffs, NJ: Harry N. Abrams, (1981).

The J. Paul Getty Trust. *Beyond creating: The place for art in America's schools.* Los Angeles (1985).

Gilligan, C. *In a different voice: Psychological theory and women's development.* Cambridge: Harvard U P, (1982).

Gombrich, E.H. *Art and illusion: A study in the psychology of pictorial representation.* Princeton: Princeton U P, (1969).

Gouldner, A.W. *The future of intellectuals and the rise of the new class.* New York: Seabury P, (1979).

Hamblen, K.A. Modern fine art: A vehicle for understanding Western modernity. *Bulletin of the Caucus on Social Theory and Art Education,* (3) (1983): 9-16.

_____ The culture of aesthetic discourse (CAD): Origins, contradictions, and implications. *Bulletin of the Caucus on Social Theory and Art Education,* (4) (1984): 22-34.

_____ A descriptive and analytical study of art criticism formats with implications for curricular implementation. *American Educational Research Association Arts and Learning SIG Proceedings, 3* (1985): 1-13.

_____ The Feldman approach: A catalyst for examining issues in art education. *Bulletin of the Caucus on Social Theory and Art Education,* (6) (1986): 79-86.

_____ Approaches to aesthetics in art education: A critical theory perspective. *Studies in Art Education, 29*(2) (1988): 81-90.

Hirsch, E.D., Jr. *Cultural literacy: What every American needs to know.* Boston: Houghton Mifflin. (1987).

Jaffe, H.L.C. Syntactic structure in the visual arts. In G. Kepes (Ed.), *Structure in art and in science.* New York: Braziller. (1965).

Kaelin, E.F. The social uses of art: A plan for the institution. *Arts in Society, 9*(3), (1972): 371-386.

Kandinsky, V. *Concerning the spiritual in art and painting in particular.* F. Golffing, M. Harrison & F. Osterag, trans. New York: George Wittenborn. (Original work published 1912). (1947).

Kant, I. *Critique of judgement.* J.C. Meredith, trans. Oxford: Clarendon. (Original work published 1790). (1952).

Langer, S. The cultural importance of the arts. In R.A. Smith (Ed.), *Aesthetics and problems of education.* Urbana: U of Illinois P, (1971).

Logan, F. *The growth of art in American schools.* New York: Harper. (1955).

Mattil, E.L. (Ed.). *A seminar in art education for research and curriculum development.* University Park: The Pennsylvania State U, (1966).

Mittler, G.A. Perceptual thoroughness as a prelude to discriminate decision making in art. *Viewpoints (Bulletin of the School of Education at Indiana University), 52*(3), (1976): 15-29.

Osborne, H. *Aesthetics and art theory: An historical introduction.* New York: E.P. Dutton. (1970).

_____ *Aesthetics.* London: Oxford U P, (1972).

Rosenberg, H. *The anxious object: Art today and its audience* (2nd ed.). New York: Horizon P, (1966).

Segy, L. Geometric art and aspects of reality: A phenomenological approach. *The Centennial Review of Arts and Science, 11*(4) (1967): 419-454.

Sharer, J. *Children's inquiry into aesthetics.* Paper presented at the National Art Education Association Annual Convention. New Orleans. (1986, April).

Silver, H.R. Ethnoart. *American Review of Anthropology, 8* (1979): 267-307.

Smith, R.A. *Excellence in art education: Ideas and initiatives.* Reston, VA: National Art Education Association. (1987).

Waddington, C.H. *Beyond appearances: The study of the relations between painting and the natural sciences in this century.* Cambridge: MIT P, (1969).

Weitz, M. The role of theory in aesthetics. In J. Margolis (Ed.), *Philosophy looks at the arts: Contemporary readings in aesthetics.* New York: Charles Scribner's Sons. (1962).

Wolfe, D. The growth of three aesthetic stances: What developmental psychology suggests about discipline-based art education. *Issues in discipline-based art education: Strengthening the stance, extending the horizons.* Los Angeles: The J. Paul Getty Trust. (1988).

Wolfe, T. *The painted word.* New York: Farrar, Straus and Giroux. (1975).

# Feminist Approaches to Art Criticism

## Kristin G. Congdon

In the past twenty-five to thirty years the feminist movement has functioned to increase discussions about women's art and women artists. Dialogue centers around one or more of the following issues: 1) the recognition and establishment of women's art history; 2) the existence of gender differentiated approaches to artistic processes, products and aesthetic response; and 3) the development of non-hierarchial approaches to understanding and appreciating art which is sensitive to women's world views with respectful regard to age, race and class. Although research, discussion, debate and analysis may focus on one issue more than another, each concern affects the other in the expanding development of feminist approaches to art. This development, at least in academic circles, necessitates and includes talk about art or art criticism.

In this chapter, I will identify and synthesize various aspects of approaching art from varying feminist perspectives in an effort to further develop needed alternatives to the currently dominant formalist approach to art criticism. In this effort, I am indebted to many fine feminist writers, folklorists, art historians, anthropologists, sociologists, art educators and artists from all walks of life. Although I strongly believe that my work here is very different from the isolated approach of formalist art criticism which functions within rigid boundaries, usually disregarding contextual information, I recognize that the proposed approach (or approaches) also has shortcomings. While this work takes a culturally pluralistic approach, as a result of my mostly North American focused spectrum of research, it reflects views from a predominately English-speaking, largely North American world. With this understanding, I invite the reader to interact with this format with a critical mind and add, edit, sort and synthesize its arguments, giving this chapter additional insight. Perhaps in the near future our society will no longer deny, degrade and ignore the cultural expressions of the majority of our people—people of color, women, the economically poor—but will embrace, enjoy, learn from and employ the understandings that result from feminist approaches to art criticism.

### Beginnings: A Recognition of the White Patriarchy's Domination

In order to begin to take a feminist perspective, one must acknowledge women's domination by white males, their second class citizenship and their status which has been framed as incomplete beings (de Beauvoir, 1952). As a reflection of their worth, their art has been seen as minor. It has been called that which is gentle, and if it is good, it is art which can co-exist with music, conversation and children (Greer, 1979). Fine art is associated with a "corporate-government-elite," which is identified with upper-class males who Hammond (1984) says "found, fund and run art museums, set standards of taste, and have a vested interest in creating, validating, and supporting art whose form and content justifies and furthers a patriarchal society order" (33). The established art world maintains control, in part, by referring negatively to the majority of women's art as decorative, traditional and craft-like. Much of it is also denigrated because of its so-called practical purpose, a charge seldom leveled against architecture, an artistic endeavor controlled largely by white males (Maines, 1979). This devaluation is rooted, to a large degree, in our sexist and racist culture. For example, Marinardi (1982) points out that quilts have been unappreciated for the same reasons that jazz was underrated for so long: because the wrong people (meaning those less valued in our society) were representing and defining American culture.

A lack of recognition leads to silencing. Quiltmakers did not choose to be anonymous; art historians simply did not make the effort to identify and record their history in the same painstaking way they attend to male artists (Mainardi, 1982). Not only are art historians, critics, collectors and museum curators responsible for the lack of attention placed on women's art, Berger (1972) points out that male artists continue to depict women differently from men in their art because the ideal spectator is "always assumed to be male and the image of the woman is designed to flatter him" (64). Clearly, women have been silenced and ignored both as artists and as viewers of art.

Not only are women unappreciated in the context of the larger society, they have also had greater difficulty in expanding their roles because resources have not been made available to them. By the 1890s, women were making gains in obtaining opportunities in education and exhibition. Some were winning awards (Walker, 1985). Today, although women are readily enough admitted to art programs, securing and maintaining faculty positions remains difficult. A 1972 report from the Women's Caucus of the College Art Association found that women made up as little as eleven percent of art history faculties and less than two percent of studio faculties in art departments in the United States (Harris, 1983). The situation is even worse than these statistics communicate: males make higher salaries, advance more readily and have greater political power in the academic setting (Hale, 1971).

Female students need role models, and they need to be taught about women's culture, an area not often entertained as viable by the male professor. Westkott (1983) writes about how important the experience is when a student discovers that her life and that of other women are not created freely but are restricted by male-dominated structures. It is a beginning point for new awareness.

Public funding in the 1980s decreased for women artists (Heartney, 1987), and representation in major exhibitions continued to be meager (Hammond, 1984; Art Alum, 1985). Berger speaks about the lack of support for women's art and women's perspectives indicating that we are all deprived by this neglect of a large and important part of history. Without the recognition and acceptance of historical perspectives from varying groups of people, a white patriarchal history is invented, justified and used to rule. A single-minded domineering perspective prevails. Heartney remarks that the decline of support in the 1980s (which had increased somewhat in the 1970s) is related to the Reagan mentality which also contributed to the defeat of the Equal Rights Amendment. When female art students do not have access to female art teachers, when they do not have an art history inclusive of a variety of women's expressions, when the visible art works created by women are degraded, when they do not have language and visual symbols recognizable as their own, when their traditional artistic forms are devalued and supportive resources are unavailable, their ability (indeed, everyone's ability) to freely create and expansively appreciate is greatly thwarted.

A feminist perspective in art must grow out of the awareness of the existing oppression of women. But it must also recognize that art is an expression of experience, of communication, of an artist who is a part of many cultural groups which bind her or him to a way of life and a particular world view. Even if one believes that a universal aesthetic exists (usually expressed in terms of formalism), work toward utilizing feminist perspectives in art requires a willingness to recognize that although individual women belong to many cultural groups at the same time, their common experience of being women binds them together in ways that may bring a common understanding to certain types of expression to which

a man may not be as readily responsive (Lippard, 1976a). Women are bound together by shared experiences which often include childbirth and child-raising and major responsibilities for homemaking and food preparation. They are also bound by oppression. It *does* make a difference to women as a cultural group that one out of every three females in the United States is raped, that one out of every two wives is abused by her husband, that one out of every four female children is sexually abused; and that eighty percent of women who work outside the home say that they have been sexually harassed on the job (Cheatham & Powell, 1986). Women's worlds are decidedly different from men's worlds which are often more aggressive, economically secure and competitive.

While most feminists acknowledge women's common bonds, there remains some disagreement about how to recognize the value of women's art in our society. This recognition would be inclusive of changes in the established art world. Some proponents of change ask that we continue to work toward assimilation; others ask that the basis of traditional art values and appreciation structures be reassessed (Walker, 1985). My preferred direction here is to work toward the development of a critical structure which includes a reassessment of many of the prevailing ideas about women's art which exists within the established art world. While I do ask that art be studied within its cultural context, I do not propose that it become (or remain) segregated from the rest of society. I agree with Rajachman (1985) who states: "We cannot do women's creativity justice so long as we consider it in an exclusively female context" (167). Men and women are so much a part of the same world that an act of oppression serves to deny and denigrate the oppressor. Everyone suffers from sexism. An oppressor may reap some benefits from a unjust position but that same oppressor must guard, continue to fight for, justify and distort reality in order to maintain the status quo. Energy expended in such negative ways is energy not spent in positive development. Those activities create and recreate the person. We are all so much a part of the same air, water and earth that it becomes superfluous in many ways to determine with clear cut boundaries which parts of women's cultures are ours and which are impositions placed on us, for the impositions may be taken in tyranny but transformed by the victim/victor into creative acts of freedom. In an effort to understand what is feminine, we must make attempts to understand women's expressions whether they are angry responses to imprisonment or delightful exchanges of creative powers.

*From a Female Perspective: Discovering Women's History*

The present women's movement asserts society's need to respond to women's needs and contributions rather then regarding them only in terms of their relationships and obligations to men (Klein, 1984). Delmar (1986) states that "feminism is usually defined as an active desire to change women's position in society" (13).

In order to make changes, women are becoming more and more involved in documenting their histories. These expressions often take form in biography and autobiography and are subjective and emotive. Unfortunately, however, it is often difficult for academic women to write with a feminist approach since the research methodologies university scholars normally value, employ and accept are those of the male-defined intellectual tradition (Westkott, 1983). Their dilemma is further complicated by continued critique and analysis from white male-oriented perspectives. Many scholars in university Women's Studies Programs feel that critical approaches to women's research will change as their history continues to be recorded. Appropriate methodologies will become apparent as the content is recorded. Documented history begins to give women the necessary role models needed for growth, making choices and societal changes (Friedan, 1963). As Shange (1977) has so aptly put it: "this is a women's trip & i need my stuff" (52). This "stuff" is varied as women's backgrounds vary. Feminism celebrates pluralism; it recognizes the ever-pressing needs in today's world to acknowledge differences related to age, class and race as well as gender. There must be many kinds of ways to be female which are valued (McFee, 1979).

Reclaiming, appropriating and actively developing history, justifying and accepting a variety of women's world views, goals and heroisms has created changes in the art world. For example, many contemporary academically trained women artists have begun to reassess their relationship to and appreciation of traditional decorative art and have incorporated many of its aspects into their own work (Nochlin, 1979; Heartney, 1987). This kind of re-evaluation is one aspect of the larger movement in which artists are attempting to find and work with that which has been uniquely female in women's experiences (Heartney, 1987). Artists involved in this kind of exploration include Nancy Spero, Judy Chicago, Miriam Schapiro, Mary Beth Edelson and Carolee Schneeman. More recently women artists such as Barbara Kruger, Sherrie Levine, Jenny Holzer, Silvia Kolbowski and Cindy Sherman are exploring the female experience as a social or psychological construct.

The importance of women's art history within the larger content of women's culture cannot be underestimated. Several researchers are uncovering, writing about and rewriting textile history, and in the process portraying women artists as strong, committed and politically active individuals (Anscombe, 1984;

Parker, 1984; Ferrero, Hedges, & Silber, 1987). The repression and subjugation of Western women painters has been carefully and painstakingly recorded by Greer. She documents how women's roles and society's expectations of women has resulted in their inability to receive a quality education, to be recognized and respected by the established art world for good work and to be granted sufficient emotional and financial support. She often gave her energy to nurture male relatives. She allowed them to sign her work or she signed her work with a male name. She struggled to find her own voice. Fortunately, many of today's women artists are writing about their experiences so that others may know about them and learn from them (Chicago, 1977; Truitt, 1982; Hammond, 1984).

An understanding of women's art and women's culture is unveiling information about who women are and what they have the potential to become. Many aspects of women's worlds are becoming acknowledged as increasingly different from those worlds created by white males. While men are expected to excel in a particular arena; women are conditioned to be adequate in many areas. Boys learn imdependence, competition and organizational skills whereas girls focus on relationships with others which involve intimacy and a greater effort toward peaceful interchange and compromise (Gilligan, 1982). That which is masculine tends to separate and that which is feminine tends to connect. Gilligan tells us these attitudes have much to do with how we problem solve and define the world. Perhaps because of these perspectives Cheatham and Powell noted that many of the women artists they have met do not have as a characteristic goal the need to get to the top in a competitive isolated manner but to use art as a way of connecting to all things and creating more fulfilling lives. Gilligan states: "Since the reality of connection is experienced by women as given rather than as freely contracted, they arrive at an understanding of life that reflects the limits of autonomy and control. As a result, women's development delineates the path not only to a less violent life but also to a maturity realized through interdependence and taking care" (172).

Compromise, the desire to make and utilize connectiveness and the appreciation of differences, contributes to a feminist desire to break down hierarchies in art forms. Artists such as Miriam Schapiro and Joyce Kozloff embrace the decorate arts in an effort to affirm their strength in history and to break down the politics of high and low art (Robins, 1984). Quilts, embroidery and other needlework have become more important and more valued by academically trained women artists and art critics. Langer (1985) states that a feminist approach to making and appreciating art also avoids the traditional male belief in the existence of and striving for the perfect object: "Instead, a woman-centered perspective replaces this dubious object and its mechanistic overtones with the more exciting and rewarding concept of experimentation. The right to fail, to be human, to keep on trying and growing is fundamental to feminism itself'' (5). The idea of perfection can be dehumanizing; it can restrict and reject artistic forms in a pluralistic society. Feminist criticism, Lorde (1984) tells us, must recognize that the form of artistic creation is a class issue. We must be aware that form may also speak to race, gender and age.

Feminist approaches to art recognize that women's lives have historically been intertwined with meeting the needs espoused by men and by mundane daily routines (Bovenschen, 1985). However, it is also recognized that these kinds of situations did not completely shut off women's creative responses. Women's spaces, so-called women's work and her traditional roles are now being re-evaluated. The house and home has traditionally been women's domain. This association is true in Native American cultures as well as in Anglo-American domestic systems. For example, the Blackfeet Native Americans recognize that the teepee belongs to the wife rather than the husband (Wolf, 1982). Class status may influence the amount of outside stimulus a woman may experience. In other words, money can buy a woman time outside the home to experience art from the established art world such as concerts, theatre or dance (Lippard, 1984). As a result of this exposure, art work may change, be more innovative and become more attached to contemporary ideas and thought. Women who work in the home and especially those who rear children know life to be made of a great deal of simultaneous activity. Life is made up of distraction (Modliski, 1982). Some artists, like sculptor Lila Katzen and Ukrainian egg decorator Ida Moffit, learned to expect interruptions and worked around them (Munro, 1979; Jones, 1979). Many artists, like Katzen, have had to learn to live without a room of their own. As a result, their art work has to adapt in form, materials and content to their working environment.

So-called women's work in the home has been substantially recognized as duplication, doomed repetition, stifling, tiresome and empty activity (Friedan, 1963; de Beauvoir, 1974). "Womanhouse," the remodeled home instigated by Judy Chicago and Miriam Schapiro responded to women's imprisonment within domestic walls (Chicago, 1977; Robins, 1984). But women artists are also beginning to reclaim and (re)affirm their experiences in the home in a positive way (Hammond, 1984). Female novelists recognize the power of housework, at times, to be therapeutic. Toni Morrison's character Sethe in *Beloved* (1987) folds laundry and kneads dough to calm her sorrow. Mary Frank sees beauty in it: "I love the gesture of work, watching someone do work they do well or with experience, with certain essential gestures, nothing

wasted. Watch someone washing clothes, lifting things, even cooking. Stirring or sifting" (Munro, 1979, 290). Artists from all walks of life are now acknowledging the artistic inspiration given to them by females in their homes. Alice Walker (1983) credits much of her achievement to her mother who always took the time to grow beautiful flowers, and Beverly Pepper remembers with joy her grandmother's rose garden and rose jelly (Munro, 1979). Louise Nevelson, Georgia O'Keefe, Elaine de Kooning and Miriam Schapiro all acknowledge their attachment to lace (Munro, 1979); Alma Thomas and Helen Lundeberg remember their female relatives' sewing activities as inspirational; and Jacob Lawrence attributes his early fascination with patterns of color to the bright throw rugs his mother placed throughout his Harlem home (Wernick, 1987). Women's aesthetic touches and their accomplishments deserve credit. Such inspiration as Sophie Taeuber-Arp's strong influence on the de Stijl movement as well as abstract art's debt to textile design need recognition (Anscombe, 1985).

The reassessment of women's spaces is reflected in contemporary still lifes. Rather than the classical arrangement of fruit and wine bottles, women are now responding artistically to sinks full dirty dishes, unmade beds, laundry, cooked food and canning jars. Hammond states: "Sometimes these still lifes are presented neatly put away on shelves or in drawers, but usually the objects take over, multiply, as if to say a woman's work is never done. The images fill the canvas as the chores fill the day" (30-31).

Feminist women are beginning to understand and build on their connectedness to their worlds. Feminist criticism should reflect that connectedness. The act of sewing, knotting or piecing a quilt should be seen as representative of a connecting activity (Hammond, 1984). Women want to connect to history, to tradition. Joan Snyder utilizes her Russian and German heritage in her art as Faith Ringgold builds on her African American identity (Gill, 1987; Munro, 1979).

The act of connecting also means understanding the women's movement as a collective activity and not a movement for individuals (de Beauvior, 1952). It is an economic struggle as well as a political and cultural one. Women's artistic communities must welcome within their boundaries women of all ages and from all backgrounds (Lippard, 1976a, 1984). Women should not have to continue to work in isolation. The connections must also recognize that a woman's perspective incorporates context. It can be non-competitive, subjective, and bonding. Feminist criticism is interdisciplinary. It "must by its very nature focus on such disciplines as Philosophy, Literature, Psychology, Religion, Politics and Sexuality" (Langer, 1985, 4). The best criticism opens doors, raising more questions than it answers.

At the same time feminist criticism makes

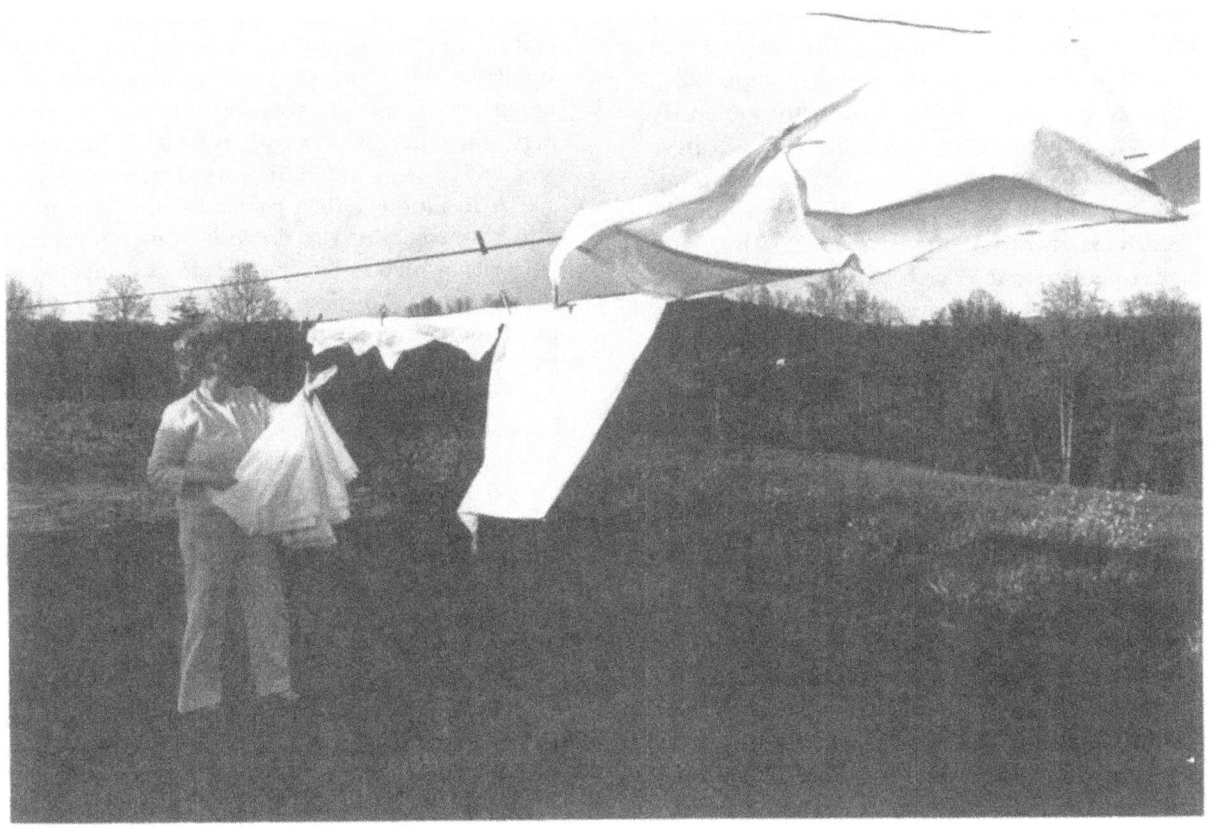

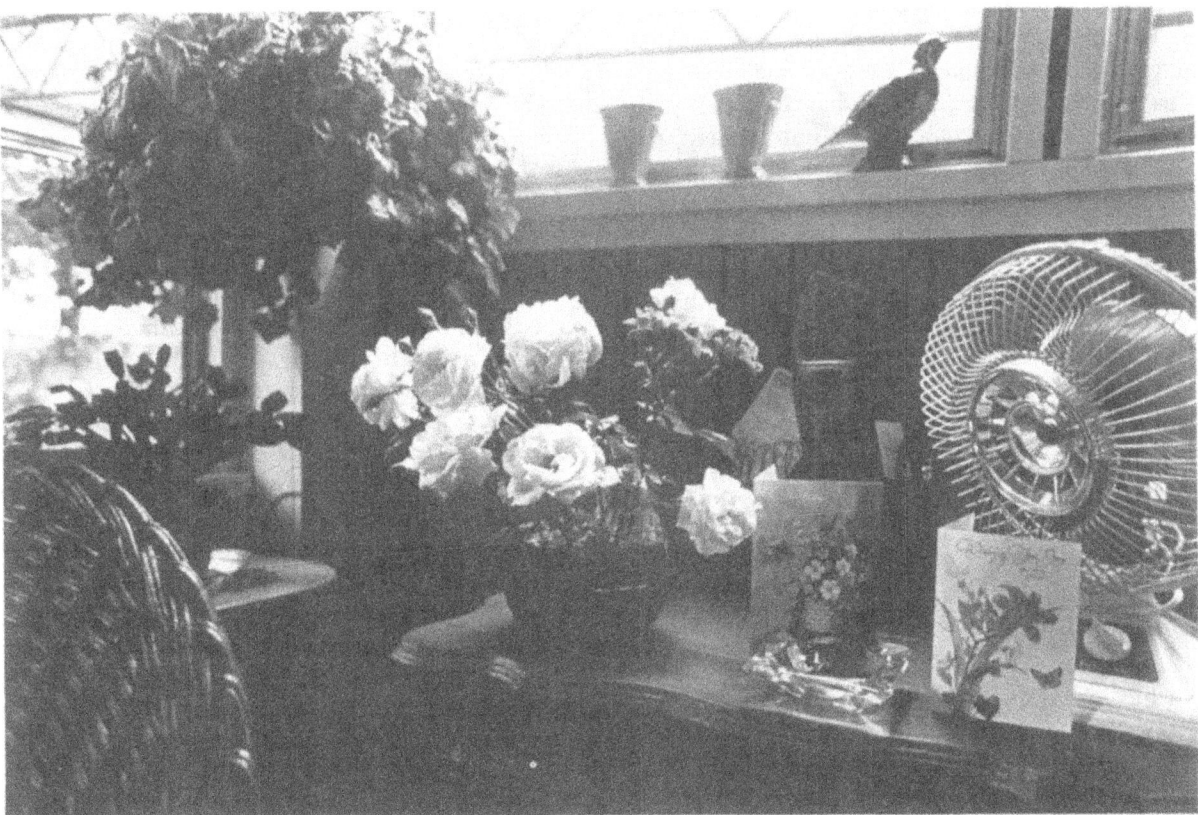

Untitled photographs by Martha V. Carden.

connections, it must act to celebrate differences. For example, artistic judgments among the Mesquakie of Iowa are not often actively debated (Torrence, 1984). They are verbally understated and generally understood. On the other hand, the Eskimos have eighteen words to describe "white," opening up possibilities to see snow which Anglo-Americans do not readily experience (Williamson, 1980): "Difference must not be merely tolerated, but seen as a fund of necessary polarities between which our creativity can speak like a dialectic" (Lorde, 1984, 111). Differences amongst women from varying cultures should be embraced as ways to enrich individual and collective visions and make pathways toward the fulfillment of our dreams. Indeed, difference is and must be the foundation for choice, a concept which touches at the heart of the feminist consciousness.

### Female Expressions/Female Centered Education

Many female artists are tuned-in to the fact that women talk about their art as they speak about their lives (Truitt, 1982; Hammond, 1984). Feminist art criticism is personal. The artist "admits that she is a person. She recognizes that her reactions, associations, likes and dislikes, are connected to who she is as much as to what she is reading (viewing, hearing, etc.)" (Bass, 1975, 43). Bass further points out that because her art is personalized, a woman will say, "this book has meant the most to me this year" rather than "this is the best book of the year" (43). The art process is so intimate for women that they often say their fears and conflicts are worked out in their art (Hammond, 1984).

Women's experiences, expressions and dreams manifest themselves in a variety of ways. Many critics and historians are beginning to take note of the similarities of expressions within this vast feminine domain of creative forces. Certain materials are associated with female works. Women have always brought their creativity into the needlework arts (Mainardi, 1982). They use cloth, thread, yarn, ribbon, sequins, beads and ric-rac as well as lint, shopping lists, coupons, kitchen shelving, patterns, wallpaper, napkins, leftovers and hand-me-downs (Hammond, 1984). Elaine Reichek chose to work with black organdy in 1976 (Robins, 1984); Joan Snyder has used lentil beans, seeds, threads and pockets in her work (Gill, 1987); and Harmony Hammond chooses to use rags which are free and given to her by anyone and everyone. Viewed historically, often—but not always—women's art has been created from natural materials rather than human-made materials (Ancombe, 1985).

The scale of women's art, generally speaking, differs from men's (Greer, 1979). It is often noted that women work on smaller formats than men. But women do not and have not necessarily worked small as a matter of free choice. However, the prevailing smallness of women's creative formats does not necessitate a minor statement. It is a white male perspective that says "bigger is better." Furthermore, women can work and have worked on a large scale.

Association with a particular size of work may also have something to do with women's association with that which is "inside" while men identify with that which is "outside": "We have broadly accepted the male concern with facade and monument, the female concern with function and environment; the male concern with permanence and structural imposition, the female concern with adaptability and psychological needs; the male concern with public image, the female resistance to specialization; the male concern with abstract theory, the female concern with biography and autobiography" (Lippard, 1976a, 74). Lippard further tells us that these concerns express themselves in certain elements which reoccur in women's art:

a uniform destiny, or overall texture, often sensuously tactile and repetitive of detail to the point of obsession; the preponderance of circular focus, inner space...a ubiquitous linear 'bag' or parabolic form that turns in on itself; layers, or strata, or veils; an indefinable looseness or flexibility of handling; windows; autobiographical context; animals; flowers; a certain kind of fragmentation; a new fondness for the pinks and pastels and ephemeral cloud colors that used to be taboo. (49)

The imagery of academically schooled women artists repeatedly reflects matriarchal history, traditional women's arts, decoration, women's sexuality and journalism (Hammond, 1984).

Even when men and women work in the same art form, there are differences. Lippard (1976b) points out that when men and women have both worked in body art, there are differences in attitudinal approach which results in a difference in expression; men's art is often far more sadistic and violent than women's.

Most all women artists view their art as connected to their daily lives, illustrating the feminist statement "the personal is political." Many artists actively use this idea to make a political statement and work for social change for oppressed people. Lippard (1984) feels this direction is taken so often because women identify with those who are disenfranchised. Miriam Schapiro has worked to acknowledge and honor those women artists who have remained largely invisible; Joan Snyder created "Resurrection" in 1977 to tell the stories of violence against women (Gill, 1987); and Judy Baca organizes the creation of murals in Los Angeles to empower the poor and change lives (Cheatham & Powell, 1986). Women artists who are academically trained and have worked with autobiographical content in the 1970s experimented with the forms of body art, video art and artists books (Robins, 1984). Women's experiences have also continued to be expressed in embroidery, sewing and chinapainting as well as knitting and crocheting.

Women artists of all kinds remain responsive to repetition, patterning and decorative elements in art. Hammond says that many artists use a grid to organize their patterns of repetition. Native Americans are well known for their use of repetition which is incorporated positively into other aspects of their daily lives. For the Zuni, rhythmical repetition is seen as a necessity (Bunzel, 1929); and the best Kwakiutl artists are often also known as the best dancers (Holm, 1965). Repetition is valued by many, not because of its ability (or inability) to discover something new but because it acts to soothe and to create a sense of certainty and security (Munro, 1979).

Feminist approaches to art criticism, especially when speaking about women's work, should take into account all of the above discussed aspects of women's worlds and their art: women's art history, a recognition and appreciation of women's art, her traditional forms, her materials, her symbols and her ways of appreciating art and viewing the world. Feminist approaches should result in the adaptation and expansion of women's ways of knowing and learning. The recent book *Women's Ways of Knowing* (Benlenky et al., 1986) states: "Educators can help women develop their own authentic voices if they emphasize connection over separation, understanding and acceptance over assessment, and collaboration over debate; if they accord respect to and allow time for the knowledge that emerges from firsthand experience; if instead of imposing their own expectations and arbitrary requirements, they encourage students to evoke their own patterns of work based on the problems they are pursuing" (229). If one begins to view the world in such a way that knowledge is seen as connected, a kind of equality amongst varying groups of people is set up. The goal becomes understanding rather than proving. For the white male, defining, analyzing and explaining the world are most important; for the female, the world cannot be so easily defined because it is constantly growing and changing. Female understanding comes from watching and learning about the world as an emerging changing process (Schaef, 1981). Rose (1986) sees these differences not only influencing what kinds of knowledge are superior but what kinds of labor are valued. She states that to understand and develop feminist ways of knowing, we must begin by looking at women's work. Women's art work should be instrumental in the development of gaining perspective on women's lives, their world views and their ways of knowing.

Feminist approaches to art criticism must incorporate and work with oral history as well as the written word. Without it we will all lose the opportunity to gain the wisdom of many groups of people. Even worse, this lack of recognition can act to deny them their existence. An elderly Nootka woman from Vancouver Island explains: "Kill a memorizer and you killed a whole hank'a history, and if you're gonna kill someone's history, well, your own might not last long, and when that's gone, you just killed all your people who were here before you all over again" (Cameron, 1981, p. 78).

Women's ways of knowing must be expressed in non-sexist and self-affirming language. This can be difficult; but as attention grows and sexist language becomes more apparent, new words, phrases and ways of naming and creating our world will be developed. Paulo Freire (1968) has made us aware of how language is used to dominate groups of people. He feels that owning dialogue is a fundamental condition of being a free person.

Frueh (1983) has gone through influential art history texts and found presently used art language is also language that can be associated with war, revolution and conquest. She recognized these descriptors as defining values of art in a patriarchal world. She states: "Artists 'destroy' precious styles, they engage in campaigns, skirmishes, military exercises, battles and conquests. We read about assaults, attacks, invasions and confrontations as well as rebels and revolutionaries" (6-7). These kinds of language usages, comparatively speaking, exclude women. An alternative to this way of speaking might be found in the chants used by the Bread and Puppet Theatre: "Art soothes pain! Art is like green trees! Art is like white clouds in blue sky! Art is not business!" (Cheatham & Powell, 1986, 137). This language is connective, inclusive, non-hierarchial. It works to expand our tastes and values and to reinforce the existence of art as a part of our lives.

Feminist language understands context, and it acknowledges and reflects the personal and the political. It makes connections, and it celebrates life. It respects differences in the use of phrases and words and seeks to understand and accept these differences. For example, the Blackfeet people talk with respect about "old ladies" as a proper term for grandmothers whereas Anglo-Americans might think that usage disrespectful (Wolf, 1982). Afro-American quilters will often say that their colors must "hit each other right" to reflect an aesthetic preference that has strong relationships to their heritage and connections to jazz (Wahlman & Scully, 1983). Using language appropriately and purposefully aligned to one's perceptions is both a sign and a tool of liberation (Hill, 1986).

*Summary*

It is at this point that a patriarchial oriented and organized paper might place the information given here in some number of summarized categories. I now find it difficult and even unnecessary to take this step even though I have done it on other occasions without too much distress. Instead of taking that route here, I choose to reemphasize the connection women's art has to life and how language about it should reflect that connection. Although a room of one's own may be desirable for many, the truth of the matter is that many women's creative spaces have an interpenetration between their lives and their art that Judy Chicago (1977) says makes it hard to determine where their art and their daily lives separate. Indeed, the women's room for many is a space without walls. In working environments, in form, in content, in function and in appreciation, women's art is an integral part of their worlds. Miriam Schapiro reports that because of her organizational methods, she was once told that she had finally learned to have a seamless life. She replied: "What a wonderful way to describe a person's life. It means your life and your art have become one" (Gill, 1986, 101).

Feminist art criticism approaches must emerge and develop as women create and learn more about their histories and envision and fulfill their futures. This approach to art (and life) may be in its beginning stages, but its potentials and possibilities, even now, seem exceptionally hopeful.

The author would like to thank Carol "Lane" Aldridge for her helpful reading of an earlier draft of this chapter.

# Works Cited

Anscombe, I. *A woman's touch: Women in design from 1860 to the present day.* New York: Penguin Books. (First published in Great Britain by Virago P, 1984). (1985).

Art Alum. To my dear Alma mater. *Women Artists News, 10*(5-6), (September, 1985): 8-9.

Bass, E. In place of criticism. *The Feminist Art Journal, 4*(1), (Spring, 1975): 42-43.

Benlenky, M.F., Clinchy, B.M., Goldberger, N.R., & Tarule, J.M. *Women's ways of knowing: The development of self, voice, and mind.* New York: Basic Books. (1986).

Berger, J. *Ways of seeing.* London: British Broadcasting Corporation and Penguin Books Ltd. (1972).

Bovenschen, S. Is there a feminine aesthetic? In G. Ecker (Ed.), *Feminist aesthetics.* Boston: Beacon P. (1985): 23-50. (Translated by B. Weckmueller).

Bunzel, R. *The Pueblo potter: A study of creative imagination in primitive art.* New York: Dover, (1929).

Cameron, A. *Daughters of Copper Women.* Vancouver, BC: Press Gang. (1981).

Cheatham, A., & Powell, M.C. *This way daybreak comes: Women's values and the future.* Philadelphia: New Society Publishers. (1986).

Chicago, J. *Through the flower: My struggle as a woman artist.* Garden City, N.Y.: Anchor Books. (1977).

deBeauvior, S. *The second sex.* New York: Vintage Books.

(First published by Alfred A. Knopf, Inc. 1952). (1974).

Delmar, R. What is feminism. In J. Mitchell & A. Oakley (Eds.), *What is feminism: A re-examination.* New York: Pantheon Books, (1986): 8-33.

Ferrero, P., Hedges, E., & Silber, J. *Hearts and hands: The influence of women and quilts on American society.* San Francisco: Quilt Digest P. (1987):

Freire, P. *Pedagogy of the oppressed.* New York: Seabury P. (1986).

Friedan, B. *The feminine mystique.* New York: W.W. Norton. (1963).

Frueh, J. The dangerous sex: Art language and male power. *Women Artists News, 10*(5-6), (September, 1985): 6-7 & 11.

Greer, G. *The obstacle race.* New York: Farrar Straus Giroux. (First published by Secker & Warburg, 1979). (1979).

Gill, S. From "femmage" to figuration. *Art News, 85*(4), (1986): 94-101.

———— Painting from the heart. *Art News, 86*(4), (1987): 128-135.

Gilligan, C. *In a different voice.* Cambridge: Harvard U P. (1982).

Hall, L. In the university. In T.B. Hess & E.C. Baker (Eds.), *Art and sexual politics.* New York: Collier Books, (1971): 130-146.

Hammond, H. *Wrappings: Essays on feminism, art, and the martial arts.* New York: Mussmann Bruce. (1984).

Harris, A.S. *Feminist Art Journal, 3.* (1973).

Heartney, E. How wide is the gender gap? *Art News, 86*(6), (1987): 139-145.

Hill, A.O. *Mother tongue, father time.* Bloomington: Indiana U P. (1986).

Holm, B. *Northwest coast Indian art.* Seattle: U of Washington P. (1965).

Jones, S. (Ed.). *Webfoots and bunchgrassers: Folk art of the Oregon country.* Salem: Oregon Arts Commission. (1980).

Klein, E. *Gender politics: From consciousness to mass politics.* Cambridge: Harvard U P. (1984).

Langer, S. Is there a feminist criticism? *Women Artists News, 10*(5-6), (1985): 4-5.

Lanning, L. & Hart, V. *Ripening: An almanac of lesbian lore and vision.* Minneapolis, MN: Word Weavers. (1981).

Lippard, L.R. *From the center: Feminist essays on women's art.* New York: E.P. Dutton. (1976a).

Lippard, L.R. The pains and pleasure of rebirth: Women's body art. *Art in America, 64*, (1976b): 73-81.

Lippard, L.R. *Get the message: A decade of art for social change.* New York: E.P. Dutton. (1984).

Lorde, A. *Sister outsider.* Trumansburg, NY: Crossing P. (1984).

Mainardi, P. Quilts: The great American art. In N. Broude & M.D. Garrard (Eds.), *Feminism and art history: Questioning the litany.* New York: Harper and Row, 330-346. [Reprint from *Feminist Art Journal*, (Winter 1973) 2 (1), (1982): 18-23.

Maines, R. Fancy Work: The archaeology of lives. In J. Loeb (Ed.), *Feminist collage: Educating women in the visual arts.* New York: Teachers College P. (1979): 78-82.

McFee, J.K. Society and identity: A personal perspective. In J. Loeb (Ed.), *Feminist collage: Educating women in the visual arts.* New York: Teachers College P. (1979): 78-82.

Modleski, T. *Loving with a vengeance: Mass-produced fantasies for women.* New York: Methuen. (1982).

Morrison, T. *Beloved.* New York: Alfred A. Knopf. (1987).

Munro, E. *Originals: American women artists.* New York: Simon and Schuster. (1979).

Nochlin, L. Toward a juster vision: How feminism can change our ways of looking at art history. In J. Loeb (Ed.), *Feminist collage: Educating women in the visual arts.* New York: Teachers College P. (1979): 3-13.

Parker, R. *The subversive stitch: Embroidery and the making of the feminine.* London: Women's P. (1984).

Rajchman, J. The postmodern museum. *Art in America,* *73*(10), (October, 1875): 110-117, 171.

Robins, C. *The pluralist era: American art 1968-1981.* New York: Harper & Row. (1984).

Rose, H. Women's work: Women's knowledge. In J. Mitchell & A. Oakley (Eds.), *What is feminism: A re-examination.* New York: Pantheon Books. (1986): 161-183.

Schaef, A.W. *Women's reality: An emerging female system in a white male society.* Minneapolis: Winston P. (1981).

Shange, N. *For colored girls who have considered suicide/ when the rainbow is enuf.* Toronto: Bantam Books. (1977).

Torrence, G. From woodland to prairie: Art of the Mesquakies. In S. Ohrn (Ed.), *Passing time and traditions: Contemporary Iowa folk artists.* Published for the Iowa Arts Council. Ames: Iowa State U P. (1984).

Truitt, A. *Daybook: The journal of an artist.* New York: Penguin Books. (1982).

Wahlman, M.S., & Scully, J. Aesthetic principles in Afro-American quilts. In W. Ferris (Ed.), *Afro-American folk art and crafts.* Boston: G.K. Hall, (1983): 78-97.

Walker, A. *In search of out mothers' gardens.* San Diego: Harcourt Brace Jovanovich. (1983).

Walker, S. Strong-minded critics: Feminist art criticism in the nineteenth century. *Women Artists News, 10*(5-6), (September 1985): 12-13, 23.

Wernick, R. Jacob Lawrence: Art as seen through a peoples' history. *Smithsonian, 18*(3), (June 1987): 56-67.

Westkott, M. Women's studies as a strategy for change: Between criticism and vision. In G. Bowles and R.D. Klein (Eds.), *Theories of women's studies.* Boston: Routledge & Kegan Paul, (1983): 210-218.

Williamson, J. *Consuming passions: The dynamics of popular culture.* New York: Marion Boyars. (1986).

Wolf, B.H. *The ways of my grandmother.* New York: Quill. (1982).

# Criticism of Computer Art: The Implications of Interactivity

## Linda F. Ettinger

The term "computer art" strikes many people as dichotomous. The frequently heard phrase that "computers don't make art—artists do," while on the one hand curtailing thoughtful discussion, also suggests provocative assumptions and attitudes about art and computing. One assumption is that the term "art" refers to an object. Another assumption is that the term "artist" refers to a particular type of individual. A third assumption is that computers are somehow independent entities that have the power to "do" things on their own. A fourth assumption is that "making art" involves only two primary components: an artist and a resulting art object; a viewer or audience is often considered secondary and separate. A fifth assumption is that people, whether they agree or not with the intent of the phrase "computers don't make art" at least agree on the meaning of the individual words.

The phrase and the attendant assumptions provide an entry point to this chapter on the criticism of computer art. It is written for those who feel that computer art is something different from other kinds of art—perhaps something that should not really be categorized as art. It is also written for those who feel that computer art does indeed fit within a larger category of art but are not sure why and would like to explore someone else's thinking on the topic. And it is written for those who believe that the essence of art is grounded in dynamic inquiry about our world and that art world constructs, in order to be most useful, must be equally grounded and dynamic.

The purpose of this paper is to examine computer art in a manner that shifts attention away from focus on art as object and on artist and art critic as particular specialized individuals. Instead I focus on an aspect of computer art—interactivity—that requires a change in the ways in which we define art, artist, art critic and audience. My strategy is threefold. I present examples of computer art that do not fit comfortably within traditional definitions of the term "art." Therefore, I begin with a discussion about how we define and categorize as a way to broaden existing definitions. Next, I select things people are saying and doing in the area of computer art and examine how

these differ from attitudes and approaches we in the art world have come to expect. In particular, I examine the ideas and experiences of three authors: Franke, Krueger and McHale. Franke, a scientist/artist who teaches Cybernetic Aesthetics at the University of Munich in Germany, wrote what has become a landmark book on the topic of computer art titled *Computer Graphics/Computer Art* (1971). Krueger wrote the book *Artificial Reality* (1983) while a member of the Computer Science Department at the University of Connecticut. It is a celebration of contemporary interdisciplinary thought regarding the potential relationships among computer technology, art and society. McHale, an artist and sociologist at the Center for Integrative Studies at the University of Houston, wrote "The Future of Art and Mass Culture" (1979). In his article, which has received far too little attention, McHale anticipates changes that might occur in "the cultural configurations of 'an information society' more dependent on visual communications" than societies dependent upon oral communication or print (63). In other words, he examines conditions for a world in which art provides a primary way to interact. I conclude by exploring the value of interactivity as a dynamic process in our society with the educational potential to change our conceptions of participants in the art construct, including artist and critic.

### On Definition

Fratto (1978) and Lakoff (1987) suggest that the ways humans define and categorize may be primary cognitive modes. From where do definitions come, and what purposes do they serve? Hanson (1969) states: "A useful term cannot apply to everything. Some logical or conceptual boundary must appear somewhere....At the command 'Define your terms!' we look to existing boundary rules, in texts or lectures, or else we formulate new ones on the spot" (25). Historically, our definitions of art have come from individuals defined as experts in the field. Day-to-day experiences of individuals not necessarily deemed "expert" also become part of specific definitions. As such, definitions of art and the usefulness they hold in any given context are measures of a degree of historical relatedness and a reflection of complex cultural and social associations and assumptions.

Toulmin (1972) provides a helpful examination of the "problem of intellectual evolution" or on what occasions and by what processes people are willing to change existing definitions (343). In a discussion related to the philosophy of science, Toulmin compares the view of *justification* to the view of *discovery*. Each refers to a formal system of how we sort, define, classify and evaluate experience or information. The view of justification involves the development of a priori frameworks against which we can predict what will fit—things that cannot be justified are not considered. The view is based on a belief that objects and experiences have inherent properties. As a result, it tends to maintain the status quo and appear exclusive. Suspicion of the power of justification arose in the philosophy of science with the number of anomalies identified that would not fit in prescribed frameworks. Acknowledgement of anomalies led to the development of another view— that of discovery. The context of discovery involves development of frameworks against which we can compare: things that do not seem to fit are analyzed as anomalies, or discoveries, with the potential to expand existing perspectives. This view concentrates more on dynamic flexible characteristics and promotes an emergent growth of knowledge. The issue of evaluation is integral to this discussion. In each case, there is an existing tradition and some kind of innovation. By what process are some things selected to be included and others not? On what occasions do humans change their ideas? The justification position assumes an underlying framework of truth: an explanation of the world, whether complete or not, that provides a constant measure for all eventualities. The discovery position, on the other hand, assumes an underlying framework of adequacy: a construction of the world in a given time and place, subject to continual revision.

The difference can be summarized with a perspective gained from the study of cultural anthropology that suggests we are not "in the world" (for example, the world of art) but rather in one understanding of it. Learning any organized body of knowledge involves learning a language of theory and the scope of application of that theory. Within the context of discovery, the problem of change and expanding ideas becomes not just one of warring camps but one of uniting different world views.

More recently, theorists who propose a social construction of reality (Foucault, 1984; Geertz, 1973; Lakoff, 1987; Lakoff & Johnson, 1980; Parker & Pollack, 1981; Ricoeur, 1981) view the process of definition as the study of "entire domains of experience and not in terms of isolated concepts" (Lakoff & Johnson, 1980, 117). Rather than basing definition on examination of the inherent properties of experiences and objects, a metaphorical view of definition is proposed which seeks to understand the interactional properties of experiences and objects—how things function in peoples lives. Alpert (1990) elaborates in relation to definitions of art:

A society's inclusions and exclusions of meaning are an expression of its beliefs, prejudices, and political organization— its ideology. The full meaning of any word is not encompassed by any set of (graphic) letters. The meaning of "a-r-t" also comes from what [I view] it is not: [for example] "art" is not "a-c-t" or "a-r-m" or "a-r-t-i-s-a-n." Thus, the meaning of a word carries with it some ghosts of what it is not ([I believe] it is this, not that) and its meaning(s) change in relation to other words and meanings in its proximity. [We can extend this argument further, so that] when I say "art" I may be thinking of something like a "painting" on a canvas. I am, at some level [which may be conscious or unconscious], simultaneously thinking about what is not art: [for example, I may believe that] art is not pornography, or art is not politics, or art is not advertising. (2)

Lakoff provides an additional perspective: "Most categorization is automatic and unconscious, and if we become aware of it at all, it is only in problematic cases" (6). Fortunately, computer art provides such a case.

### Changing Definitions of Art and Artist

Definitions of art as a special category imply related definitions of artist as a specialized individual. Each is socially determined and includes attention to patterns of education, work environment and social milieu. As I have demonstrated elsewhere, the social/ cultural separations inherent in traditional categories of art and artist are not always reflected when particular profiles of individuals working in creative ways with computers are examined (Ettinger, 1990; Ettinger, 1981; Ettinger & Jones, 1981). Questions addressed in this section focus on the relationships that exist between conceptions of art and artist. In particular, I focus on interactional properties of computer art that allow conceptions of art and artist to be constructed that are very different from those with which we are familiar.

In order to think about the ways in which the category computer art promotes reflection on conceptions of art and artist, it is helpful to begin with an existing definition. Franke provides a definition of computer art that has been quoted frequently: "A work of computer art will be understood here as being any aesthetic formation which has arisen on the basis of logical or numerical transposition of given data with the aid of electronic mechanism" (7). Franke's definition encompasses many possibilities and allows inclusion of not only computer images and objects that resemble conventional drawing, painting, photography and sculpture, but more importantly, also such things as electronically mediated, three dimensional video environments, interactive displays and multi-media events. However, from a distance of nearly twenty years, Franke's definition may hinder development of innovative conceptions of art and artist in that it continues to focus attention on computer art as object. Such a focus results in an all too common attitude that asks why artists should use computers to arrive at visual effects costing much less in traditional media. If the goal is merely the creation of an art object, a positive response may sometimes be difficult to justify.

But computer art both promotes and allows a different focus. Another departure point for a definition of computer art is provided by Krueger (1983), who writes that "the best way to integrate the computer and the arts is to focus on the aesthetic process rather than on producing a finished work of art. Emphasis should be on exploring the universe of alternatives that the computer can provide" (186-187). This "universe of alternatives" refers to the creative design of various kinds of interactive electronic environments. In other words, the value of computer art may rest in the human need that is attended to and the aesthetic experience that may be derived from a situation, i.e., a particular art context or environment. Attention is focused on the ways people act and interact within the art context, not on an object. Emphasis is placed on individuals' evolutionary and reciprocal processes of making and experiencing.

As a way to focus attention on a context of experience, rather than on an art object, Krueger (1983) introduces an idea he terms the "Responsive Environment" as a new model for art. He writes:

The Responsive Environment was conceived as a new art form. It represents a unique melding of aesthetics and technology in which creation is dependent on a collaboration between the artist and the participant. The artist composes a network of aesthetic response relationships. The participant explores this universe....The art form is the composed interaction between human and machine, mediated by the artist. (xiii)

The characteristic that differentiates computer art as defined by Krueger from most other forms of art is that it incorporates the role of audience in a dynamic and integral way allowing an individualized construction of the definition and experience of art. In other words, this kind of art is not passively experienced but can be manipulated by an audience in simple or complex ways. And as audiences participate in the work they function simultaneously in ways that are like the artist.

To more clearly examine the potential of such art experiences, Krueger (1983) presents *Metaplay*, a responsive video art environment exhibited in a traditional space at the Memorial Union Gallery in 1970 (18). *Metaplay* was an attempt to integrate visual, aural and responsive conditions. The art work consisted of a large room in which participants' actions were monitored by a computer: "Traditional criteria of art, beauty, and responsive subtlety were set aside. The focus was on the interaction itself and on the participant's awareness of the interaction" (18). Krueger describes the setting:

The sequence of events started with a group of six to eight people entering the darkened Environment. The lights were brought up and their projected video images became visible. The typical audience reaction at this point was surprising. Often, faced by the large screen where the only active element was their own image, people would sit down and watch. Large screen video projection was apparently undreamed of by many of the participants. We therefore allowed at least a minute for time just to appreciate the phenomenon. After the initial awe was overcome, one of the interactions would ensue. These were terminated by the lights dimming and the artist writing 'Good-bye', or the equivalent. (25)

One of the more popular interactions was learning to control the movement of one's own reflection, resulting in a path on the video screen described as "drawing." The initiating artist, sitting in a room some distance away from the gallery, was able to see and interact with the reflection of the image of the audience. The artist could draw, for example, on the reflection of a hand. Through an interactive and responsive process, artist and audience learned to control the way lines were drawn. Only the simplest rudimentary drawings were possible, but "neither the facilitator nor the audience was ever concerned by the limitations of the drawings. What excited people was the interacting in this peculiar way through a video-human-computer communication link spanning a mile" (Krueger, 1983, 25). The innovative ingredient in this kind of art experience—and the one that appeals to me most as an art educator—is an apparent heightened sense of commitment and responsibility felt among participants, artist and audience alike. Once these elements begin to be present in any experience, individuals build an investment and a sense of ownership. Art, defined in this light, becomes an inquiry model, a tool for the exploration and critical examination of cognition as human practice. At this point, the distinctions between "artist" and "critic" also begin to dissolve.

In a more recent example, Makkuni (1989) presents an electronic sketchbook project. He explains:

The electronic sketch book of Tibetan Thangka painting project is conceived as a way of using computing and video representations to preserve Thangka imagery and the cultural context in which it is created, and as a way to use these presentations to reveal the process of composing Thangkas. The project is a collaborative effort between Senge Lama, one of the last two living artists of the 'Karma Gadri' style of Thangka painting, Xerox researchers, the curators of the Asian Art Museum of San Francisco, and the Tibetan community. The sketch book, according to its designers, has two roles: a passive preservation role and an active dissemination role. In the passive role the sketch book takes form as a chronicle, an audiovisual diary of Thangka imagery like its traditional predecessors expressed by manuscript illuminations and narrative paintings. In the active role, the sketch book is a medium of transmission, connecting the Thangka master and beginning painters mediating between painters and the records in the diary in electronic form, and re-integrating the historical practice with contemporary tools. (227-228)

Because the computer allows recording of both the programming used to develop the sketchbook and the compositional process of making a Thangka painting, Makkuni writes "video representations introduce into the craft environment a medium that is fundamentally about process. Along with static diagrams and sketches, the sketch book collected action sequences in which craftsmen create Thangkas. Beginning painters or spectators can replay the scenes and experience them, almost as if they were actually present with the master, and thus learn the craft by re-enacting process" (234). Here, too, the unique characteristics of computer art are presented for consideration, including the ability not only to document visual information but also to interact with and manipulate it. If the interaction properties of this electronic sketchbook were critiqued, attention could focus on the ways that people interact with the sketchbook, allowing examination of the social context of aesthetic experience.

Another kind of responsive environment is the cybernetic jewelry made by Reed (1988): "Although jewelry has historically been equated with hardware, the advent of the single-chip CMOS microcomputer allows a redefinition in terms of software. A radically different new kind of jewelry is presented, based on liquid crystal display (LCD) graphics controlled by an on board microcomputer" (27). Reed defines an "information age jewel," informed by the character of the interactive video. Simplified geometric images, represented on an LCD, are able to change in response to external conditions. Reed states:

The interactive nature of computer technology makes it fairly simple to use data input from external sources, such as switches, keyboards, or sensors, to modify the execution of the program, and thus the visual appearance of the jewel. Visual output in such a system could be determined by brain waves and barometric pressure, for instance, combining to alter program execution. (30).... At the far reaches of conjecturing, we may anticipate such things as the application of artificial intelligence principles and non-invasive nerve signal receptors to create a 'bionic paradigm', which will blur the distinction between the jewel and its wearer/operator. (33)

Reed's computer jewelry is an excellent example of the ways in which the computer is highlighting the shifting of traditional categories concerning the definition of art and artist. Is this "cybernetic jewelry" most at home in the area of medicine, aesthetics or self-help psychology? Is there a need to place it in any one of these categories more than another? Does cybernetic jewelry suggest another way of conceptualizing art and artist?

*Changing Definitions of Art Critic and Audience*

Just as the computer is impacting the ways in which we categorize and define art and artist, it also affects the ways in which we think about the art critic. Questions addressed in this section focus on the changing roles of the critic in relation to computer art. In particular, I focus on the shift of the larger category of audience from a peripheral role to a central one, i.e., an integrated position.

Assisting varied audiences with ways of experiencing or understanding art has been a shared responsibility, assumed in recent history by a relatively small number of individuals defined as experts, including art educators, art historians and art critics. But computer art has not generated a large part of the critical (or historical) discussion in traditional art world literature. A cursory review of eighteen pages of the Art Index from November 1984 to October 1989, scanning the descriptors computer graphics, computer industry, computer input-output equipment, computers (advertising, archaeological applications, architectural, engineering and planning applications, design applications, museum and art gallery applications, photographic applications, typesetting and printing processes) reveals only one article specifically devoted to some aspect of computer art, one article in a search of three key journals including *Art in America*, *Artforum*, and *ARTnews* (Gardner, 1985). It has been suggested that computer art is too young to judge, that this fledgling visual form must mature before it can be fairly evaluated in terms of its merits. However, this argument is based on a justification point of view as described earlier and seems to be a poor position, one that only leads to a blinded view of current events. During this same time period, no fewer than twenty-seven articles on the topic appeared in one journal alone, *Leonardo: Arts, Sciences, and Technology*. Even twenty years ago Franke stated that "nowadays it is almost impossible to keep track of the literature on computer art" (71); but this literature is not found where artists and art critics have traditionally been trained to look. Computer art of the type described by Krueger is more likely to be encountered in a video arcade, an interdisciplinary research center, a city planning office or Disneyland than in an art museum or art gallery. Talk about computer art is more likely to be found

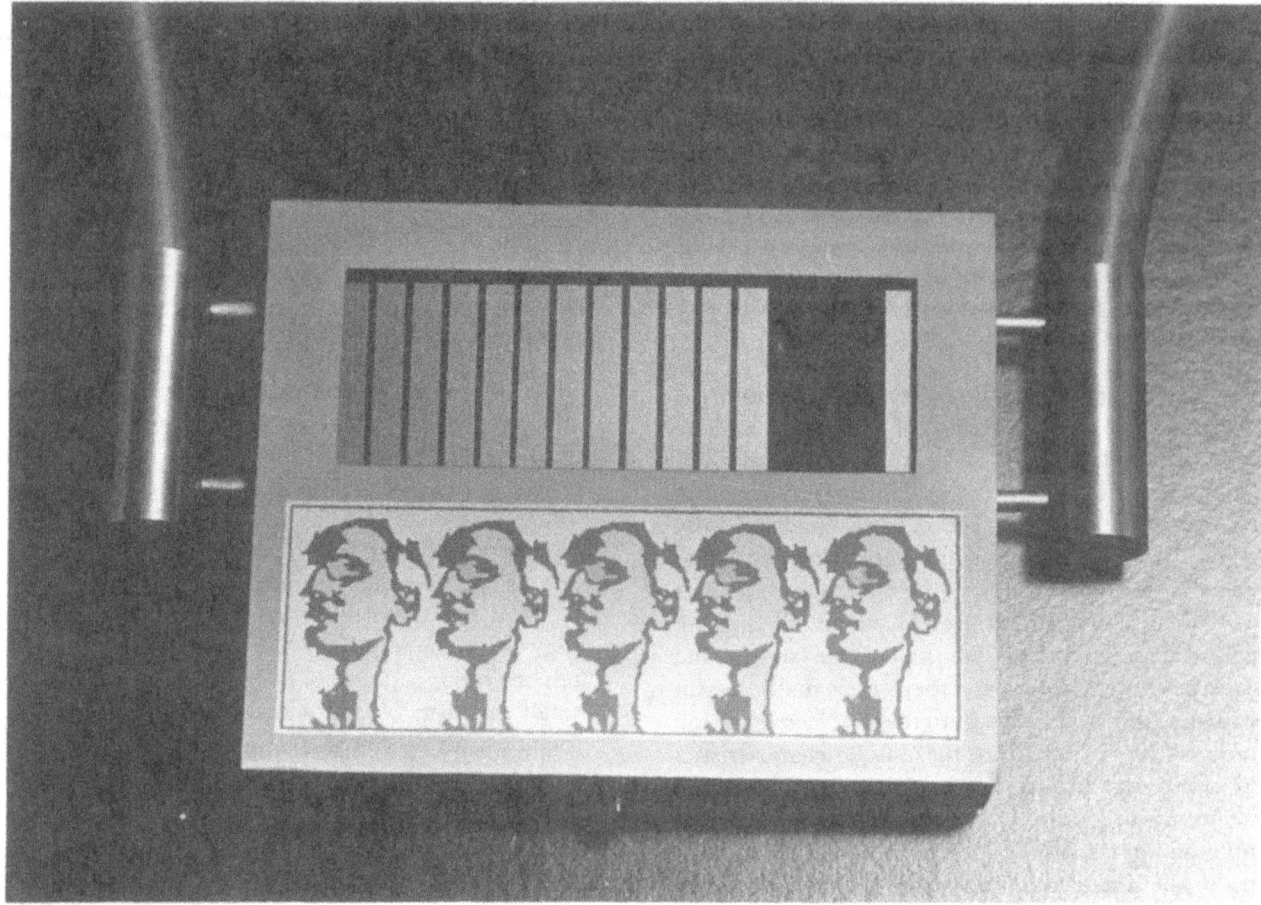

"Alien Day: Cybernetic Neckpiece." Photograph by Vernon Reed.

in journals and other forums that address questions of technology and in new journals eager to expand a narrowly conceived art market.

The reasons for this situation are not mysterious. Along with changing definitions of art and artist comes a need for expanded terminology in order to engage in critical dialogue. Examination of formal qualities of art as defined in the nineteenth century is not sufficient for critical investigation today. For example, Krueger (1983) lists "responsive environs," "intimate technology" and "artificial reality" as important aesthetic concepts for consideration within a larger electronic environment. Other authors refer to the dynamic visual qualities of graphic computer art including rotation, interpolation, transformation, iteration, real-time, animation and interaction (Rivlin, 1986; Kerlow & Rosebush, 1987). Each of these terms refers to an aspect of computer art with unique meanings and associations. Two examples of computer art selected from the 1988 Association for Computer Machinery, Special Interest Group: Graphics (ACM SIGGRAPH) Film and Video Show catalog exemplify the situation. Haxton (1988) of the Center for Computer Art and Animation, William Paterson College, describes "The Art Dream" as
Center for Computer Art and Animation, William Paterson College, describes "The Art Dream" as:

a fantasy journey through a series of 20th century paintings. A modern art book opens, and the paintings on each page become 3-D. In reality, these paintings are 2-D. In "The Art Dream," the viewer sees a 3-D world through the use of computer generated models derived from the original paintings.... "The Art Dream" was produced with Alias I software on Silicon Graphics IRIS computers. (12)

Sabiston (1988) of the Visible Language Workshop, MIT Media Laboratory, describes "Beat Dedication" as:

a personalized rock video for my ten year old brother with a new drum set. It's the story of a stainless steel puck drummer and his arch-enemy, the Killer Volkwagen Fly. The animation can be computed to accompany any song. My soundtrack interpreter reads MIDI information from a synthesizer and uses it to generate animation keyframes; hence, the drummer's movements are automatically synchronized to the music. (13)

Not only new terms but new attitudes must become part of the criticism of these kinds of works. For instance, each of these examples was produced by a group of people rather than an individual. Critics need to be able to talk about collaboration as central to this type of creative process. Although collaboration as a part of process in the visual arts is not new, as clearly evidenced in the areas of architecture and theater, acceptance of the values and attitudes reflected in the collaborative process has yet to become an integral part of the world of fine art (Ettinger & Hoffman, 1990). An appropriate model is suggested by McCormick, DeFanti, and Brown (1987) in a special publication on scientific visualization. They recommend "a new initiative in Visualization in Scientific Computing to get visualization tools into 'the hands and minds' of scientists" (vii). Their strategy requires an acceptance of the notion of teams of individuals, including visual artists, as necessary to address all kinds of inquiry, including art, in a multidimensional manner.

At the same time, questions of identification and attribution of computer art come up. If computer art is created by groups of people, who can lay claim to ownership? Who is credited with the idea? Whole new areas of art law have developed around these questions. Jones (1989) addresses the complexity of just one issue: "Extensive use of digitally scanned images of painting, photographs, film and video assure that many creators of computer imagery deal directly with issues such as appropriation, blurring of authorship, dematerialization of the art object, and questioning the relation of 'original' to copy" (36).

Linehan (1976) writes of the changing criteria for evaluation of computer art. His concern is with a shift from "a stable, non-changing piece of material to a changing, progressively dematerializing expression of an aesthetic idea" (6). Linehan asks: "As physical structure dematerializes into conceptual structure, there are inherent problems for the critic. What is to be criticized, the fading ghost of matter, or the emerging aura of concept?" (6). Linehan also proposes that critical dialogue of this kind of art should not be based on nineteenth century formalist criteria, but should utilize what he describes as "means-end criteria" in order to examine an aesthetic system as a complex experience:

A systems design method demands an elaborate plan—one in which goals, objectives, and the interaction of components is specified. Options within the system are clearly delineated, and the interaction of components is specified. The systems artist (acting like an aesthetic manager or an aesthetic systems engineer) leaves 'tracks' throughout the planning process in the form of flow charts, computer programs, and testing results. Consequently there is data on which the design process can be determined and evaluated.... While ultimately it is the 'aesthetic outcome' which needs to be evaluated by the critic, a systems view would argue the necessary interconnectedness of outcome with the design and planning process. (8-9)

## Conclusion

The purpose of this essay has been to focus on a particular characteristic of computer art—the aspect of interactivity—in a way that highlights the potential of computer art to change definitions of art, artist, critic and audience. I have viewed the category of computer art, in the words of McHale, "as one aspect of the transformative changes through which we are passing on our way to the future" (63). People are becoming more and more familiar with various forms of high technology that have been designed and structured as mediators in many areas of daily experience (i.e., banking, communicating, cooking). Computer art requires a new conceptualization, one that focuses on art as connected experience rather than art as isolated product. Nadin (1989) posits: "Against the background of the digital (i.e., of the information and symbol-processing paradigm), we arrive at the realization of the need to consider art in its interrelations with all other products of human activity" (46).

We have emerged from a time when art is defined and categorized as something separate from society. Computer art offers the opportunity to view art as integrated and connected with other social structures. In the creation of art in the form of Krueger's "Responsive Environs," networks of possibilities are composed. Each decision an artist makes in the development of a responsive environment is recorded by the computer and can be reviewed, analyzed and re-directed. Krueger (1985) states: "An obvious next step invites the audience to participate and actually influence events" (150). This potential implies a new relationship among the categories of artist and art critic. People can participate in an active dialogue not possible with other forms of art. By focusing attention on one's role within a larger environment, participants personalize the experience and formulate meaning; they function as creators. The experiencing of an art environment can be recorded and reviewed as part of an interactive process. Although one individual may start any given interaction, the continuing dialogue becomes the creative purview of all. In other words, participants function as artist and critic. Previously distinct roles blend in a way that all parties can assume creative control and make aesthetic decisions based on their own interests and insights.

Just the tip of the iceberg of the potential for this kind of experience to have a powerful effect on people's lives is evident when we look at the large numbers of individuals today who enjoy video games. Turkle (1984) examines dynamic participation and what she terms the "holding power" of interactive video games. She sees interactive computing as compelling because a condition is established which "creates the condition for other things to happen" (14). Turkle compares the idea of holding power to the concept of "flow" as described by Csikszentmihalyi: "Psychologist Csikszentmihalyi studied people's inner states while pursuing activities that appear to contain rewards in themselves—chess, rock climbing, dance, sports, surgery. He discovered that central to all of them is an experience which he calls 'flow.' Its most marked characteristic is the 'merging of action and awareness' " (338). Forman (1987) is also interested in the phenomena of interactive video and whether it promotes the making of more deliberate choices, specifically among young children. He states: "Interactive video is now available to millions of children. Is it better than anything it replaces? Can we identify unique aspects of the video medium itself that represent an advantage over previous media?" (233). Forman answers this question in the affirmative, focusing on the attitude of reflection he says video environments promote. Through observation of children interacting with one another and a video game and children interacting with one another and a setting of real objects, Forman concludes that children tend to pause, reflect, experiment, review, analyze, evaluate and cooperate more frequently in the video mediated situation. In particular, he suggests that use of the "record and replay" mode encourages the kind of contemplation and reflection that has been described as supportive of critical thinking. He concludes:

We are only in the beginning stages of understanding the advantages of interactive video media....How interesting it would be for children to see a rerun of their own shadow as cast in profile or with their face to the light source. They could slow it down or speed it up to gain a better understanding of how their own body moves when kicking, batting, or doing a cartwheel. These are but a few derivations from self-object distancing that have implications for the education of young children. (242)

When individuals categorized as scientists, mathematicians, engineers, artists and viewers learn to work together to produce what they and others readily describe as aesthetically pleasing visual images, our cultural notions of what art is, who artists are and the role of art critics are brought into question. I agree whole heartedly with McHale's position that "the future of art, therefore seems not to lie so much with the creation of enduring masterworks but, in part, with the exploration and definition of alternative social and cultural directions" (62). As an art educator, I have witnessed the kind of alienation that can result from art defined and categorized as an exclusive visual object, produced and interpreted by specialized experts with limited appeal for a narrowly defined audience. Rather than accept this situation as "the way art is," I look to other definitions in which art is viewed as a central part of people's lives. Critics of computer art, at this point primarily the producers and consumers of various kinds of electronic imagery, have the opportunity to examine this art as a dynamic and integrated component of a larger information-based society.

# Works Cited

Alpert, L. Feminist art criticism: Issues, assumptions, & lived experience. *Controversies in Art & Culture, 3*(1), (1990): 1-12.

Ettinger, L.F. Portrait of a secondary teacher. *The Computing Teacher, 9*(2), (1981): 49-50.

Ettinger, L.F. *Why manager's need visual education: How oral histories inform curriculum design.* Manuscript in progress. (1990).

Ettinger, L.F. & Hoffman, E. Quilt making in art education: Toward a participatory curriculum metaphor. *Art Education, 43*(4), (1990): 40-47.

Ettinger, L.F. & Jones, B.J. Portrait of a high school student. *The Computing Teacher, 9*(3), (1981): 55-57.

Forman, G.E. Computer graphics as a medium for enhancing reflective thinking in young children. In D.N. Perkins, J. Lochhead, & J. Bishop (Eds.), *Thinking: The Second International Conference,* Hillsdale, NJ: Lawrence Erlbaum Associates, (1987): 233-243.

Foucault, M. In *The Foucault reader.* Rabinow, P., (Ed.). New York: Pantheon Books. (1984).

Franke, H.W. *Computer graphics computer art.* London: Phaidon P. (1971).

Fratto, T.F. Undefining art: Irrelevant categorization in the anthropology of aesthetics. *Dialectical Anthropology, 3,* (1978): 129-138.

Gardner, P. The electronic palette. *Art News, 84* (2), (1985): 66-73.

Geertz, C. *Interpretation of cultures.* New York: Basic Books. (1973).

Hanson, N.R. *Perception and discovery: An introduction to scientific inquiry.* San Francisco: Freeman, Cooper & Company. (1969).

Haxton, D. The art dream. In A. Slate (Ed.), *ACM SIGGRAPH'88: Film and Video Show Catalog,* (1988): 12.

Jones, B.J. Computer imagery: Imitation and representation of realities. *Leonardo Supplemental Issue, ACM SIGGRAPHII1989,* (1989): 31-38.

Kerlow, V. & Rosebush, J. *Computer graphics for designers and artists.* New York: Van Nostrand Reinhold. (1987).

Krueger, M.W. *Artificial reality.* Reading, MA: Addison Wesley. (1983).

Krueger, M.W. *Videoplace*: A report from the artificial reality lab. *Leonardo, 18*(3), (1985): 141-151.

Lakoff, G. *Women, fire, and dangerous things: What categories reveal about the mind.* Chicago: U of Chicago P. (1987).

Lakoff, G. & Johnson, M. *Metaphors we live by.* Chicago: U of Chicago P. (1980).

Linehan, T. An investigation of criteria for evaluating computer art. *Computer Graphics and Art,* (1976): 6-9.

Makkuni, R. The electronic sketch book of Tibetan Thangka painting. *The Visual Computer, 5,* (1989): 227-242.

McCormick, B.H., DeFanti, T., & Brown, M.D. Visualization in scientific computing. *Computer Graphics, 21*(6). (1987).

McHale, J. The future of art and mass culture. *Leonardo, 12*, (1979): 59-64.

Nadin, M. Emergent aesthetics—aesthetic issues in computer arts. *Leonardo Supplemental Issue, ACM SIGGRAPHI/1989*, (1989): 43-48.

Parker, R. & Pollack, G. *Old mistresses: Women, art and ideology.* New York: Pantheon Books. (1981).

Reed, V. Cybernetic jewelry: Ornament for the information age. *The Visual Computer, 4*, (1988): 27-34.

Ricoeur, P. *Hermeneutics and the human sciences.* (J.B. Thompson, Ed. and Trans.). Cambridge: Cambridge U P. (1981).

Rivlin, R. *Graphic visions of the computer age: The algorithmic image.* Redmond, WA: Microsoft P. (1986).

Sabiston, B. Beat dedication. In A. Slate (Ed.), *ACM SIGGRAPH '88: Film and Video Show Catalog*, (1988): 13.

Toulmin, S. *Human understanding: The collective use and evolution of concepts.* Princeton: Princeton U P. (1972).

Turkle, S. *The second self: Computers and the human spirit.* New York: Simon and Schuster. (1984).

# The Poetics of Green Esthetics:
## Situating "Green Criticism" in the Postmodern Condition

## jan jagodzinski

*A Global Vignette*

The prospects of living in the "Greenhouse World" of the twenty-first century are almost too horrible to contemplate. Consider the following: Gaea's ozone level continues to erode; two large holes or 'tears' in the stratosphere have now been discovered, eliminating part of the Gaea's protective shield against the sun's deadly ultra-violet radiation.[1] If the percentage of carbon dioxide in the atmosphere continues to increase, then by the year 2050 Gaea's annual average temperature will climb anywhere between five and fifteen degrees Fahrenheit, affecting every organism on her surface. Large tracts of the east and west coast of North America will be submerged under water, not so much because the glacial ice will begin to melt but because the oceans will rise as the warm water begins to expand. Presently, a species becomes extinct every thirty seconds. The great forests on her skin are dying, thousands of forest fires are visible from satellite pictures sent from the Amazon rain forest. When Gaea's human population doubles in the next few decades to eight billion, food shortages will become an acute problem; presently, sixteen percent of the world's population goes to bed hungry.

Depending on which accounting system is used, between fifty and eighty percent of all scientific experimentation in the United States is military-based. Between eighty and ninety percent of the world's resources are used up by Japan and America, the leaders of the capitalist spearhead. Whether one calls it *new age politics* (Satin, 1978), an *Aquarian conspiracy* (Ferguson, 1980), *postmodern science* (Rifkin, 1984), *ecofeminism* (Griffin, 1988), *ecology for freedom* (Bookchin, 1981), *Green Peace ethics* (Porritt, 1984) or *ecosophy* (Drengson, 1983), these responses form the strands of a global political consciousness which argues for alternate ethical, political, economic and esthetic solutions to the domination of scientism, capitalism and communism. The nuclear, ecological, gender and racial issues continue to shrink spaceship Earth. Globally, the hegemony of the two superpowers is breaking up as nations under their sway begin to find their own cultural identity. The standard of living and the meaning of progress and development in these countries is no longer measured in terms of Gross National Product, indicating the material wealth a country is able to consume, rather social values and social services are becoming the new indicators of the "good" (Nicaragua, for example). The U.S. and Japan are not held up by Eastern Europe as *the* progressive "democratic" models of leadership. Patriarchy, too, is under question as women become more and more conscious of their oppression. Globally in terms of outright numbers these movements are marginal. However, in terms of potential impact the growing "ecological" myth is attempting to displace what Lyotard (1984) has termed the "grand narrative" of the West: progress, production, profit, capitalism, domination through centralization, the scale of bigness and massive accumulation (i.e., multinationalism, nuclear power). What I have described above is certainly an alarmist view, one which is meant to shock and stun and hold the reader's attention, for the bell toll has been sounded, a solitary note that continues to reverberate around the entire earth. As Suzuki recently called it, in a five-part series of radio broadcasts on the CBC, it is *A Matter of Survival.*[2]

*Esthetic Ecosophy:*
*Green Criticism and Deep Ecology*

It has been fashionable to be aware of semiology and deconstruction whenever cultural critique is attempted. The play of signs within language has put phallogocentrism to flight, cynicism becoming a common response to authority as we begin to recognize the rhetorics of representation used throughout the economy of signs. Just as physics has lost its paradigmatic status as the queen of the sciences, philosophy, as the search for Truth, has undergone a similar displacement. In a previous essay, "Toward an Ecological Aesthetic: Notes on a 'Green' Frame of Mind" (1988), I argued for the need of a new myth and the role that a particular strand of feminism played in that vision. Keeping this in mind, what follows is an attempt to steer an imaginative course between phenomenology and structuralism (Silverman, 1987), a course which is itself overlaid by a deconstruction of the masculine and feminine positionalities. *An aesthetic ecosophy of deep ecology is proposed.*

In the early 1970s, Naess (1973) made a distinction between "shallow environmentalism" and "deep ecology." This definition has been further extended and developed by him (1984) as well as a new generation of thinkers in the 1980s: Devall and Sessions (1985), Devall (1979, 1980, 1984). Tobias (1985), and Sessions (1987). Whereas former environmental groups were "anthropocentric" and failed to sufficiently challenge the values of advanced industrial societies, this later movement was an attempt to "level" the separation between Nature and humans at the apex of creation. A "biospherical egalitarianism" or a "soft anthropometricism" has been promoted that would extend equal rights to all living things. A greater sensitivity to the degrees of encephalization, that is, to the degree that a living organism can willfully change its ecological niche, is required. Whales and porpoises, after all, have greater encephalization than sharks. How human beings are to relate to each species requires our attention at the level of an ecosophy. What should be the impending harmony or equilibrium with all creatures "big and small"? Further, how can we change not only our dominance over things but develop a sense of self that goes beyond the possessive individualism of the Englightenment—the individual bent on "having" and "experiencing" it all? Holistic thinking and self-realization, by being locally and globally interlinked and interrelated to the Other, including the nonhuman, requires walking a "path" of least resistance, one that "does not tear the rice paper" as the *koan* states, a path which would have minimal impact on the Other's being (Snyder, 1974). It calls for a new ascetic way of life, one which is mindful of the use value of all consumables in relation to the well-being of the living Earth. To ecosophize such a possibility is to both essentialize and, at the same time, to deconstruct the language of formalist criticism as it pertains to green esthetics and green consciousness in our current historical moment. The jargon of this project is difficult to avoid. My overall intention is to present six econtological esthetic realms in terms of deep ecology and a green poetics in order to demonstrate how they interrelate us to living systems. My project attempts to re-write the familiar aesthetic language of line, color, texture, size, mass and space which, from a modernist perspective, is often translated as a functionalist aesthetic free of social analysis for the economic exploitation of natural resources.

The first three dimensions relate to the local *immediate environment* and are associated with the *oikos* as the feminine pre-Oedipal levels of aesthetic experiences.[3] The next three are global. These relate to the *demos* and are associated with the Oedipal masculine realm. Characteristically these realms have been separate spheres, critiqued by many feminists as the separation between nature/culture and public/private. The values of the masculine realm have dominated Enlightenment rhetoric and encouraged dominance over the Other. It is hoped that green criticism is able to deconstruct this hierarchy by enacting, a by now familiar ruse: "to act locally and think globally." It is this imaginative global vision which projects such politics out of the realm of mere resistance. Underlying this personal vision is also the conviction that ethical and political "ground" might be formed from a green poetics. Criticism which oscillates between the local and the global must have a base that paradoxically floats on the water of life. The myth must tie together the material of the human body with all other bodies throughout the Earth. To make the esthetic dimension a meaningful lived experience, rather than a modernist category of experience confined to the picture frame or stage, these six econtological dimensions shall be described as they permeate lived life. I am suggesting, therefore, that there are at the very least six levels of ethical and political ways of being "green." We may operate on one or more of these levels depending on the site/cite/sight we find ourselves in. Each of these dimensions is informed by a binary opposition which is characteristically masculine and feminine. The tension of this opposition always calls on us to problematize the "difficulty" of life, the difficulty of choices in the historical context that we live in today. I perceive these binary oppositions, therefore, to be the extreme states of the body which inform experience (*Erlebnis*), holding our esthetic "skin" in dialectical tension, neither side of the opposition entirely erasing nor transcending the other, as ends and the questioning of those ends. Lived esthetic experience occurs in this dialectical gap between these binary oppositions. It is the space of play, of risk, and creativity—the poetics of green consciousness.

*An Esthetic Daydream:*
*The Poetics of Green Esthetics*

*Three Pre-Oedipal Realms of Esthetic Experience*

*The Esthetics, Ethics and Politics of Line:*
*Lived Experience of Directionality and the tensions of being both lost and found*

The spacial-temporal experience of "line" is continually informed by the body's negotiation between becoming *lost* and finding a *direction.* Human journeys are always packed by ambiguity, paradox and, above all, surprise. It is the feeling that new vistas, new elevations, new edges are always presenting themselves as each step is taken. Constructing an argument during a conversation, following a melody in music, creating a path through the dance of the body, all have a ground from which they began, a paradoxical point of origin that cannot be found but exists originally in chaos, in nothingness. As such, all lines, all directions, are *traces*. They are the whispers of conversations past, of memories linked together, held in a mist of relationships. Lines are segments, fragments whose ends trail off into the extremes of their own horizons. Each representative instance of creative freedom and intuitive exploration begins with a point and a direction. *Line is directionality*. It is a crisscross informed by both the feminine and masculine presence, held in binary tension through the interaction of the horizontal and the vertical within the labyrinth of thought. Line is always hesitant, formed from the chaos of differences.

When one thinks of the energy transfer of the life line, the complementarity which must occur between opposites to generate life, then the telephone wire and the electric cord are analogous to Nature's umbilical cord, the root, the blood vessel; all are instances of the transference of life—the need to exchange a message across and between borders, frames and barriers where the inside now has become the outside and the outside now has become the inside. When there is no purpose or meaning to life, one's existence becomes directionless, empty, lifeless. The borders are closed. Noise sets in. Thermic death is always possible when no breathing is allowed. Such are experiences when circumstances do not allow the risk to take place, no gasp permitted.

Putting one's consciousness "on the line," walking on the edge or on a tight-rope, is the esthetic experience which animates us. Tightrope walkers, downhill racers, mountain climbers and car racers continually put their life on the line since at any time the human risk-taking may snap. In conversation, it is only through the question that a "way" may be created, the journey activated, an intentional arc bridged with the Other. Yet, the question may stun the body in its rhetorical force. In music, the creation of "noise" indicates that one has become lost, but this clamor and violence of noise points us to the very limits of our previous harmonics. It indicates the strains of human emotion and social response (Attali, 1985). Order and Noise are the obverse sides of the same coin. Mistakes, on the other hand, surprise both the player and the listener from the well-defined path. They are the lived life between tonality and atonality. The "rap" song of life can always be found, but this inner song— *inner Klang* as Kandinsky (1912) called it—can be silenced if we are led to believe that a proper musical vocabulary is necessary for its reception (McClary, 1985). For it is the tone, the tension (Latin: *tonus*—tension; Greek: *tonus*—the act of stretching)

of the voice, of the line, which helps to communicate our inner "soul." It is the "pitch"—as when one throws out a message—which gives a line that must be grasped and authentically heard. The singer and poet give voice (*Sagen*) from and to the depths of this Being. Falsetto, soprano, baritone, bass and silence, the cadence of the human voice reveals the tonality of the experiences which hide behind its calling.

The voice should maintain the oral tradition of leaders, peace-makers, prophets and visionaries. Their voices should lead us "out" to dialogue. Since all conversational journeys start from a point (in the double meaning of the term: as a direction and as a starting mark), friends of the Earth must make a moral choice as to which line shall be taken. Such a choice, claimed Fromm (1981), might lead to civil disobedience for the cause of justice. The heretic must expose and unveil. Green leadership requires a conscious awareness as to the direction the journey will take. The *oikoumental* good to be achieved must be informed by the tradition chosen.[4] The ethics of line, of direction, requires an inescapable eschatology, a philosophy of history as *progress in social relationships* as opposed to enlightened progress in technological and material innovation.

How should environmentalists throw out lifelines to the Earth in their care? Should their bridges be different depending on the location? How then do we walk the earth gently? It seems we might learn something from indigenous populations. To cite/ sight/site one instance: when an oil pipeline was to be put in the MacKenzie River Valley in the Northwest Territories, the "carrying capacity" of the land was going to be affected. The Deni Nation hired their own anthropologist to study the land and the effects on fishing and trapping. These calculations contradicted those of the oil company's anthropologist. Justice Minister John Berger, to help settle the dispute, hired a government anthropologist who produced a third set of figures entirely in discord with the other two. Justice Minister Berger put a two year moratorium on the decision. Today the pipe line is being built. The traditional maps of the MacKenzie territories held by the Elders will become disrupted. A whole lifestyle will change. The politics of line, of direction, are the most difficult to determine. As a democracy, we believe that our government representatives have a direction. That direction has, since the Enlightenment, been one of economic growth, technological progress on the grounds that our Gross National Product reflected a standard of living that corresponded with a nation's happiness. But, as the above case highlights, such is not the case. What might be other alternatives? Can we find yet other ways?

One such posture is that of responsible "anarchy."[5] For a politics of direction it is crucial that the point itself, the *arche*, be questioned, otherwise line falls into nihilism and anaestheticism. Responsible anarchy is a deconstructive move, for it requires both that which is found, the law of the line, and that which is lost, as the claim of the Other. Yet, this is not enough, for there is a need to transgress ends, to have ends and to be aware of those ends. Deconstruction is therefore a double gesture. The politics of line is that we can do justice to that which is off-line, to defend the rights of the different, not those of the same. To claim responsibility of the Other is also a double gesture. When the lifeline is thrown out to the claim of the Other, it is done in recognition that their claim has been excluded. It is the experience of *difference*, of those "lost," not physically lost, but "absent" because they are not recognized in the Canon. Perhaps no other culture today is and was as sensitive to the ethics of line as the Australian Aborigines. Chatwin (1987) describes the "song lines" of their culture where their entire landscape had sacred meanings, where the names of children referred to certain birthing spots, where boundaries ended when a tribe's song stopped, only to be picked up by those living in the next territory. In our post-industrial society, borders are to be policed and guarded. They have lost their magic. If such borders are weakening, their re-territorialization is on economic grounds in order to compete in a larger market and not for symbiotic reasons to enrich life.

I remind the reader that it is from Gaea that we derive the subject of geography, the study of the lines of the Earth. Further, the study of *geomancy* is the divination by lines, while geology and geodesy are yet further derivatives. The grid of lines that encircle the Earth, latitudes and longitudes, were charted during Imperialist expansion. Perhaps the equator still holds a certain fascination. Certain points on the globe were magic in their "magnetism," but few of these points and lines are left. Certainly the mountains are there, as is the equator. Both the South and the North Poles continue to draw exploration and fascination. Yet it is above these very points that the very "tears" as "tears" in the stratosphere have been found. There is need to re-enchant the Earth, as Berman (1981) calls it. We are in dire need of a new geometry. East and West are arbitrary directions which need to be deconstructed, much as Said (1978) has done. The Mercator map has been shown to underemphasize Africa, the "dark continent" and overemphasize Europe, the "white continent;" hardly surprising given the context of its making. Rarely do we realize that the racism behind color forms such representations of the Earth. The satellite pictures of Gaea were the first to decenter the naivety of maps. A new projection is badly needed and we may indeed be on the edge of it given the changes in Eastern Europe and the emergence of new Western European alliances like that of both East and West Germany and the

lowering of trade borders throughout Europe in 1992. This then draws me to the next esthetic-ethical dimension.

## The Stain of Color and The Shade of Moods

A jump beyond living a line mentality is to consciously recognize the place of mood in our lives. A mood is like a blanket that covers us when we reflect upon a conversation that has been completed. It is a recalled memory that vivifies life. What is the color of the blanket that covers Gaea today? Her mood has been disturbed, from once Green to muddy Brown. Color stains the boundary of a thing. It binds and sustains the emergent properties. It completes their presence through harmony. It is the line turning to make a shape that conveys a self-contained totality, a thick idea which then presents itself in a certain shade or tint, as soprano, bass, baritone. This can only happen when the journey has been completed, fulfilled, as when the artist has said "Enough! This stands on its own." This color circle occurs when children "round" their dance movements, when rocks are placed in a circle to form a boundary and children call it their place. When any space is bounded, as in a circus ring, a wedding ring or a bell's ring, a centering of attention presents itself. The lived environment should also be perceived as a ring, a pitch, a place to center oneself; and periods could be colored fragments that make the day. Yet, there are stains and noises on the surface of Gaea's skin: human-made oil spills, industrial pollution, forest fires.

Personality is exposed color; and I ask, how has Gaea's personality changed? The tension between the binary oppositions of hot and cold, between laughing and crying, the extremes of our body's psychological and physiological tolerance, can only be maintained by "blanket" spaces. The blanket forms a canopy, a temporary space like a tent or igloo. The Earth's biosphere has been its canopy, one that has sheltered her and us from the harsh realities of the cosmos, yet now that canopy is at risk. The canopy of the great rain forests has been altered through corporate greed; there are now surveillance satellites and "space" junk which mar the trust for global communication. Spying, as the new patriarchal Eye, adds to the hermeneutics of suspicion. The glaze is one of surveillance.

What are the ethics of color? Has color lost all sense of spiritual symbolism as it once had among many indigenous peoples? Has it been appropriated only in the name of power and dominance—the colors of gravity denying eros? White, the color of the most powerful racial skin, has come to symbolize the clinical mind, the germ free, dust free, environment of high technology, the operating room and, of course, the labor room. What colors is our Earth undergoing? A thoughtless blending of all colors gives us a mud brown; its fragrance is not that of the living Earth, rather it has the stench of waste and decay. Does coolness and indifference by multinationals prevail? By 2005, industrial nations have called for a twenty percent reduction of carbon dioxide. Every year, since 1984 Mercedes Benz has violated the U.S. federal gas mileage standards. It has paid out $26 million in fines, but what is money when Exxon can spend $2 million just to run a full-page ad in American newspapers to cover up the environment damage of the oil spill by the Exxon Valdez.[6] The harmony of colors as in *difference* rather than as *in*difference can only bring about enrichment, for the dominant colors in Western Tradition have always been White and Gold. Racism celebrates clarity, purity—the intensity of the diamond instead of coal, and the unrefined stones at the common stock.

Take any area of the forest. Study the myriad shapes and colors of interconnectedness. What are the ethics of keeping it alive while recognizing its death? We are beginning to realize today that to keep life we must go to the margins to preserve it. Middle-sized frogs are dying north and south of the equators.[7] Niches which seem far away are affected by pollutants issuing from the centers. We need only think of acid rain and nuclear fallout to realize that there are no distances; there are only points, and these points are slowly changing colors; muting, fading as the "blood" is sucked out of them. Green has become symbolic of this "blood." With red as its complement, the edge between them shimmers in revival.

*Texture: The Lived Experience of the Home and Familiarity*

Texture forms the third level of the esthetic dimension. Texture is the conversation with "things" to enable one to know them intimately. It is the language of poetry, the adjectives and adverbs that form the ground of distinction. Texture is our personal communication with Nature's dialogue: it is the experience of craft which intimately binds our consciousness with Gaea's material consciousness; it is the potter in conversation with clay; it is the weaver in conversation with fibre; it is the lapidary maker in conversation with stone; it is the crafts tradition that is the very fabric of technology.[8] Texture touches. It is found within the palm of the hand and at the tips of the fingers. One cannot get closer to the Earth than through the touch of the hand. The grasp of the fingers presents an immediate response. The greatest amount of grey matter in the brain is dedicated to the hands. They play, they sensitize, they touch. *Texture is the exposed history of the "thing" embodied on its patina, worn like our skin.*

A home away from home suggests a cared for place. The dialectical tension between the binary opposition requires that we embrace everything we touch to make it a part of ourselves. We must avoid "breaking" or "marking" things. Historically, these appear to be signs of dominance. Repair embodies the ethics of texture, for in the art of repair there is mending, healing and love to keep a thing's essence alive. Texture is therefore deconstructing of our waste and decay. It is recognizing our own abjections. What we consume and dispose, both physically and mentally, allows us to grow. What we excrete from our minds and our bodies may be re-used and placed in new contexts. It is through our failures that we learn who we are. Repair is nurturing and healing. All living things require nurturing and healing if their life is to be preserved. Everything new demands that it be approached with a "soft" instrumentalism, gently prodded and closely felt.

Unquestionably, natural material leaves the mark of character. Leather, clay, wood, wool and organic fibers bear the wrinkles and blemishes left on them. They possess consciousness; plastics do not. Synthetic plastics do not take on a patina, a life; one is merely able to keep it longer and keep it looking like new longer, like a silicon breast. The experience of texture is left for the very rich—those who can afford to buy antiques, vintage cars and wines and purchase historical houses in need of restoration. The connoisseur, the aesthete, becomes our artistic expert in residence. Art preserves its élite status of "excellence." Rather than recognizing that the dimension of lived aesthetic experience is available for all, we have relinquished our power of discrimination to those who can claim extraordinary refinement. Yet everywhere we may find signs of creative "adhocism" (Jencks, 1973). What has been demeaned as folk, primitive and naïve art is where human creativity flowers through personal solutions to psychological and physical problems. Rather than *haute cuisine*, home-cooked meals and handed-down recipes provide the identity of a distinctive style, that "little bit extra" as is often said: natural brewed beer, organic food, the family restaurant which provides a distinctive taste.

All this, when compared with consumerism and fast food take outs, shows how impoverished this dimension has become. When you slurp through a straw from a MacDonald's plastic cup, it is a very one-dimensional experience. It becomes iconic of western functionality. You do not examine the color of the liquid you are drinking, nor would you want to for fear of being repulsed. Slurping it through a straw hardly makes the liquid linger in my mouth. Coke and Pepsi have manufactured our loss for the taste of pure water (the ramifications of this for health reasons are just too staggering to contemplate). Nor does grasping a plastic waxed paper cup hold a pleasant experience. Japanese tea ceremonies, Viennese coffee houses, and British pubs are reminiscent of what we have lost. Spaces now are meant to be occupied for a short time. Conversations are kept brief in such garish surroundings. If all this were otherwise, MacDonald's and companies like it would be out of business.

Western capitalism has denied us the textural dimension of the esthetic experience. Western capitalism has generated wants rather than needs, the *simulacra* of the commodity sign (Baudrillard, 1983). The corporate sector continues to commit the "sin" of gluttony. Waste is not recycled for further growth; rather, a consumer mentality of needless production is propagated. The history of things is eliminated. Repair, as the nurturing back to life of a thing, is being eliminated. Built in obsolescence is one way; throwing the thing away is another. As Jameson (1983, 1984) points out, in a post-modernist society everything is a pastiche of everything else. The self, as reflected by a well-defined artistic style, is gone.

*Three Oedipal Realms of Esthetic Experience*
*Size: The Lived Experience of Scale*

The question of size, of design, of theater, requires that the esthetic dimension reach out to a wider audience. The question of scale becomes important. The binary oppositions between the mega and the micro, between the megalithic and the miniature, inform the tension of a centered self who tries to mediate the superego through the psychological proportionality of things. This is a standing up to the Father. Both things and people larger than Self must be accommodated by the individual psyche. Miniatures, for example, allow for the reduction of things to a surveyable scale. Psychologically, they provide the control of structures too large for the body to handle proportionately. Miniaturization allows for the reduction of things to the level of endearment. The impulse to keep a fish tank, to practice the ancient Chinese art of *feng shui* (Rossbach, 1983) or the ancient Japanese art of *bonzai*, to collect stamps of countries around the world, to wear medallions, badges, lockets and wristwatches, to model cars and buildings, to use coins, are all substitutions, surrogates and reminders of the larger institutional and personal values that they represent. They offer a form of transportable presence of the larger whole. Miniatures are engulfed by the body. Their size, where they appear on the body as ornament, and at what distance they are viewed determine their relative importance. One might think of cut precious stones as representative of the extreme care and intricacy of miniature production. One has to look at the subtlety of detail to appreciate their worth. All miniaturization is suggestive of fine tooling, fine control, flashes of brilliance and exquisiteness. We have all experienced moments when many mirrors,

many sides, have been presented so that we feel a "grasp" of an issue.

In the pre-industrial world, the craftsperson provided the proportionality of things to clients as use value. Inequalities among the classes were perpetuated through such things as shoe length, materials used and, of course, the time of production required. Customization rather than standardization was the measure of proportionality. Production was limited, but quality prevailed. In *Modern Times*, to hark back to Chaplin's delightfully funny filmic satire, we live in a mega-society where the standardization of things is based on an ideal individual, a faceless individual. The ideal man, woman, child, family in a particular age cohort becomes the target of industrial design (Papanek, 1974). Vast sectors of people with disabilities and the aged are overlooked. Particular ethnic needs are leveled. Young army recruits become testers for many of the products designed by industry.[9] Again, the best designed "goods," like clothing, houses, and cars, are extremely expensive and out of reach for the general populace. Rather, the overproduction of goods which offer variations in cosmetic change of design proliferate. Research becomes advertising, selling the same thing in a different package rather than authentic product re-design for human use or as the old adage goes, putting the same old wine in new bottles. Designer water, like Perrier, exemplifies the irony of the age. Million year icebergs are next to be "bottled." This mega mentality of post-modernism has dwarfed the individual. We are stuffed full of overchoice. This is customization, but it is customization driven by the values of the market place, by innovation, not by human needs.

Perhaps no one more than Sale (1982, 1984, 1985) and Schumacher (1973) have made us aware of the ecological necessities of scale. Sale, in particular, speaks of harmony in relation to scale. Prior to the rise of our post-industrial state, he notes, there has always been an intuitive sense of size operating in human settlements. Archaic villages, Greek city states, medieval municipalities, New England towns and religious communities were all governed by a self-governing human unit beyond which it would not grow. "Harmony through division" was practiced.[10] Sale applies the four determinants of civilization (scale, economy, politics and society) to the notion of bio-regionalism—bio-regionalism being a territory that is "naturally determined" through the attributes of flora, fauna, water, climate soils and landforms and the human settlements and cultures these attributes have given rise to. These boundaries are fluid and identifiable, and Sale (1984) identifies them from the largest to the smallest: eco-region, geo-region, vita-regions. An economy of preservation, conservation and accommodation of a steady state to reach "climax" would be maintained.

*Mass: The Lived Experience of Gravity*

Mass, as the fiftl. esthetic dimension, is informed through the binary oppositions of gravity (permanence) and lightness (moveability). Our minds quiver from the pull of tradition and the hope of utopia. Such quiverings are out of body experiences which we try to comprehend. At the level of mass we recall archetypes that lie between heaven and hell, between good and evil. Gravity means denseness and compactness. It means weighty concerns—the lure of well trod traditions. We are creatures of permanence. Our *raison d'être* is left in things which endure through time. Perhaps it is our way to push back death, to leave something of ourselves behind. It is perhaps the impulse of the funerary arts. We preserve the traces of ourselves through mummification, embalming statues and images built in effigy, yet paradoxically, there is a mindfulness that we ultimately belong to Gaea.

"Things" of mass embody the meanings, the summation of the history, of a people and a culture. They can, as in an autobiography, also embody the summation of one person, a leader. Together, they represent the sculpture, the music, the great epics, the great literature of any period. They are our civilizational archetypes, emerging as symbols of unification, binding desperate groups together. Such symbols possess power over us and are encrusted with the weight of their sacredness; they are holy. They push on our backs and propel us forward on well worn paths already travelled by our predecessors. Turned into orthodoxy, the wisdom within these "texts" becomes stultified. The fetishization of this power creates domination, maintains rigidity, oppression and prevents flexibility.

The "body's" remembrance of mass may be extended through the corridors of time to a moment when birth and development are continuous and non-divisible, to a place where gravity, which informs Gaea, embodies the memory of our planet (Lovelock, 1979). There is speculation in the "new science of life" that all living things are shaped by morphogenetic fields which have been formed through the discourse of past forms of a given species (Sheldrake, 1981). Punctuated evolution occurs. New species come into existence only when that link with their past is broken and a dissipation of the structure occurs (Prigogine, 1980). The "tradition" or archetype which informs that species no longer serves its creation, its evolvement. Today, we as a species, *homo sapiens sapiens*, are undergoing a similar dissipation. Feminists have raised the issue as to whether our current archetypes are one sided—heroic and male. Could and should other archetypes inform our species if we are to continue to live on the skin of Gaea?

The ethics and politics of mass suggest that sacred spaces, special places, are needed to harbor traditions if their dialogues are to be kept alive. Historically, the paleolithic caves, the Delphic oracles, the academies, the universities, the mosques, the churches have provided for the word to be read and interpreted. Characteristically, the (re)interpretation of traditions has taken place within times of crisis, and only when a *critical mass* was achieved did human consciousness change (Jaynes, 1976). What should the responsibility of green leaders be if they hold such power to shape a tradition? What should be the role of our organic intellectuals? Einstein and Oppenheim struggled with such questions, as did Joan of Arc. How should power be delegated? Who should conduct the new orchestration? Or should it now be understood that "orchestration" as a unification be changed to polyphony and cacophony, thus allowing many voices to be heard? Should the tradition of leadership itself be questioned? Perhaps the new polyphony is to be found within each autobiography, the entire tradition improvised through responsible anarchy.

The poetics of mass for green consciousness is immense. Bodies of knowledge, Foucault's articulation of "discourse" as traditions that answer questions of profound enigmatic human concerns, were the achievement of the humanities (Dreyfus & Rabinow, 1982), yet it is these imaginary discourses that are dissipating, breaking up. What is needed, in Castoriadis' (1984) sense, is a new social Imaginary, and this Imaginary can only be formed by the decentering vision to the peripheries which have been left out. It requires the examination of cross-cultural solutions to the universals of power, equality, peace and death if alternatives are to be found. The ethics and politics of a mass esthetics have been stripped of this transcendent potential. Current attempts to view knowledge as a hermeneutic enterprise require that it be radicalized (Gadamer, 1975; Caputo, 1987, 1988). All knowledge stands within a historical conversation which shapes our collective myth, and women of all persuasions are trying to take part in that conversation, to add to its gravity by lightening its current structure.

*Space: The Lived Experience of the Cosmos*

It may well be, that we are on the edge of cosmological change: the move from a male centered view that has held our attention since the "birth" of the sun gods, to a decentered Cosmos which becomes more and more of a possibility as Voyager leaves our solar system. The implications of such an upheaval have yet to take full effect, but the aporias have been reached. Theorizations that go beyond the speed of light are wanting: an absence of Light? What can that possibly mean? How can the Dark be "written" in? Such a question leads us again to the mystery of life and death, back to myth of a new emerging Imaginary. The dialectics between the darkness and the open eye, mediated only by the membrane of our blinking, is intriguing. It is light and vision, the central metaphors of the Enlightenment which hold us prisoners of our own mind. The "Big Bang" and the impossibility of explaining those first few nanoseconds, by the likes of Stephen Hawkins, creates new heights of irony for we are dealing with a sexual male metaphor of the worst kind. Hawkin, the leading contemporary cosmologist who invented a mathematical system virtually *ex nihilo* to help explain the origin of the cosmos, uses a wheelchair, his body deteriorating by a chronic neurological disorder. Such pathos is difficult to avoid. Only through the wizardry of high technology has he been able to sustain his writing and speaking. This raises a question: how is metaphysical thought shaped through the technology lived experiences as gendered and embodies subjects?

The esthetic dimension of space as embodied in the architecture of a culture forms the final analysis. More than a canopy or shelter, it is an envelope which symbolizes the mythology of a culture. It forms the highest and most spiritual creative dimension. Topple the Tower of Babel and you deconstruct the sacred ground it rests on. Unearth the deified archetypes and you expose the soul of a tradition. Destroy the gods and goddesses and you destroy the very core of beliefs which both blind and bind a culture. Architecture provides the (re)newing experiences for a people. It is the place for spiritual bathing. In it one experiences the sublime, the awe and the mystery of the universe. Stonehenge, the pyramids, mastabas, churches, synagogues, temples and, today, our space science centers are such (re)newing baths into which one becomes baptized into a culture's cosmology. The architect as the composer of unearthly music must capture the highest aspirations, the collective unconscious imagination, and give it spiritual form. Today the global envelope, Gaea, is emerging to compete against the current cosmology. Opposing this are the postmodern multicorporation buildings with their pastiche of styles that allude to the greatness of the past.

All of the previous esthetic dimensions are subsumed under this collective vision. It is informed through binary oppositions of an envelope and the open air, between participation and ostracism, between the Earth and the Cosmos. Exile, both physical and psychological, is perhaps the most difficult cross to bear because it demands, not only that we struggle with the paradox of having to reject an entire tradition which bore us but also to realize that a new forthcoming space needs to be created. Perhaps such feelings inform the explorations of the adventurer, the astronaut, the inventor, the star-gazer. On their journey, they take something along to remind them of the culture they once knew. If they return, they do so with reluctance. Their Mother culture is now perceived through a new body. The esthetics of space

requires coming back full circle, starting the journey of line once more, perhaps hungry, shelterless and thirsty, yet being in full knowledge that such a journey must be taken because the current world-view must be rejected, a new cosmos projected. Such are the birth pains of ideology-critique. Such are the pains and joys experienced by a Galileo or a Lilith (Phillips, 1984). Perhaps the ecological and feminist movements will provide the new cosmology for Spaceship Earth?

*Speculations of Practice:*
*The Postmodern Spirituality*

Is there an emerging cosmology; a postmodern spirituality which would take us into the twenty-first century with renewed hope? Griffin (1988) believes so, as so do many others for the geopolitics of local and global politics are intimately related. The effects of Chernobyl, the burning of the Brazilian jungle rain forests and the pollution of sulphur dioxide into the air are felt immediately, globally. The local/global dichotomy should become a new ampersand, "local & global," which signifies the possibility of such an enfolded space. Reversing the binary oppositions it clearly means "supplementing" architecture with the notion of *dwelling*, space with the notion of *place*, and figure with *ground*, both in the literal and figural sense as Mother Earth, Gaea (Seamon & Mugerauer, 1985). As opposed to the semiological and poststructuralist musing of so many postmodern theorists, there has been the attempt to reinstate experience and environmental hermeneutics into the architectural discourse in order to recover the "lived body" (Mugerauer, 1985). The late philosophical writings of Heidegger, Bachelard and Merleau-Ponty have been the major influences.[11] The theorizations of Norberg-Schulz (1971, 1980) are representative of such developments. He has developed the notion of a *genius loci*, or the "spirit of the place," which *is not* to be reduced to some identifiable systemic code. Rather, in Christopher's Alexander's (1979) words, it is a "quality without a name." The *body* is brought back and "inhabitation" becomes a "lived" experience (Jager, 1985). As contrasted to the description of a door in semiotic terms which relies on the door's meaning as an architectural "word" in a system of architectural signs (Seligmann, 1982), the meaning of door for Lang (1985) is an embodied experience. He speaks of what it is like to experience the "threshold" that a door provides in the passage of the body from the inside to the outside and vice versa. The description of such "lived experience" requires great sensitivity. *Genius loci* becomes an intangible atmosphere which includes the topographical patterns, textures, natural and climatic conditions such as light, wind and sound.[12] Regional and local differences are recognized. Buildings and sites are envisioned as "living" bodies. The word "building" refers us to the Indo-European base *bhu*, meaning "to dwell," and is related to the English "to be." In phenomenological discourse they are anthropomorphized.

In the broader context, the question becomes how are we to *dwell* on the planet Earth. The implications for this require that a new cosmology be born and a new relationship with Nature be found. Quite clearly one strand of the search for this new spirituality with Nature has been, and is being, developed by ecofeminists. Freer (1983) provides a summative statement:

Patriarchy has divorced us from the earth and turned our attentions skyward. Modern technology has alienated us from our bodies and made us dependent on machines and chemicals. The Christian church, and other patriarchal religions, viciously suppressed pagan religions and gave us no rites or rituals with which to revere the earth. The gruesome threesome of patriarchy, male religions and technology have dishonored the mother and countenanced the rape and pillage of the planet until she can barely support life. In the midst of this destruction the children of Gaea are experiencing an immense spiritual hunger, a fearsome dread of isolation and meaninglessness. The tragedy of such inner emptiness is apparent to anyone who has ever experienced, however fleetingly, the celebration which is life. (131)

Together, the implications of this ecofeminist position, Green Party politics and the movement of women's spirituality constitute the major fronts for change in land reform and housing (Capra, 1984; Spretnak, 1982). Ecological groups throughout the world have proposed an entire rethinking of agriculture; they have supported the use of "soft" energy devices which would harness the sun, wind and water; they have politically organized themselves to fight for the removal of both nuclear and chemical dump sites; they have tried to remove nuclear weapons (Greenham Commons) and prevented nuclear plants from being built; they have made suggestions for changing public transportation systems and have rethought the whole issue of scale and the human environment (Kumar, 1984; McRobbie, 1981; Sale, 1982; Schumacher, 1979). For feminists, like Merchant (1983), "the death of nature" has meant the loss of organismic metaphors and the mechanization and instrumentalization of medicine through male hands especially in gynecological professions. Merchant's thesis is suggestive of the possible recovery of midwifery and gynecology under women's "hands," a move which of course begs the whole issue of who controls women's bodies. In terms of the question of architecture, the redesigning of hospitals and birth centers might be one direction where her thesis has found fruition (Bishop & Marks, 1981).

On the whole, ecofeminism and Green Party politics have attempted to deconstruct the binary oppositions between consumption/waste and production/recycling by providing complementary solutions.

It, too, is an antihumanistic alternative in the form of its anti-progressive stance. Schumacher's (1973, 1979) theorizations in particular have been influential. By introducing eastern ideas, notably Buddhist "economics," he was able to theorize a way to meet local production needs through the utilization of local resources making economics manageable at the community level. Green Party politics supports this "holistic sense of our embeddedness in nature and the interconnected character of all phenomena, which is parallel to the principles of Native American, pre-Christian European (i.e., Pagan), Taoist and Buddhist traditions" (Capra, 1984, p. 54).

The return is to re-enchant the world. In Turner's (1969) sense, to recover "liminal spaces" which have been lost so that certain spaces take on a symbolic and ritual value, a value different from that of a sports stadium, a movie-theater or a mega shopping mall. Arguelles' *Earth Ascending*, (1984) and LaChapelle's *Earth Wisdom* (1970) each in their own way attempts to re-enchant geometry. Part of such re-enchantment certainly will mean the displacement of vision as the hierarchical sense. Paradoxically we must become "blind" in order to see again. The use of sound for healing and for having one's "being" immersed communally has become more and more important as knowledge from oral/aural indigenous cultures is recovered (Schafer, 1985). Since the enlightenment tradition, the dominance of vision as the most objectifying of the senses, has locked the human imagination into the metaphors of sight for objective and materialist analysis. The change to aural metaphors suggests the possibility of increasing our sensitivity to the effects of our environment, our buildings and our furniture on our bodies (Leitner, 1978). It may also be possible to rethink the symbols that have always held us.

As the integration of eastern mysticism takes place with western technology on both sides of the border, one can only hope that the emergence of a New Age will recover the best of both worlds.[13] This surely must lie on the horizon since postmodernism has brought the globe to a listless state. Given the best possible scenario, one which closes its eyes for the moment to the total annihilation and destruction of Mother Earth through nuclear destruction or green house strangulation, what might the new Age Communities be like? Bookchin (1982) speculates that

the rudiments of an ecological society will probably be structured around the Commune—freely created, human in scale, and intimate in its consciously cultivated relationships—rather than clan or tribal forms that are often fairly sizable and anchored in the imperatives of blood and the notion of a common ancestry....On a still larger scale, the Commune composed of many small communes seems to contain the best features of the *polis*, without the ethnic parochialism and political exclusively that contributed so significantly to its decline. Such larger or composite Communes, networked confederally through ecosystems, bioregions, and biomes, must be artistically tailored to their natural surroundings. We can envision that their squares will be interlaced by streams, their places of assembly surrounded by groves, their physical contours respected and tastefully landscaped, their solids nurtured caringly to foster plant variety for ourselves, our domestic animals, and wherever possible the wildlife they may support on their fringes. We can hope that the Communes would aspire to live with, nourish, and feed upon the life-forms that indigenously belong to the ecosystems in which they are integrated. (344)

Currently such cooperative communities as Paolo Soleri's *Arcosanti* (Arizona), Another Place (New England), Auroville (India), Findhorn (Scotland) are the lone exemplars practicing, however imperfectly, this perceived New World Order values of interconnectedness, redistribution, complementarity, heterachy and indeterminacy.

*Closing Vignette*

There is certainly a danger of romanticism when speculating about green consciousness and its relationship to esthetics, ethics, politics; the danger is a form of a new biologism, a renewed organicism which, in the past, has been used quite effectively by the Nazi party (Pois, 1986). Today we are seeing an increasing rise of fascist mentality as the purity of nationalism and sovereignty become contentious issues as borders begin to break down, and more and more immigrants from impoverished countries flood into the industrialized world. Such fascist mythology has been shaped historically by a male discourse—the pursuit of "The Holy Grail" (Whitmont, 1982). I am unsure of the full implications of the above proposal, but yet feel somewhat less apprehensive in that it leans heavily toward releasing repressed feminine values so that a dialectical tension and balance between the "masculine and feminine" principles might be "restored." The overcoming of a male psychosis—the contempt for women—requires a postpatriarchal world that, I believe, is consistent with green poetics. It requires a recasting of what is meant to be a humane being. Perhaps it means a re-writing of the Nietzsche's Dionysian myth, as Whitmont (1982) and Evans (1988) have done, ridding him of his own misogyny so that a fascistic regime will not appropriate his works again. Their proposals seem extreme yet such visions are required to escape the pull of the male inflated rational ego. Evans, being gay, has had to rework patriarchal masculinity while Whitmont has carefully proposed a new theophany.

What has been presented, therefore, is only an hypothesis, an explorative imaginary representation. Throughout the essay the assumption has always been that the whole enterprise of the Enlightenment has been misguided despite such brilliant social theorists like Habermas (1981) who wish to save it.[14] The form

of rationality and reason that took hold held the seeds of its own destruction. We are feeling the power of that failed vision in the phallocrats who run the corporations today. Our break with Nature has dehumanized us, alienated us away from a reverence toward material because we have overlooked the body and elevated the mind, a direct result of the embourgeoisification of the social order. Understandably, the gender issue haunts this entire attempt to reconstitute our relationship with Nature (Griffin, 1978).

From whence is the politics of this ecological discourse to emerge? The roots of deep ecology and green consciousness draw their strength from alterity, but it is backward looking in its glance, pre-Enlightenment in its disposition—aboriginal, pre-industrial, non-urban, native—the primal mind. Here, art and society were intimately related; and this integration is what has allowed me to identify a possible green poetics. But there is the inevitable danger of believing that we have fallen from grace, kicked out from the proverbial Garden of Eden (Luke, 1988). The haunts of the "noble savage" come to mind, as if there was a pristine time of endless plenitude and innocence. We are fond of pointing to indigenous peoples who have to work little to meet their daily needs, the rest of the time spent in socialization. Such a picture represses the "evil" side to their culture—racism, slavery, sexism. With no suburbs to escape to, there remains the romantic escape into the past. Likewise, as we look to the East for alternative representations, we decontextualize the very religions we draw from. Is it possible to just extract and incorporate their values without the excessive baggage that comes along with it? No doubt China had the same question when it began to incorporate Western technology. Much of the deep ecological politics falls back to "resistance" strategies of individual moral choice, reform environmentalism at the local level. It is ecotopian in its view. Yet, we live in changed times. It appears that our notions of an *avant-garde*, a small elite that will lead the way, has been misguided. They recapitulate dominance and hierarchy. If esthetics, ethics and politics are to be consonant, it appears that the personal cannot be separated from the political. Lifestyle, as many feminists claim, must be congruent with one's political style. The *Greenham Commons* example, as one among many, seems to indicate that the form for change is responsible anarchy, civil obedience which is sometimes essential (Fromm, 1981). It must occur in uncoerced terms, formed by each body throwing its resistance into the larger whole. Out of ourselves a new visionary myth will be generated. As its articulation unfolds more and more people(s) will recognize its direction. This is not the life work of a generation but of many generations. Like the six dimensions which have been outlined, it begins with a journey, a quest toward an unknown vision, yet it is pregnant with insight. Perhaps the child has already been born and awaits in the birth canal?

# Notes

[1]This essay builds upon and expands on a previous work of mine, "Toward an ecological aesthetic: Notes on a 'green' frame of mind," in D. Blandy & K. Congdon (1988). The older term "esthetics" rather than "aesthetics" is used throughout to distinguish the former term from its paradigmatic status as part of a philosophical discipline established by Baumgarten in the eighteenth century. Esthetics will denote the perception of everyday life whereas aesthetics will be confined strictly to the tradition of fine arts.

[2]David Suzuki's *A Matter of Survival* was aired on Canadian Broadcasting Corporation radio in November, 1989.

[3]Julia Kristeva's writings are important here as someone who has had similar musings in her belief that the pre-Oedipal experiences may be disruptive of the Symbolic Order. As a seminal work in this regard see *Desire in language* (1980) and *Powers of horror* (1982). This second book deals with the inadequacies of the first.

[4]The "okioumenal" rather than the more familiar term "ecumenical" is used to outdistance this essay from the Christian notion of world-wide values. Oikoumenical values would also be world-wide but would go beyond the one identifiable religious tradition. An ecological perspective which treats the Earth as oikos, a home, would be more in keeping with the spirit that lies behind this word.

[5]I will be referring to Jacques Derrida's responsible anarchy as developed by John Caputo (1988).

[6]This is but one of the many startling insights as to how corporations are cashing in on the "green revolution." See McGregor-Brown (1989-1990).

[7]As reported on the CBS news June 24, 1990.

[8]The reader will have noticed that the goddess Gaea is evoked as another name for the Earth. This name is used, following the work of Lovelock (1979), to indicate that the whole Earth is a system and possesses consciousness. This is in direct oppostion to the Enlightenment tradition which treated the Earth as dead raw material to be exploited and used for technological gains. Since this system interconnects all "things" through forms of consciousness we have yet to un(cover), it is fitting that the Earth have a name. Gaea is the Greek name of the Mother Earth; she was the oldest of the Divinities. The Olympian gods under Zeus took over her ancient shrines, yet they swore oaths by her name because they knew they were subject to her law (Walker, 1983).

[9]Papanek (1974) exposes the biases of ergonomic configurations of design which disregard the needs of special populations for the sake of economic efficiency and profit.

[10]Sale (1982) has dubbed this "the Beanstalk principle."

[11]Especially Heidegger's essay, "Building dwelling thinking," in *Poetry, Language, Thought* (1971), Bachelard's *Poetics of Space* (1964), and Merleau-Ponty's *The Phenomenology of Perception* (1962).

[12]A well developed example of this approach is provided by Violich's (1985) intuitive "reading" of four Dalmation towns and Brenneman's (1985) description of the loric and sacred spaces on the holy wells of Ireland.

[13]An integration of sorts has already taken place in the New Age Science. To mention but a few: Sheldrake's (1982) development of morphogenetic fields in biology, the whole development of the chaos theory in science (Gleick, 1987); Prigogine's (1980) work on dissipative structure, Mandelbrot's (1977) mathematical studies of the irregular patterns of Nature and of course the whole development of microphysics which has become a recent playground of metaphysical thought (Briggs & Peat, 1984).

[14]Jürgen Habermas (1981) and perhaps Blumenberg (1983) represent the more persuasive attempts today to totalize history and provide a grand theory in the tradition of Marx and Hegel. Other historians, notably the French post-structuralists like Foucault and Derrida think this is an absurd task. From the standpoint of this essay, a fundamental rethinking of eschatology would need to begin with the re-examination of patriarchy in the spirit of Lerner's (1986) and Whitmont's (1982) historical reformulations as our spiritual discourse has been shaped by male patriarchs. Goldenberg (1982) and Daly (1973) have made such a critique of the Judeo-Christian religious tradition from a feminist viewpoint. They argue that this tradition should be replaced. Other feminists, like Fiorenza (1985), argue that the Judeo-Christian tradition, once reformed, may still be able to speak to women today. For the purposes of this argument, the esthetic roots to Nature belong to a pagan era, prior to the Chalcolithic or Copper period. An exploration of pagan spirituality, as developed during the so-called "magical" phase of human consciousness (Gebser, 1985), is in order. This seems justified on the grounds that no "afterlife" conceptualizations, as yet, had been spawned. These came with male "sun" religions. The Egyptian religions have a great reverence for Nature. All deeds are to be done in the "present" so the Nature could be revered.

# Works Cited

Alexander, C. *The timeless way of the building.* New York: Oxford UP. (1979).

Argüelles, J. *Earth ascending: An illustrated treatise on the law governing whole systems.* Boulder, CO: Shambhala. (1984).

Attali, J. Noise: *The political economy of music.* B. Massumi, trans. Minneapolis: U of Minnesota P. (1985).

Bachelard, G. *Poetics of space.* M. Jolas, trans. Boston: Beacon P. (1964).

Baudrillard, J. *Simulations.* P. Foss, P. Patton & P. Beitchman, trans. New York: Semiotext(e) Inc. (1983).

Berman, M. *The re-enchantment of the world.* Ithaca: Cornell UP. (1981).

Bishop, J. & Marks, B. A Place of birth: The changing structure of obstetrical care. *Heresies, 3*(3), (1981): 48-50.

Blandy, D., & Congdon, K.G. (Eds.). *Art in a democracy.* New York: Teachers College P. (1988).

Blumenberg, H. *The Legitimation of the modern age.* Cambridge: MIT. (1983).

Bookchin, M. *The ecology of freedom.* Palo Alto, CA: Cheshire Books. (1981).

Brenneman, Jr., W. The circle and the cross: Loric and sacred space in the holy wells of Ireland. In D. Seamon & R. Mugerauer (Eds.) *Dwelling, place and environment: Towards a phenomenology of person and world.* Dordrecht: Martinus Nijhoff. (1985): 137-158.

Briggs, J.P. & Peat, D.F. *Looking glass universe: The Emerging science of wholeness.* New York: Simon & Schuster. (1984).

Capra, F. *Green politics.* New York: E.P. Dutton.(1984).

Caputo, J.D. *Radical hermeneutics: Repetition, deconstruction and the hermeneutic project.* Bloomington: Indiana UP. (1987).

Caputo, J.D. Beyond aestheticism: Derrida's responsible anarchy. *Research in Phenomenology, 18,* (1988): 59-73.

Castoriadis. C. The imaginary institution of society. In J. Fekete (Ed.), *The structural allegory: Reconstructive encounters with the new French thought.* Minneapolis: U of Minnesota P. (1984): 6-45.

Chatwin, B. *The songlines.* London: Jonathan Cape.(1987).

Daly, M. *Beyond god the father: Towards a philosophy of women's liberation.* Boston: Beacon P. (1973).

Derrida, J. *Of grammatology.* G.C. Spivak, trans. Baltimore: The Johns Hopkins UP. (1974).

Devall, B. Ecological consciousness and ecological resisting: Guidelines for comprehension and research. *Humboldt Journal of Social Relations, 9,* (1979): 177-196.

—— The deep ecology movement, *Natural Resources Journal, 20,* (1980): 295-322.

—— The development of nature resources and the integrity of nature. *Environmental Ethics, 6,* (1984): 293-323.

Devall, B. & Sessions, G. *Deep ecology.* Layton, UT: Peregrine Smith Books. (1985).

Drengson, A.R. *Shifting paradigms: From technocrat to planetary person.* Victoria, BC: Light Star P. (1983).

Dreyfus, L.H. & Rabinow, P. *Michel Foucault: Beyond structuralism and hermeneutics.* 2nd ed. Chicago: U of Chicago P. (1982).

Evans, A. *The god of ecstacy: Sex roles and the madness of dionysos.* New York: St. Martin's. (1988).

Ferguson, M. *The acquarian conspiracy: Personal and social transformation in the 1980s.* Los Angeles: J.P. Tarcher. (1980).

Fiorenza, E.S. *In memory of her: A feminist theological reconstruction of Christian origins.* New York: Crossroad. (1985).

Freer, J. Gaea: The earth as our spiritual heritage. In Caldecott, L. & Leland, S. (Eds.), *Reclaim the earth: Women speak out for life on earth.* London: Women's P. (1983): 131-135.

Fromm, E. *On disobedience and other essays.* New York: Seabury. (1981).

Gadamer, H.G. *Truth and method.* G. Barden & J. Cumming, trans. London: Sheed & Ward. (1975).

Gebser, J. *The ever-present origin.* N. Barstad with A. Mickunas, trans. Athens: Ohio UP. (1985).

Gleick, J. *Chaos: Making of a new science.* New York: Penguin Books. (1987).

Goldenberg, N. *The end of god.* Ottawa: U of Ottawa P. (1982).

Griffin, S. *Woman and nature: The roaring inside her.* New York: Harper & Row. (1978).

Griffin, D.R. (Ed.). *Spirituality and society: Postmodern visions.* New York: State U of New York P. (1988).

Habermas, J. Modernity versus postmodernity. *New German Critique, 22,* (1981): 5-18.

Heidegger, M. Building dwelling thinking. In M. Heidegger, *Poetry, Language, Thought.* A. Hofstadter, trans. New York: Harper and Row. (1971): 145-161.

Jager, B. Body, house and city: The intertwinings of embodiment, inhabitation and civilization. In D. Seamon & R. Mugerauer (Eds.), *Dwelling, place and environment: Towards a phenomenology of person and world.* Dordrecht: Martinus Nijhoff. (1985): 215-226.

jagodzinski, j.j. Toward an ecological aesthetic: Notes on a "green" frame of mind. In D. Blandy & K.G. Congdon (Eds.), *Art in a democracy.* New York: Teachers College P. (1988): 138-164.

Jameson, F. Postmodernism and consumer society. In H. Foster (Ed.), *Anti-aesthetic: Essays on postmodern culture.* Port Townsend, WA: Bay P. (1983): 111-125.

Jameson, F. Postmodernism, or the cultural logic of late capitalism. *New Left Review, 146,* (1984): 53-93.

Jaynes, J. *The Origins of consciousness in the breakdown of the bicameral mind.* Toronto: U of Toronto P. (1976).

Jencks, C. *Adhocism: The case for improvisation.* New York: Doubleday-Anchor. (1973).

Kandinsky, W. *Concerning the spiritual in art.* New York: Dover. (1977).

Kristeva, J. *Desire in language: A semiotic approach to literature and art.* L.S. Roudiez, Ed. T. Gora, A. Jardine, & L.S. Roudiez, trans. New York: Columbia UP. (1980).

Kristeva, J. *Powers of horror: An essay on abjection.* L.S. Roudiez, trans. New York: Columbia UP. (1982).

Kumar, S., (Ed.) *The Schumacher lectures,* vol. II. London: Bond & Briggs, (1984).

LaChapelle, D. *Earth wisdom.* Silverton, CO: Finn Hill Arts Publishers. (1970).

Lang, R. The dwelling door: Towards a phenomenology of transition. In D. Seamon & R. Mugerauer (Eds.), *Dwelling, place and environment: Towards a phenomenology of person and world.* Dordrecht: Martinus Nijhoff. (1985): 201-214.

Leitner, B. *Ton: Raum/Sound: Space.* New York: New York UP. (1978).

Lerner, G. *The Origins of patriarchy.* New York: Oxford UP. (1986).

Lovelock, J.E. *Gaia: A new look at life on earth.* Oxford: Oxford UP. (1979).

Luke, T. The dreams of deep ecology. *Telos, 76,* (1988): 65-92.

Lyotard, F.J. *The postmodern condition: A report on knowledge.* G. Bennington & B. Massumi, trans. Minneapolis: U of Minnesota P. (1984).

Mandelbrot, B. *The fractal geometry of nature.* New York: Freeman. (1977).

McClary, S. Afterword: The politics of silence and sound. In J. Attali, *Noise: The political economy of music.* B. Massumi, trans. Minneapolis: U of Minnesota P. (1985): 149-160.

McGregor-Brown, I. The greening of corporate America. *Adbusters*, (1989-1990): 52-53.

Merleau-Ponty, M. *The phenomenology of perception* C. Smith, trans. New York: Humanities P. (1962).

McRobbie, G. *Small is possible.* New York: Harper & Row. (1981).

Merchant, C. *The death of nature: Woman, ecology, and the scientific revolution* San Francisco: Harper & Row. (1980).

Mugerauer, R. Language and environment. In D. Seamon & R. Mugerauer (Eds.), *Dwelling, place and environment: Towards a phenomenology of person and world.* Dordrecht: Martinus Nijhoff. (1985): 51-70.

Naess, A. The shallow and deep, long-range ecology movement: A summary. *Inquiry, 16,* (1973): 95-100.

Naess, A. Intuition, intrinsic value and deep ecology. *The Ecologist, 14,* (1984): 210-214.

Norbert-Schulz, C. *Existence, space and architecture.* New York: Praeger. (1971).

Norbert-Schulz, C. *Genius loci: Towards a phenomenology of architecture.* New York: Rizzoli. (1980).

Papanek, V. *Design for the real world.* New York: Granada. (1974).

Phillips, J.A. *Eve: The history of an idea.* San Francisco: Harper & Row. (1984).

Pois, R.A. *National socialism and the religion of nature.* New York: St. Martin's. (1986).

Porritt, J. *Seeing green: The politics of ecology explained.* Oxford: Basil Blackwell. (1984).

Prigogine, I. *From being to becoming: Time and complexity in the physical sciences.* San Francisco: W.H. Freeman and Co. (1980).

Rifkin, J. *Algeny: A new word—a new world.* Harmondsworth: Penguin. (1984).

—— *Biotechnology or brave new world?* Videodisc. Edmonton: University of Alberta Health Science Media Services. (1988).

Rossbach, S. *Feng shui: The Chinese art of placement.* New York: Dutton. (1983).

Said, E. *Orientalism.* New York: Vintage. (1978).

Sale, K. *Human scale.* New York: Perigre Books. (1982).

—— Mother of all. In S. Kumar (Ed.), *Schumacher lectures*, vol. II. London: Blond & Briggs. (1984): 219-150.

—— *Dwellers in the land: The bioregional vision.* San Francisco: Sierra Club Books. (1985).

Satin, M. *New age politics: Healing, self and society.* Vancouver: White Cap Books. (1978).

Schafer, M. Acoustic Space. In D. Seamon & R. Mugerauer (Eds), *Dwelling, place and environment: Towards a phenomenology of person and world.* Dordrecht: Martinus Nijhoff. (1985): 87-98.

Schumacher, E.F. *Small is beautiful: A study of economics as if people mattered.* London: Briggs & Briggs. (1973).

—— *Good work.* New York: Harper & Row. (1979).

Seamon, D. & Mugerauer (Eds.). *Dwelling, place and environment: Towards a phenomenology of person and world.* Dordrecht: Martinus Nijhoff. (1985).

Seligmann, C. What is a door? Notes toward a semiotic guide to design. *Semiotica,* 38(1/2), (1982): 55-76.

Sessions, G. The deep ecology movement. *Environmental Review, VII,* (1987): 105-126.

Sheldrake, R. *A new science of life: The hypothesis of formative causation.* London: Granada. (1981).

Silverman, H.J. *Inscriptions: Between phenomenology and structuralism.* New York: Routledge & Kegan Paul. (1987).

Snyder, G. *Turtle island.* New York: New Directions. (1974).

Spretnak, C. (Ed.). *The politics of women's spirituality: Essays on the rise of spiritual power within the feminist movement.* Garden City, NY: Anchor. (1982).

Suzuki, D.A. *Matter of Survival.* Montréal: Canadian Broadcasting Corporation Transcripts. (1989).

Tobias, M. (Ed.). *Deep ecology.* San Diego: Avant Books. (1985).

Violich, F. Towards revealing the sense of place: An intuitive 'reading' of four dalmatian towns. In D. Seamon & R. Mugerauer (Eds.), *Dwelling, place and environment: Towards a phenomenology of person and world.* Dordrecht: Martinus Nijhoff. (1985): 113-136.

Walker, B.G. *The woman's encyclopedia of myths and secrets.* San Francisco: Harper and Row. (1983).

Whitmont, E. *The return of the goddess.* New York: Crossroads. (1982).

# Two Futures For Vernacular Architecture

## Howard Davis

Architecture is both an art and a profession. As an art, it may be a medium of self-expression for its maker, a way of interpreting the world, a way to realize things that are beautiful. Like the other arts, it is subject to critical models, is influenced by other fields and responds to prevailing trends. As a profession, architecture must be responsible to its clients and to society; its practitioners may need to temper their urges for self-expression with the reality of what people need. In this sense, what architects do becomes criticizable not only through means that are self-referential, or limited to people who are within the profession or who understand its language, but by lay people and society at large. Criticism itself may therefore have several layers to it, ranging from the intellectual interpretations of an architectural historian to the responses of the "person on the street" to the self-criticism of the architect her—or him—self. Moreover, any of this criticism may influence action: it may help shape the next building by the same architect, put the architect out of business or start a trend shared by other architects.

Since criticism in architecture may help to influence action, it is difficult to separate the issue of criticism from the question of artistic influence. A critical model may be intimately tied with the design and production activity itself. Twentieth-century architecture, like movements in other centuries, has been marked by strongly formed ideologies and diverse, often consciously-chosen, influences. These influences have included the modern technology of mass-production, the iron and steel engineering technology that emerged in the nineteenth century, the writings of social reformers and political revolutionaries, the work of the Arts and Crafts movement, the architecture of ancient Greece, American grain elevators, the vernacular architecture around the Mediterranean, cubism and abstract expressionism. Any of these influences may work as criticism in that it may set a goal or a standard against which new work is measured.

The purpose of this essay is to examine one such influence—vernacular architecture—in its role as a critical model for modern architecture up until this point and for the future. In this chapter I shall argue that vernacular architecture, the study of "buildings of the everyday world," has two possible interpretations and therefore two possible effects on action, two possible futures.

One interpretation is that vernacular architecture should be looked at primarily in terms of *what* is built—the particular forms, arrangements of spaces, construction details and ornament that are characteristic of such buildings. Using this interpretation, architects who wanted to make use of vernacular architecture as a model for their future work would copy and interpret vernacular buildings and places, within the context of their present methods of practice, with the hope that such work would lead to positive change.

The second interpretation is that vernacular architecture should include an understanding of *how* things are built—construction and craft practices, the social relations surrounding the building activity, the flow of money, the legal and regulatory framework surrounding building production—and how these human process-oriented factors affect what is built. Using this interpretation, architects and others who wanted to make use of vernacular architecture as a model for their future work would need to understand how vernacular environments were actually formed and how to translate such understanding into actual, present-day conditions. This interpretation does not preclude an understanding of the beauty or functionality of vernacular architecture—it only requires that one see those qualities as goals and results of a human system of production.

My argument is simply that a critical interpretation of vernacular architecture in which it is seen as a style or as a particular set of forms cannot have a future that is useful to the development of the built environment without a corresponding interpretation that sees it also as a human process.

*Buildings of the Everyday World*

The usual definition of vernacular architecture has to do with buildings that are built by hand with local materials taken almost directly from nature deeply rooted in a cohesive traditional culture. Places that come to .mind are the whitewashed villages of Greece, the thatched mud huts of equatorial and southern Africa, the stone villages of Ireland and the

45

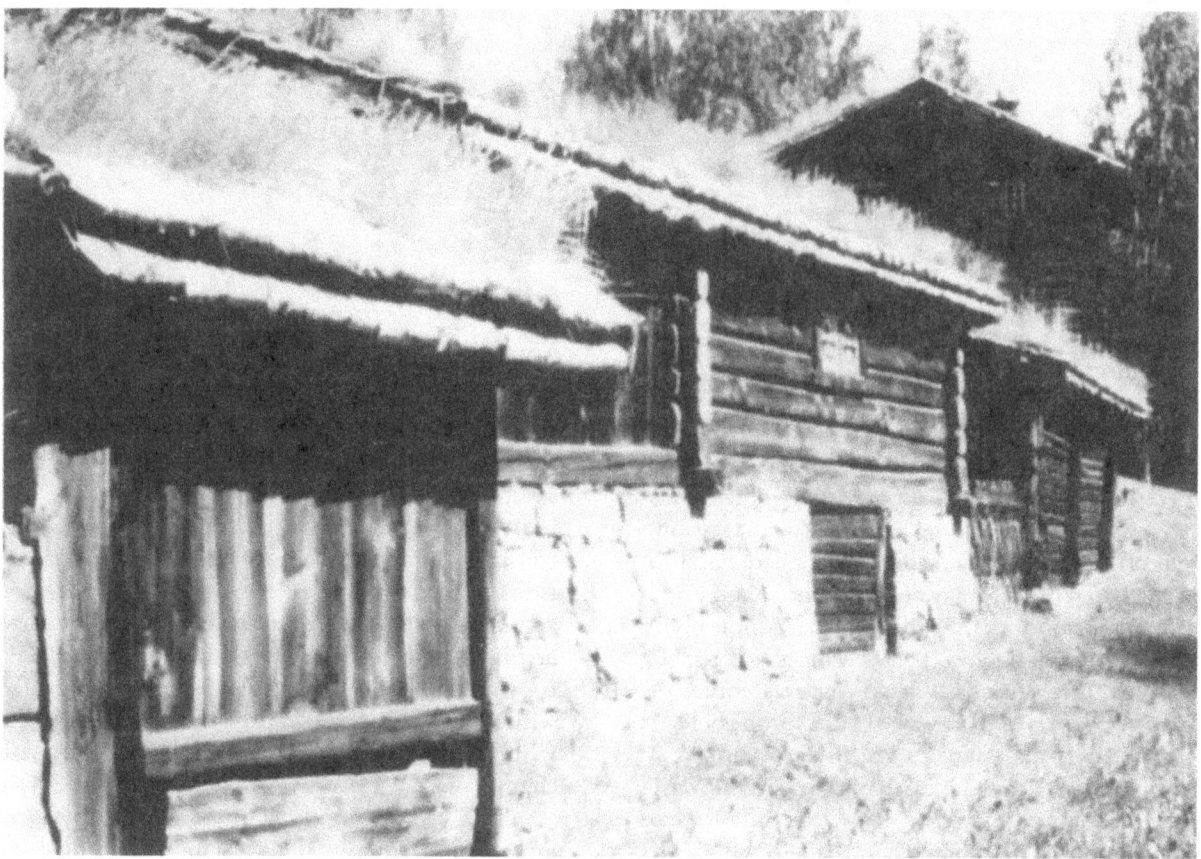

Fig. 1. A traditional Norwegian farm building in the folk museum at Lillehammer. Note the log construction and the sod roofs. (photograph by Howard Davis)

Native American pueblos of the American southwest. These places and others like them have stood the test of time; they house (or housed) cultures that are strongly defined; the buildings are direct expressions of need, social organization, climate and available construction technologies.[1]

These buildings are important for several reasons. First, as opposed to the relatively few buildings that are consciously designed by architects, they have traditionally comprised most of the buildings in the world. As such, they are not curiosities but represent an important phenomenon that is worthy of study in its own right: the shelters and workplaces of billions of people. Second, their close ties to their local culture makes them an effective tool for understanding that culture—a tool that has been amply taken advantage of by cultural geographers, anthropologists and historians. Third, and most relevant to this chapter, they have had a strong influence on architectural design, since architects have seen in them values that they feel are important in their own work.

The vernacular buildings of primitive and traditional societies often exhibit a close connection between their formal and functional aspects, a sense of absolute purposefulness at the same time that the buildings may be highly symbolic of the social institutions that they house.[2] Consider for example

the traditional Norwegian farm complex (Fig. 1), as it existed from the Middle Ages up until relatively recent times. In the absence of villages and towns in a country without a feudal past, these farmsteads represented the typical unit of settlement in the Norwegian countryside (Bugge & Norberg-Schulz, 1969; Lloyd, 1969). In some parts of the country they were arranged around two adjoining yards—one for living quarters, workshops and crop storage, the other for animals and feed. Buildings were always made of logs; they tended to be very simple, often consisting of only one room. In the case of work buildings or animal buildings, they had only one purpose. The family's house would have a main room with an open fire in the center and a smoke hole in the roof. There would be a long table and bench along one wall; family members would sleep in that room, or in the case of slighter larger houses, in smaller rooms immediately adjacent. The yard around which dwelling houses and workshops were arranged had as its focus a small building, the most elaborately ornamented in the whole farm, that was used for the storage of crops and occasionally for guest quarters as well.

These buildings were very simple and primitive by modern standards. But they represented a powerful reality to the people who inhabited them. The building grouping itself, with buildings clustered together for

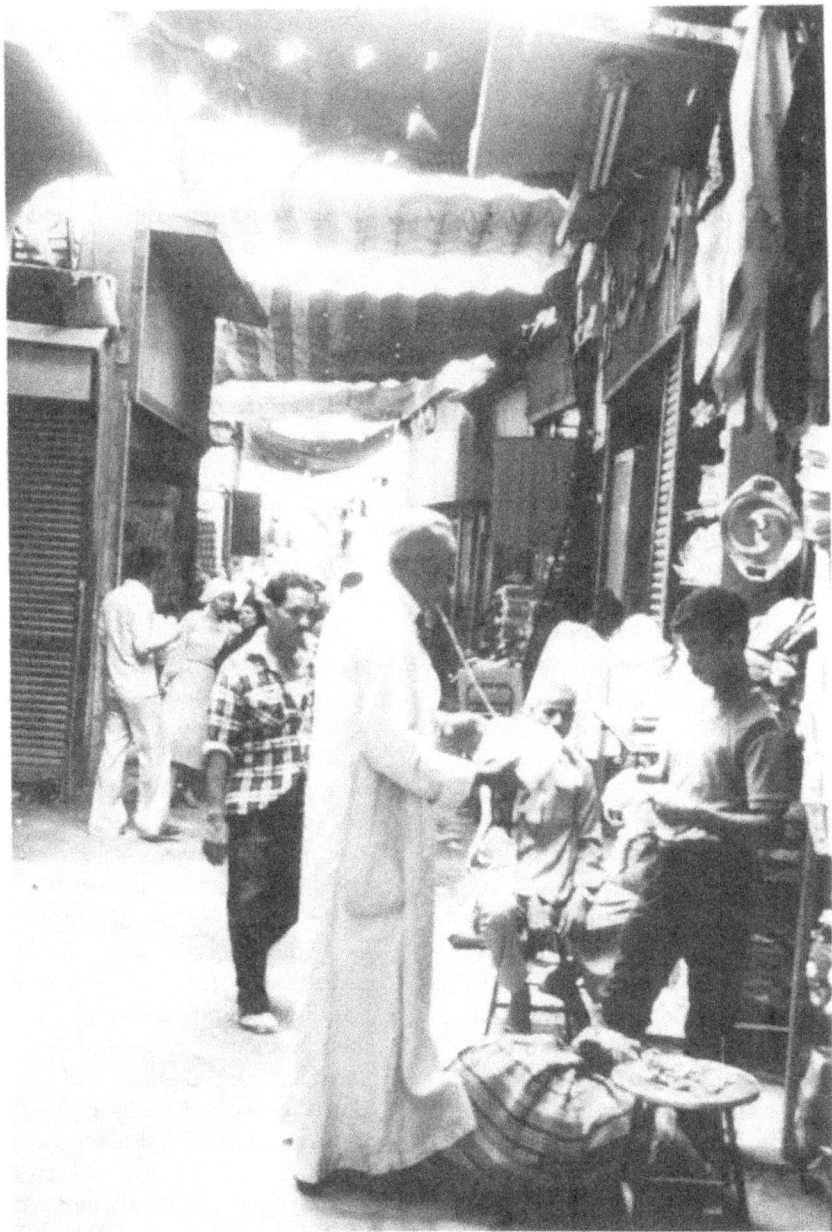

Fig. 2. A market street in the medieval section of Cairo. (photograph by Howard Davis)

protection and convenience, provided for a symbolic "homecoming;" while the individual buildings, separate from each other for reasons of construction and to reduce the chance of fire spreading, helped give a strong identity to each sub-unit of the family and to daily work. The function of protecting the crop—the wealth of the farm—was given the highest symbolic importance in the building lavished with the most ornament and the most care in its construction. In the harsh life of Norway, this rough place was nevertheless a picture of unity and order, with the fire at the hearth, and the farm representing the ongoing reality of every family.

In the Islamic cities of North Africa, in a very different climate and culture, people made their existence with different forms of settlement.[5] Here the basic unit of habitation was traditionally the brick-and-plaster courtyard house, often in a different part of the city from the work place, shielded from the street with high windowless walls and labyrinthine entryways (Fig. 2). Family life happened in and around the courtyard; streets in residential quarters tended to be used only for passage and not for daily work. But the reality of peoples' lives carried them through the city on complex daily paths that included the house, the mosque, the market. Society itself was enormously intertwined, not a collection of independent units as could be found in the Norwegian countryside; and the form of the city, with its networks of narrow streets and mosques marking the social, political and religious center of each quarter, reflected this complexity. These places represented an equally strong reality and an equally strong unity. To the person living in these places, they represented the entire world; and even though life was difficult by our modern Western standards, these places and the life lived in them were complete.

The reality and material strength of these kinds of places has been appreciated by writers and scholars, written about in travelers' accounts of the nineteenth century and studied in this century by anthropologists, cultural geographers and social historians (Glassie, 1968; Lane, 1986; Morse, 1972; Noble, 1984; Warner, 1962). The field of anthropology, which until relatively recently concentrated on primitive societies, brought the habitations of people ranging from the South Sea islanders to the Native Americans of the Southwest to the attention of readers and began to make connections between peoples' lives and the places in which they lived.

Beginning in the 1930s, American academic scholarship in vernacular architecture, or the architecture of the everyday world, began to blossom. To a large extent this scholarship was not done by architects or even by architectural historians, groups whose interests at the time tended toward the monumental. Initially, it was done almost exclusively by cultural geographers, anthropologists and folklorists who saw vernacular architecture as the built record of cultural diffusion and as a means of understanding cultures through an understanding of their artifacts. This work, the beginning of which is often credited to the geographer Fred Kniffen and his article "Louisiana House Types" (1936) has yielded many fruitful results, not the least of which is an understanding of how American house types have changed over time and across geographic distance.

In more recent years historians, with whom the study of the history of everyday life has gained a good deal of legitimacy, have begun themselves to study vernacular architecture, and this academic legitimacy has started to make inroads into the discipline of architectural history which had been traditionally tied to art historical scholarship. Architectural history has begun to see the everyday built environment—the buildings which make up 99% of those built in the world—as worthy of its attention.[4]

What is emerging is a new definition of vernacular architecture, a widening of the class of buildings that may be the object of vernacular architecture studies. Buildings that have nothing whatsoever to do with architectural style, that are totally "indigenous" in the sense of the early Norwegian farm, Eskimo igloo or the cave dwellings of Cappadocia, are relatively few. More numerous are examples like that of the New England farmer who decided that he wanted a Greek revival front on his house after he saw one in town, or of the English architect C.R. Ashbee, who consciously used vernacular forms from rural England in his house designs, or Greek shipowners' houses of the mid-nineteenth century in which neo-classical motifs and symmetries were added to traditional village houses, built with local techniques and by local craftsmen (Fig. 3). These buildings all straddle the boundary between "vernacular" and "non-vernacular." Including them in our definition of vernacular architecture represents a realization that societies are not static and that influence may come from different directions. The igloo has a good deal in common with the simple English parish church, even though the church may have been influenced by an imported style and built by a professional. *Both of them represent the most likely products of their cultures at the particular time they were built*, and what they have in common is their sense of inevitability or their ordinariness within their respective contexts.

As the boundaries between vernacular architecture and non-vernacular architecture become increasingly blurry, it is becoming clearer that the world of building is, in fact, a continuum ranging from the humblest hut to the greatest cathedral. At the beginning of *An Outline of European Architecture*, Nikolaus Pevsner (1963) wrote a statement that helped give legitimacy to the traditional art-historical view: "A bicycle shed is a building. Lincoln Cathedral is a work of architecture" (15). The difference between two such buildings is indeed extreme, particularly in terms of their aesthetic content and symbolic meaning. These "artifacts" are about as different as artifacts can be. But if we look at two such buildings in terms of the human processes that made them, the difference is not nearly as clear. For in between the cathedral and the bicycle shed may be a smaller church built by some of the same masons as the cathedral, a rectory that shared craftspeople and styles with the church, a smaller house that did the same with the rectory, a service building that did the same with the house. If we look at the world of building in terms of *process*, we find that it is indeed a continuum with continuities of style, craft, materials and ornament. For this reason it can be argued that traditional scholarship in architectural history represents an arbitrary exclusion of important buildings, processes and ideas.

Such continuities are beginning to be recognized within the discipline of architectural history. But even as the boundaries between vernacular architecture studies and traditional architectural history become blurred, most writing and scholarship about architecture—vernacular and otherwise—is still concerned with the artifact itself rather than with

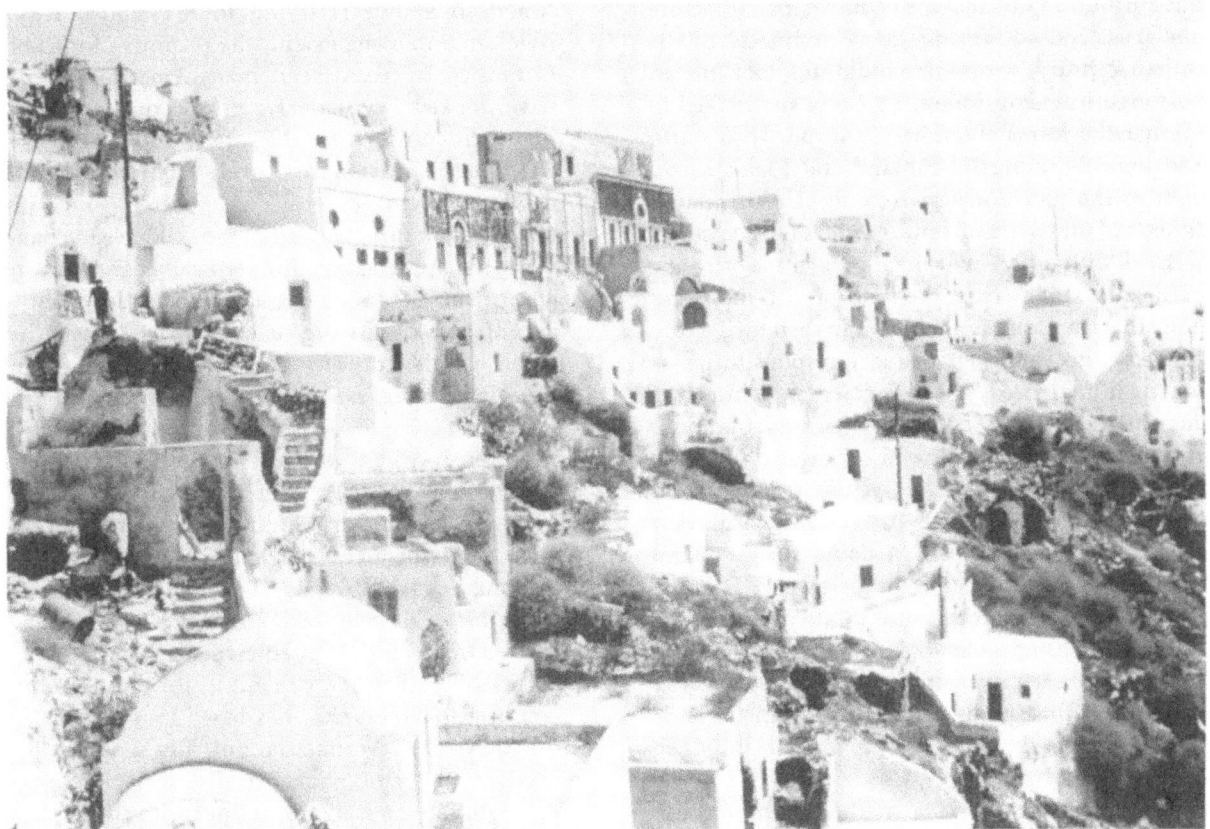

Fig. 3. The village of Oia on the Greek island of Santorini. The houses at top center with classically inspired facades were built by ship owners in the nineteenth century. (photograph by Howard Davis)

understanding, in a detailed way, the process that caused the artifact to be made. It is well understood by architects and architectural historians that much of the vernacular architecture of the world was not designed by professionally trained architects at all but was, instead, built by builders and lay people using commonly understood knowledge and techniques. However, it is not yet very well understood that the architectural design process, happening on a drawing board in an office, is fundamentally different from the building process that occurs in the growth of traditional vernacular environments. This difference is fundamental to the character that traditional vernacular buildings take on and, as I will argue, basic to a reasonable future for vernacular building.

This difference raises the possibility of a new definition of vernacular architecture that recognizes the continuum of building and takes into account the processes through which buildings are made. Suppose we define the vernacular buildings of a culture simply as: those buildings that are most likely to be built at a particular time. Such a definition would accommodate the igloo and the parish church, the rural builder who incorporates the work of an urban architect and the architect who is influenced by the local builder. Such a definition recognizes the

continuities of the building world. This definition might also include many modern buildings that some people feel are indeed vernacular but which do not fit into the romanticized visions of others: tract developments and gas stations, strip development and mobile home parks. All of these buildings are "the most likely thing" to be built in a particular place, although some require imported knowledge and technologies.

Indeed, it may be much more useful to look at vernacular architecture not in terms of a particular class of artifacts but rather in terms of a particular sort of process. As we shall see in the following sections, the definition of vernacular architecture as "the most likely buildings to be built" in a particular place at a particular time is the most helpful definition for the purpose of trying to design a reasonable future for the built environment as a whole.

### Modern Architecture and the Vernacular: The Two Futures

Modern architecture, at least up to the mid-1970s, was seen by many of its practitioners to be a direct expression of needs, an "honest" use of construction materials, all free from the stylistic shackles of architectural history.[5] These are all qualities that one might attribute to much of the vernacular architecture of the past. Indeed, among many architects of the twentieth century, vernacular buildings took on an almost mythical significance. Le Corbusier looked to the vernacular forms of southern Europe, Alvar Aalto to the wood buildings of Finland and Frank Lloyd Wright to the native materials of the United States. Architects of the twentieth century who saw themselves concerned with a non-stylistic approach to form saw in vernacular architecture the kind of directness and honesty that they were searching for in their own work. Architects who saw their primary responsibility as satisfying human needs saw in vernacular architecture a smooth relationship between form and function. Both interpretations allowed architects to use vernacular architecture as a kind of "palette" from which they could pick and choose building forms that seemed to meet their needs. In doing so, they used the vernacular as justification for their work. The first future for vernacular architecture would continue this tradition of architects who look primarily at the form of buildings for their inspiration—of seeing something in a building that seems to meet the aesthetic and/or functional needs of their own project and then copying or modifying it.

Some architects working in the late nineteenth and early twentieth centuries also saw vernacular architecture as *process*. The process they saw stressed the activity of building, the relationship of the craftsperson to craft and the individual and social benefits that might come from a process-oriented attitude to building. These architects included some of those who were working in the Arts and Crafts movement. In a curious way the craft-centered ideals of the Arts and Crafts movement continued (along with a very different style of building) in the German Bauhaus. The Arts and Crafts ideals were revived again, with still different building forms, with the communal "back-to-the-land" movements that accompanied the social protests of the 1960s and 70s; and they have been revived yet again, most recently, with various projects throughout the world that draw on the abilities and energies of local communities. The second future for vernacular architecture would continue this tradition of seeing architecture as a human process—of seeing the beauty of the world as something that must emerge from all the people who are living in it.

### The First Future:
### Vernacular Buildings as Product

There have been, at various times over the last century or so, movements in architecture that have relied greatly on the vernacular for their visual, aesthetic and even functional content. These have included certain aspects of the Arts and Crafts movement in England and America, the Garden City movement, various

American architects trying to re-establish regional styles and, to some extent, the primitive forms of Le Corbusier. In recent years many American architects have looked consciously to the past, often the nineteenth century, for their inspiration.[6]

These movements and architects are not necessarily linked either by ideology or direct professional influence. What they all have in common is a deep appreciation for vernacular architecture *as an artifact*: they see in it an aesthetic simplicity, an appropriateness to the place, and the possibility of using architecture to help restore local identity. Buildings that "look like" vernacular buildings are the result (Fig. 4). Much of this work is quite accomplished and will last in the history books. It includes the work of earlier architects, such as C.F.A. Voysey in England or John Gaw Meem in New Mexico, and of current architects, such as Geoffrey Bawa in Sri Lanka or Abdelwahed El-Wakil in the Arab world. They have all designed buildings of great power derived from vernacular antecedents.

Geoffrey Bawa, for example, the most prominent architect in Sri Lanka, has based much of his work on the local vernacular of his island: broad overhanging roofs, open walls to let the breezes through, integration of buildings with the landscape, the intensive development of gardens surrounding buildings, the use of locally produced materials. Bawa has designed schools, houses, hotels and even the new Parliament building in Colombo. His work has served as a model for many architects, particularly those in the Third World, who see the importance of reviving local building traditions as one means of asserting local identity in a post-colonial world. Some of Bawa's buildings almost seem as if they were actually vernacular, not designed by an architect at all; others are clearer re-interpretations of local traditions.

Similarly, in a completely different climate, architects in the Middle East and North Africa are relying on vernacular forms to attempt to revive traditional culture in that part of the world. These architects have been inspired by the work of Hassan Fathy, an Egyptian architect who over the course of several decades until his death in 1989, worked with the ancient mud-brick techniques of the Nile Valley and with simple rectangular vaulted volumes, plastered over and whitewashed (Fathy, 1973; Steele, 1988). These architects include Abdelwahed El-Wakil, riding the wave of the Islamic revival with the design of new mosques in traditional configurations, and Charles Boccara and Elie Mouyal in Morocco, designing houses with traditional materials and finishes.

Such work constitutes a "design model" of a future vernacular architecture. Much of it is highly accomplished, a serious attempt to introduce a new design attitude to the enormous amount of building

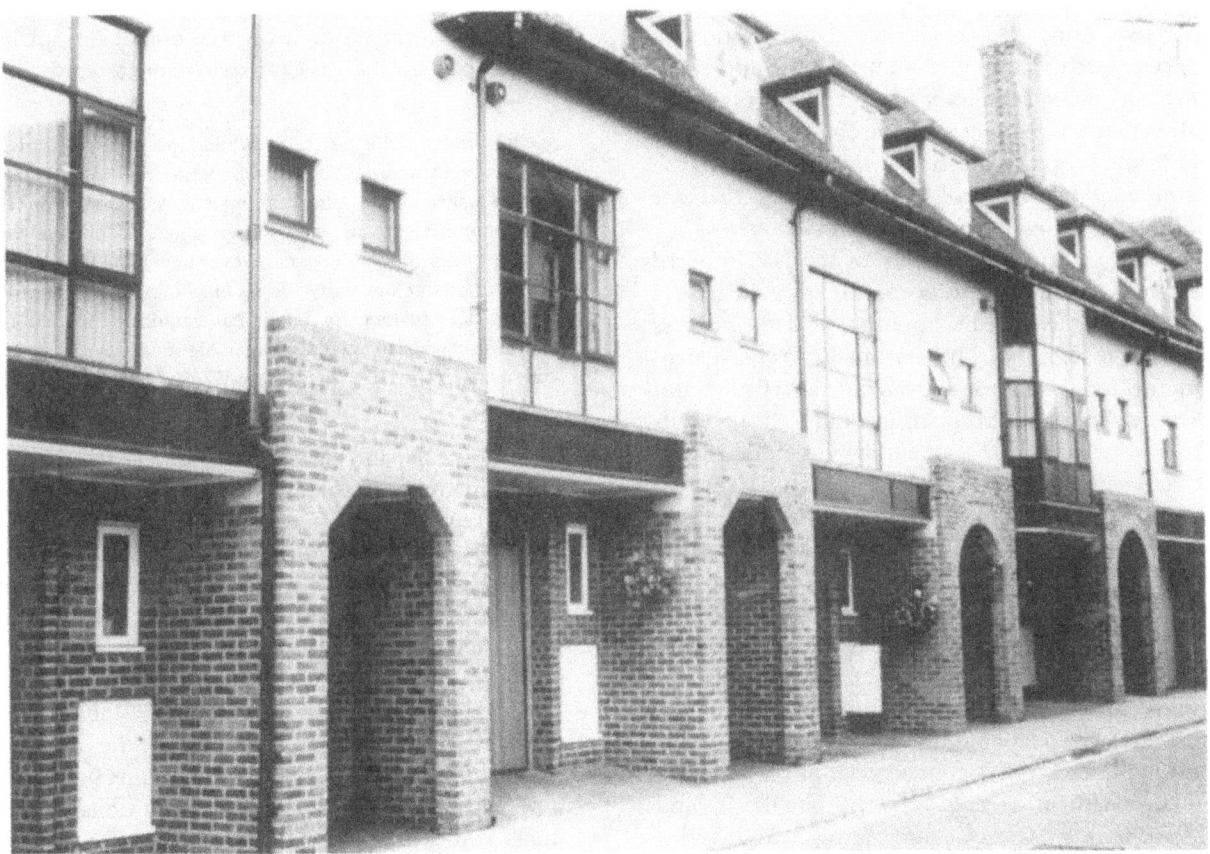

Fig. 4. New houses in Winchester, England, showing modern use of vernacular details such as brick arches, divided windows and pitched roofs with dormers. (photograph by Howard Davis)

that is taking place in developing countries. As an architectural model it seems to assume, above all, that it is primarily architects who are responsible for the form of buildings and that the large quantity of building that has to take place would happen by other architects designing similar buildings. But given the fact that architects are directly responsible for only a small percentage of the buildings in the world, the "design model" may be doomed to failure. Most buildings are not built by professional architects or with reference to academic architectural history. They are built out of habit and as a result of the easiest and most expedient construction processes. In the countries where these professional architects work, the vast majority of building occurs unaffected by their work. Typical are buildings with concrete block walls and wooden or sheet metal roofs, economically expedient but without much reference at all to pre-colonial local traditions. The "design model" of vernacular architecture seems to have little effect on the bulk of building activity.

Instead, in these places, the professional architects who are working with traditional vernacular forms and motifs are often criticized for being elitist. Very often their buildings are done for either institutional clients or for wealthy private clients and much less

often as ordinary housing. Although these buildings are understood to be beautiful, they are also often seen to be unresponsive to the needs of the majority of the population and are considered irrelevant to the problem of providing a large number of houses at low cost.

There is indeed a real gap between the amount of building that needs to take place and the ability of architects who are working with any particular style or way of building—even if it looks as if it is "vernacular"—to have a serious impact on the character of this building. The problem is that what these architects do is not really vernacular architecture at all—it only *looks like* what they believe that vernacular architecture *should* look like, if it indeed existed. Even though the individual building may be quite beautiful, and perfectly suited to human needs, it is not the building "most likely to happen," and there is no clear mechanism to guarantee its proliferation. The legitimate desire to instigate a new vernacular architecture through the design model may be doomed to failure.

*The Second Future:*
*Vernacular Building as Process*
This is where a "process model"—as opposed to

the "product" or "design model"—becomes important. And it is here that the definition of vernacular architecture as the buildings "most likely to be built" emerges as important. The process model implies that the changes that are most worthwhile making and the projects most worthwhile undertaking *are those which increase the probability that the buildings most likely to be built are good ones.*

In the architectural history of the last hundred years or so, there have been models of architectural production in which the importance of the process model was recognized. The Arts and Crafts movement in architecture is often seen from only a stylistic point of view, including buildings using "natural" materials such as wood and stone and reminiscent of traditional and vernacular forms. The movement flourished in California, for example, where the climate and ready availability of good grade lumber lent itself to the informality and ability for visibly good craft that this style implied. Such buildings are associated with the architects C.F.A. Voysey, Charles R. Ashbee and Richard Norman Shaw in Britain, Charles and Henry Greene, Julia Morgan and Bernard Maybeck in the United States. Today, buildings and objects designed by these architects can command great prices and have been imitated in recent years by architects and architect/builders who are attempting to re-instill a sense of craft in building.

But the Arts and Crafts movement also had a strong social and political component to it. The pace of industrialization and urbanization reached a fever pitch in the nineteenth century, and to try to counter it or ameliorate it various movements sprang up to promote the virtues of natural lifestyles or to abolish the economic system that seemed to be at the root of the evils of urban life. It was certainly the case that cities were crowded, polluted and dirty; that the countryside seemed to be getting swallowed up by mines and coal-belching factories; and that people were being forced to leave their traditional lives and occupations to become anonymous workers in the great industrial machine. It is no wonder that there arose concurrently machine-destroying movements, labor unions and revolutionary labor movements, back-to-the-land movements, anarchist movements, urban reformer movements.

One of the most characteristic features of the new form of industrial production was the alienation of work from its product, the removal of the worker from creative control over the work. This was different from traditional craft in which the craftsperson, although working within a very strongly defined tradition, was also able to respond directly and immediately to local conditions and the contingencies of construction. The hand of the maker was allowed to show in the finished building. From the point of view of production, the Arts and Crafts movement promulgated the idea that

beautiful artifacts could only be the result of non-alienated work. William Morris, one of the spiritual leaders of the Arts and Crafts movement, wrote that

> We do sorely need a system of production which will give us beautiful surroundings and pleasant occupation, and which will tend to make us good human animals....We do most certainly need happiness in our daily work, content in our daily rest; and all this cannot be if we hand over the whole responsibility of the details of our daily life to machines and their drivers. We are right to long for intelligent handicraft to come back to the world which it once made tolerable amidst war and turmoil and uncertainty of life. (Stansky, 1985, 65)

The Arts and Crafts movement was perhaps overburdened with romantic notions of medieval craft and certainly did not manage to change the machine-oriented course of industrial production. But as a social/economic ideology, its emphasis on *the system of production* as a whole as the source of beautiful things has an important relationship to a defintion of vernacular architecture as those buildings most likely to be built. The proponents of the Arts and Crafts movement were trying to specify the conditions under which good art (and good buildings) would be built as a matter of course, the conditions of labor under which the things most likely to be built would be good.

For all of its popular aspirations, the Arts and Crafts movement and the system of handicraft that it seemed to represent may appear to us today to be elitist and impractical, especially when seen in comparison to the vast quantities of people that need to be housed and the vast numbers of buildings that need to be built. Indeed, this reversion to numbers was one of the prime arguments of those who made the case, in the first decades of the twentieth century, that only a factory-based mass-production approach to housing could satisfy the world's needs (Conrads, 1970). The architectural propaganda that accompanied the introduction of the modern movement in architecture argued that the new style was the natural result of factory-based production and that the old system of handicraft could not come close to the efficiencies of factories and machines.

The architectural ideology that rejected the old craft-based system was well intentioned in its desire to deal efficiently with large quantities of building and to do it in a way which provided "healthful" environments with light and air and connection to green spaces. Our present attitude toward the production of the built world, whether or not it is an influence of architectural polemics, is based largely on issues of quantity and efficiency of production. The built result has often not been as appealing as the pictures that the architectural polemicists drew. Repetitive houses in large tract developments, districts of huge apartment towers in most major cities of the world, large numbers of building components manufactured in factories, then delivered and assembled on the site—all of these things are typical features of the modern environment.

The emphasis on mass production that was part of the ideology of the modern movement and which guides most building practice today seems to be at complete odds with the ideals of the Arts and Crafts movement. Although the Arts and Crafts movement saw itself as the seed of a new vernacular architecture, the true vernacular that has come to dominate the twentieth century is one of repetitive, centrally controlled construction.

But there is, apart from centrally controlled mass production, another mode of production that guides much ordinary building in the world. In this country, for example, a large percentage of people are involved in the construction or reconstruction of their own houses, often without the help of architects. This activity is very often a matter of economic necessity, and it leads to buildings that are considerably more ordinary and everyday than buildings designed by architects. In its own way, it makes maximum use of the available local building culture, as did the vernacular building of the past, and as it is occurring in the Third World.

It is in the Third World, comprising most of the population of the earth, in which by far the vast majority of housing is produced either by people themselves, or by workers and laborers under the immediate direction of the homeowners (Figs. 5 and 6). These builders, working within the local economy, demonstrate this alternative mode of production most forcefully. Very often this building activity is part of what is known as the "secondary economy," the economy that falls outside of government regulation and established corporate institutions. It is a rich and human economy with people dealing directly with the workers who are building or modifying their houses. Honest competition is helping to set standards of quality as well as prices. Thousands of individuals are involved in the building process and therefore in the growth and shape of cities. This is very different from the centralized control of large building firms, of government departments and from the arm's length relationship to building that people in developed countries endure. This represents a real vernacular, most similar in terms of *process* to the vernacular building of the past, and it is these situations that must be looked at carefully, for the possibility of any kind of positive change in the way the bulk of building gets done.

The second future, then, is one based on human process and one that builds on the everyday energies of people and on the capabilities of local economies. This future is not as easy to achieve or even conceptualize as the "design model" which can deal only with a relatively small number of buildings. However, if the process model is achieved, it would be much more pervasive and effective and allow for more of society to be involved in the production of its built environment.

Such a future could only come about through a gradual and systematic change in the system of production with which buildings are built. Such change is not confined to architectural practice and might incorporate community groups who are seeking to assume responsibility for their own physical surroundings or the development of pilot projects involving user participation in design and construction (Fig. 7). Such initiatives are being taken in various places. They include recognition on the part of some governments in the Third World that "informal" ways of providing housing are here to stay; the development of cooperative housing movements in many countries of the world ranging from Scandinavia to South America; projects by various architects in which clients design their own houses and apartments; the development of locally-based operations for the development of building materials in various places in the world.[7]

In traditional society, the knowledge of how to make things beautiful was not as separate from everyday social processes as it is in the modern world; the "process" orientation to the making of the built world was not necessarily incompatible with the idea that the buildings produced as its result might be beautiful and fit places to live. The second future for vernacular architecture, the "process model," represents a recognition that, ultimately, the beauty of the world comes from people. As much as it may be within the ability of architects to make beautiful buildings individually, the making of places on a large scale that are beautiful and fit for human habitation has to be taken care of by society at large.

## Conclusion:
### The Political Dimension of Vernacular Building

Both the "design model" and the "process model" of vernacular architecture represent critical interpretations, either one of which can be used as a basis for action. The design model may inspire architects to design buildings that are similar to the vernacular buildings that they see or learn about. This approach, while it may result in buildings that are well-designed and well fit to their purpose, does not have the capability of leading to widespread improvement to the great amount of building that is taking place in the world. The "process model," on the other hand, recognizes that society at large—and not just architects—produces the bulk of the built environment and that improvement to the built environment as a whole can only come about through widespread

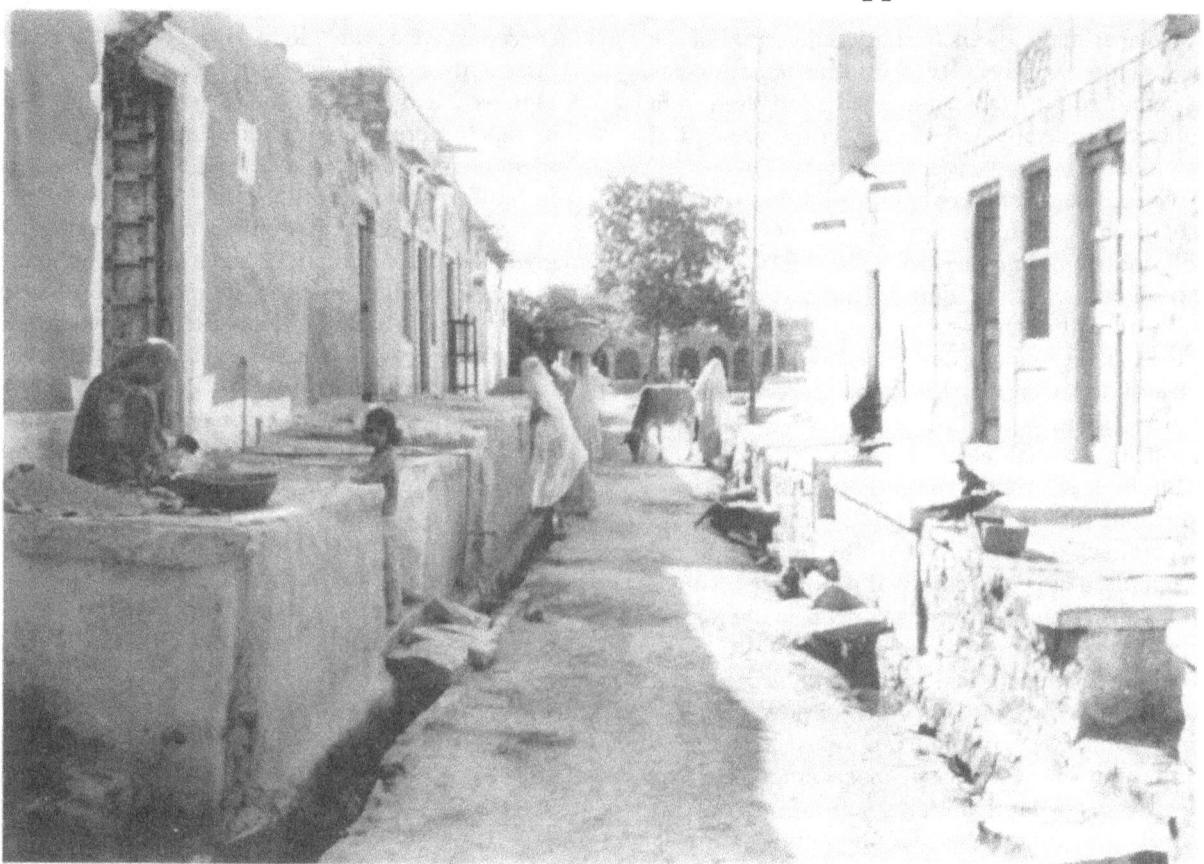

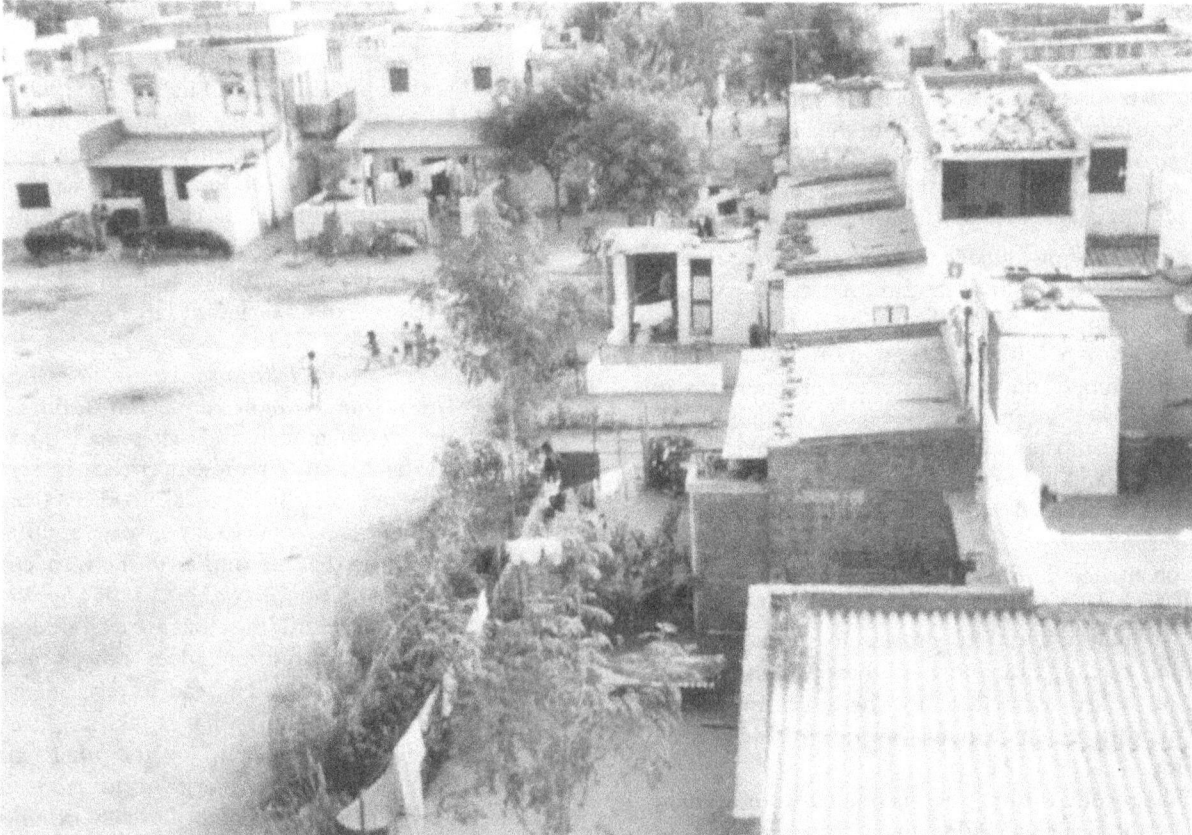

Fig. 6. Government-built mass housing in Ahmedabad, India, showing additions to houses carried out without government assistance in the "informal" economy. (photographs by Howard Davis)

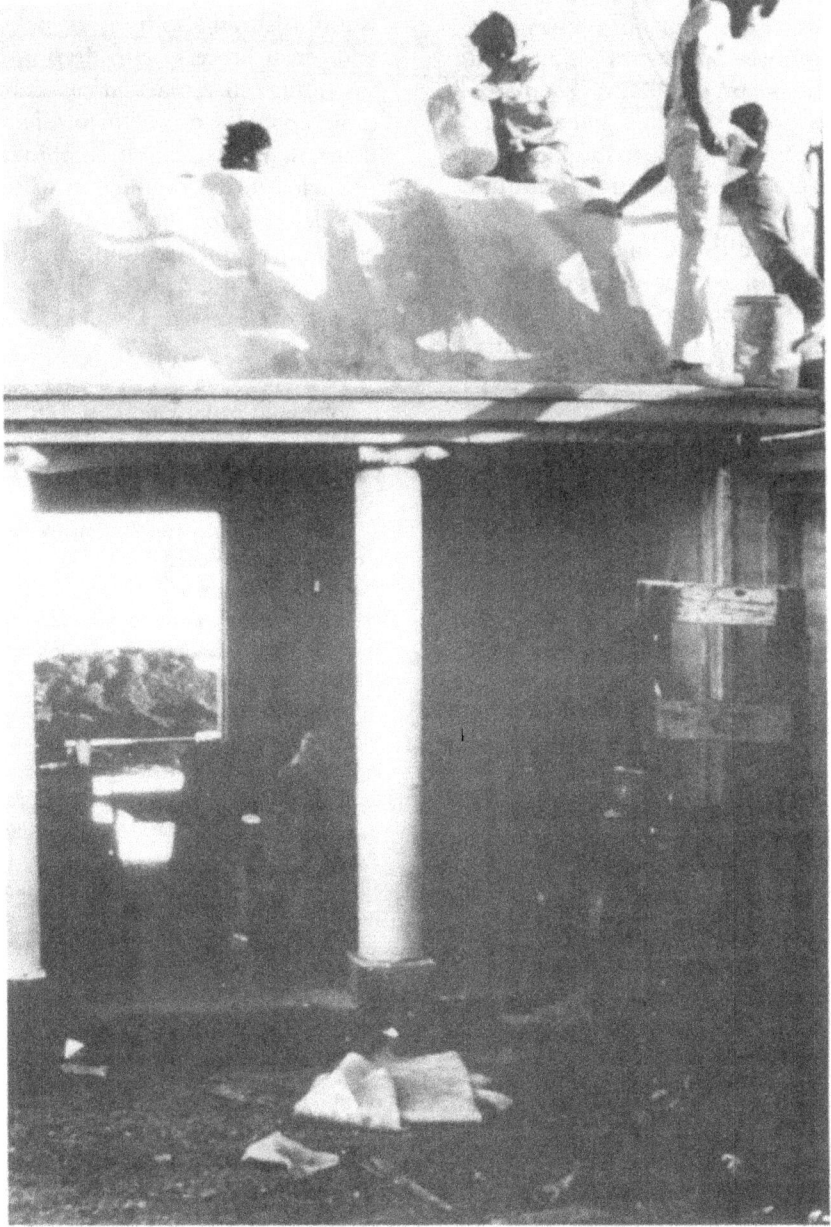

Fig. 7. Finishing the roofs in an experimental housing project in Mexico. See Alexander et al. (1985). (photograph by Howard Davis)

changes in the social processes that surround building production.

The idea of vernacular architecture as process, indeed as a process of human empowerment and freedom, raises much more general political questions, not the least of which is: "Who controls the shape of the built world?" It was perhaps more fashionable in the 1960s and 70s than today to talk about political decentralization, but in the years since then, communities of all sizes—ranging from neighborhoods in American cities to national and ethnic groups in Europe—have actually managed, as the result of long and persistent struggle, to regain control over their own lives. The idea of vernacular architecture

as local, and as widespread in society, might be helped by such movements.

What might be a simple and straightforward connection between vernacular architecture and local politics has itself had a rather confused history in this century. Although twentieth-century architecture made ample use of the vernacular for its own purposes, the most well-known current of modern architecture— the so-called International Style—was opposed to ideas of nationalism and localism. This architecture of steel and glass and concrete was to be universal in geography and universally applicable to rich and poor alike. It was seen to be the logical extension of modern methods of factory production into the realm of the construction industry, which had been (and still is) seen as the most regressive of industries, dependent on a myriad of independent craftspeople working in the mud and rain of the site. Such a method of production was compared unfavorably to cars, washing machines and all other necessities of life that could be produced in factories, under one management, using scientific techniques of mass production and efficiency. The new architecture was to change all that, and in so doing, would help solve the vast housing problems that were among the most visible by-products of nineteenth-century industrialization and twentieth-century wars.

With some exceptions, the proponents of this new style of architecture did not align themselves with the forces of Fascism that were beginning to take over Europe. Indeed, the Nazi regime—which forced the closure of the most visible institution of the new architecture, the Bauhaus—saw itself as the guardian for just the sort of folk and national architecture that was so opposed by the leaders of the modern movement. These turned out to be very strange alignments indeed: totalitarian regimes promoting a kind of building that had its natural origins "from the bottom up" in the soil, and democratic governments and institutions promoting a kind of building that might be exactly the same all over the world.

The history of such alignments has only added to the difficulty that proponents of vernacular architecture have had in making their usually apolitical point, and the unfortunate association of Nazi ideology with vernacular architecture in general has been a recurrent, if minor, theme in post war architectural thought. This theme cropped up again, most recently, as a response to Prince Charles' pleas for a new direction for architecture in Britain, an architecture based on human values, a sense of place, the use of traditional materials and forms. To anyone familiar with the horrors of much of postwar building in Britain, even if he or she is also familiar with the good intentions of the architects and the financial and bureaucratic constraints under which they labored, it is difficult to deny the validity of Prince Charles's observations. Yet a prominent architectural critic writing in one of the most prestigious British journals saw fit to compare Prince Charles' statements with Nazi ideology about architecture (Pawley, 1990). But what is to be gained by such groping? It seems much healthier to see the political associations that have been attributed to vernacular architecture as the unfortunate and erroneous remnants of troubled times and to look instead toward projects and initiatives that make real links between buildings and human organizations and politics.

If, as a critical model for the production of the built world, vernacular architecture is seen from the point of view of product alone, then it is likely that attempts on the part of architects to re-introduce

vernacular forms will be elitist in one way or another. But if it is seen also from the point of view of human and social process, with deep understanding of how the wonderful vernacular places of the world actually came about as matter of ordinary everyday activity, then it may be possible to combine a genuinely popular approach to the production of the built world with the idea that the places in which people live should be beautiful and sustaining of their lives.

# Notes

[1] The literature on vernacular architecture is extensive, ranging from popular world surveys to technical accounts of buildings in particular places. Three good surveys that can lead the reader further into this literature are Guidoni (1978), Moholy-Nagy (1957) and Oliver (1987).

[2] The use of the word "primitive" is not intended to imply a derogatory judgement.

[3] A good introduction to Islamic architecture is Michell (1978). Domestic architecture in the North African Islamic city is dealt with in Petherbridge (1978), Hakim (1986) and Akbar (1988).

[4] Domer (1989) points out that "articles in journals and monographs about vernacular architecture topics and material culture from university and private presses have increased dramatically in the last ten years. Interest in common buildings has spread from the early cultural geographers such as Fred Kniffen to folklorists, specialists in American studies, anthropologists, museum curators, landscape historians, art historians, preservationists, architectural historians and architects who find inspiration in the frank authenticity of vernacular forms and images. Membership in the Vernacular Architecture Forum in the United States is increasing about 15% a year. England, Germany and other European countries have strong organizations as well with enthusiastic members and money in the bank" (56).

[5] These concepts are basic to some of the most well known polemics of the modern movement. In *Towards a New Architecture*, Le Corbusier (1960) wrote: "The history of Architecture unfolds itself slowly across the centuries as a modification of structure and ornament, but in the last fifty years steel and concrete have brought new conquests, which are the index of a greater capacity for construction, and of an architecture in which the old codes have been overturned. If we challenge the past, we shall learn that 'styles' no longer exist for us, that a style belonging to our own period has come about; and there has been a revolution" (250). And Walter Gropius (1965), in *The New Architecture and the Bauhaus*, wrote that "a breach has been made with the past, which allows us to envisage a new aspect of architecture corresponding to the technical civilization of the age we live in; the morphology of dead styles has been destroyed; and we are returning to honesty of thought and feeling" (19).

[6] Among the more well-known of these architects are Robert A.M. Stern and the team of Andres Duany and Elizabeth Plater-Zyberk. Duany and Plater-Zyberk have attracted considerable attention for their design of the new town of Seaside, on the Gulf coast of Florida, which incorporates into a town planning code vernacular elements from nineteenth- and early twentieth-

century American towns. For an acount of this project, along with related urban planning initiatives, see Ellis (1988).

[7]For details of some of these projects, see Hatch (1984), Alexander et al. (1985), Benjamin (1985) and Spence (1987).

# Works Cited

Akbar, J. *Crisis in the built environment: the case of the Muslim city.* Singapore: Concept Media. (1988).

Alexander, C., Davis, H., Martinez, J. & Corner, D. *The production of houses.* New York: Oxford UP. (1985).

Benjamin, S. India: formal versus informal housing. *The Architectural Review, 178*(1062), (1985): 32-37.

Bugge, G. & Norberg-Schulz, C. *Stav og laft i Norge.* Oslo: Norske Arkitekters Landsforbunds. (1969).

Conrads, U. *Programs and manifestoes on 20th-century architecture.* Cambridge: MIT Press. (1970).

Domer, D. The old and new of vernacular architecture—a review essay. *Journal of Architectural Education, 42*(4), (1989). 45-56.

Ellis, J. U.S. codes and controls. *The Architectural Review, 184*(1101), (1988): 79-86.

Fathy, H. *Architecture for the poor: an experiment in rural Egypt.* Chicago: U of Chicago P. (1973).

Glassie, H. *Pattern in the material folk culture of the eastern United States.* Philadelphia: U of Pennsylvania P. (1968).

Gropius, W. *The new architecture and the Bauhaus.* Cambridge: MIT Press. (1965).

Guidoni, E. *Primitive architecture.* New York: Harry N. Abrams. (1978).

Hakim, B. *Arabic-Islamic cities: building and planning principles.* London: Routledge & Kegan Paul. (1986).

Hatch, C.R. (Ed.). *The scope of social architecture.* New York: Van Nostrand Reinhold (1984).

Kniffen, F. Louisiana house types. *Annals of the Association of American Geographers, 26*(4), (1936): 179-193.

Lane, E.W. *An account of the manners and customs of the modern Egyptians: written in Egypt during the years 1833-1835.* London: Darf. (1986).

Le Corbusier. *Towards a new architecture.* New York: Praeger. (1960).

Lloyd, J. The Norwegian laftehus. In P. Oliver (Ed.), *Shelter and society.* London: Barrie & Jenkins. (1969): 33-48.

Michell, G. (Ed.). *Architecture of the Islamic world.* New York: William Morrow and Company. (1978).

Moholy-Nagy, S. *Native genius in anonymous architecture.* New York: Horizon. (1957).

Morse, E. *Japanese homes and their surroundings.* Rutland: Charles E. Tuttle, (1972).

Noble, A. *Wood, brick & stone: the North American settlement landscape* (Vols. 1-2). Amherst. The U of Massachusetts P. (1984).

Oliver, P. *Dwellings; the house across the world.* Austin: U of Texas P. (1987).

Pawley, M. A precedent for the Prince. *The Architectural Review, 187*(1117), (1990): 80-82.

Petherbridge, G. Vernacular architecture: the house and society. In G. Mitchell (Ed.), *Architecture of the Islamic world.* New York: William Morrow. (1978): 176-208.

Pevsner, N. *An outline of European architecture.* Harmondsworth, Middlesex, England: Penguin Books. (1963).

Spence, R. Grass-roots tech. *Architectural Review, 181*(1085), (1987): 58-65.

Stansky, P. *Redesigning the world: William Morris, the 1880s, and the Arts and Crafts Movement.* Princeton: Princeton UP. (1985).

Steele, J. *Hassan Fathy.* London: Academy Editions. (1988).

Warner, S. *Streetcar suburbs.* Cambridge: Harvard UP. (1962).

# Part II
# Valuing Diverse Critical Expression

# Pluralism in African American Aesthetics and Art Criticism

## Paulette Spruill Fleming

The pluralistic nature of the American public school population presents some important challenges in the 1990s because of the tremendous diversity of races, languages, ethnic groups, socio-economic classes, student abilities, learning and teaching styles that must all be equally accommodated. The increased emphasis on the transmission of artistic and cultural heritage and the development of art criticism as a major component of art content at all levels adds to this challenge. Ideally, the question of "whose heritage should be taught" will be answered through an inclusive, pluralistic model for curriculum design and understanding art. However, the next relevant question becomes, "How do we address this diversity in artistic form and content within a pluralistic context?"

The purpose of this chapter is to examine African American aesthetics and cultural pluralism, particularly the relationship between language and culture and its significance in art criticism. Addressing diversity within a pluralistic context is a complex phenomena. The negative interactions that have occurred between cultural and ethnic groups has further complicated perceptions and responses to art. Fear, mistrust and negative attitudes have presented communication barriers for teachers as well as students, barriers which reflect the problems of the society and reveal the need for closer examination.

What has been referred to as a latent or societal curriculum has emerged and permeates traditional schooling (Banks, 1982; Cortes, 1981). Cortes identifies a societal curriculum as the education that is occurring outside of school and includes TV shows, newspapers and popular books among the societal factors that influence and shape students' attitudes. Banks has characterized this curriculum as "the curriculum that no teacher explicitly teaches but all students learn." This curriculum includes a universe of perceptions, misperceptions, images and aesthetic responses that are a part of the cultural baggage that teachers and students inevitably bring into the classroom and that adults bring into any art criticism activity.

In contemporary usage, "art criticism" as a term has been used to refer to a number of different categories of activities ranging from engaging in informal talks about art to learning how to justify aesthetic judgments to becoming familiar with the formal writings of aestheticians, critics and historians. Although the success of each of these activities involves a somewhat different set of attitudes, behaviors, skills and abilities, the impact of societal curriculum is powerful since cultural attitudes and perceptions shape our expectations (Brooks, 1979).

### Language, Culture, and Perception

Fanon (1968) stated that the relationship between language and culture is so strong that in capturing the language, one captures the culture. If, as Brooks (1979) has suggested, the function of language is to elicit and express meanings, then the language of African Americans is of particular significance in art criticism. If attitudes are held together by values and serve to "maintain and promote our value system and our self-identity," then it seems reasonable to infer that aesthetic attitudes are also held together by aesthetic values that maintain and promote an aesthetic value system and self-identity (Ross, 1980: 265). In other words, if we accept that language and culture are directly related, then we may also expect that youngsters may respond differently to works of art in an art criticism activity as a function of their language characteristics. While it is fairly obvious that differences in aesthetic preferences may result in differences in aesthetic response, the more subtle effect of the structure of art criticism activities on the language structure elicited may be missed.

Perhaps the most highly publicized recent development which illustrates Fanon's assertion is the question of whether "African American" or "Black" should be used to define people of African descent. I believe that both terms should be used as they speak to two different realities. "Black" is essentially a political term and a reaction to the lower case usage of "black" as a mixed word—a word that both described and evaluated at the same time. When Martin Luther King, Jr. affirmed that "Black is Beautiful," the capital "B" both described a people politically in an international context and articulated a cultural and aesthetic value—that "black" was not bad/evil/ugly.

The use of the term "African American" is more of a cultural term than a political one, although it does speak to the issue of parity as an American political reality for people of African descent. African American is less reactive and more pro-active in its orientation. While "Black" speaks to the political reality of people of African descent wherever they are found in a world proscribed by racism, African American brings Black people into the larger arena of hyphenated-Americans. The emphasis here, as with other American ethnic groups, is on the legacy of preceding generations. In the case of Americans of African ancestry, that legacy includes the Black heritage as well as African cultural and aesthetic values in a much larger sense. Included in this heritage is the strong relationship between the African American literary tradition and the visual arts which is reflective of African aesthetic values.

"African American" is more comprehensive in its focus and encompasses all aspects of the life of Americans of African descent. The use of the term "African American aesthetics" signals a reference to a long tradition of African aesthetic values preserved for generations through practical and folk art traditions and quite apart from identifiable subject and theme within a Western fine art context. For example, Spriggs (1979) speaks of a rhythmic dynamism which is not unlike the quality that is currently found the non-vocal accompaniments of dialect speakers—postures, gestures and walking.

An understanding of the significance of this interplay between language and culture is necessary in order to appreciate and respond to the art of African Americans. At the heart of talking or writing about art is the process of perception itself—learning to look at art and have something to say about what we see. Martin (1988) recalls Gayle's analysis in his book *The Way of the New World* where he asserts that "there is a black way of seeing" (377). Since perception is the process whereby we attach meaning to the information that the senses take in, notions about African American aesthetic perception have a decided bearing on art criticism.

In embracing "blackness" as a cultural and political statement, Black artists and activists in the 1960s repudiated previous negative labels and provided a unifying banner under which Americans of African origin could stand tall. Implicit in the use of the term "Black aesthetic" is the idea that there are certain immediate intuitive feelings and responses about works of art that artists and viewers within the aesthetic field of the African diaspora share (Fleming, 1991).

Coleman (1976) notes that the perceptual process involves not only the visual data supplied by the object but an interplay between object and the "character and disposition of the percipient" (4). As Weaver (1978) has pointed out, the attitude we form towards perceptual information is an essential part of the meaning we assign to it. Blackstream art reflects Black aesthetic values of the sixties and seventies and should be viewed as a significant development in the nation's history and culture (Neperud -& Jenkins, 1982). However, the African American abstract artists of this same period point to the fact that there is a wider range of expression, some of which is viewed as mainstream because it is devoid of Black subject matter.

Many of these artists still feel that "there is something black about their work and that this quality is essential to its character and success, although they are hard-pressed to put their finger on exactly what this quality is" (Jacobs, 1985: 5-6). This formalist "quality" reflects the artists' belief in an African aesthetic that they are heirs to as African Americans, an aesthetic quite apart from the instrumentalist aesthetic category addressed by Blackstream art.

*Culture, Communication and Art Criticism*

Because of the nature of cross-cultural interaction, the interplay between language and culture can potentially lead to communication problems in an art criticism context. Communication barriers can exist that must be carefully considered if art criticism is to succeed, particularly in American schools. Even in considering informal talk about art, the societal curriculum referred to earlier can have a powerful impact. Brown (1980) points out that teaching as a process of human interaction predicated on communication has mutual intelligibility as an essential key to success.

Unfortunately, nonrecipricol intelligibility often exists between the teacher and pupils in many urban schools. According to Taylor (1980), "there are certain ethnic and cultural markings in the speech of the overwhelming percentage of Black Americans" (22). These language characteristics and the youngsters who possess them have been viewed in a negative manner by society in general. For those children whose speech follows certain patterns of Black dialect, an attitude has often developed wherein they are viewed as less intelligent and less capable of performing certain kinds of cognitive tasks (Kossack, 1980).

Some parents have responded angrily to these attitudes. For example, on July 12, 1979, Judge Charles Joiner of the U.S. District court ruled in favor of eleven Black parents who brought suit against the Ann Arbor School District Board under the Equal Educational Opportunity Act of 1974. The judge's ruling admitted that while Black English is not a language barrier in and of itself, a barrier does exist because of teacher attitudes that cause Black English speakers to feel inferior (Kossack, 1980).

According to Ross (1980), these negative attitudes can influence one's readiness to respond, to do critical thinking and can impede the "behavioral intentions which govern one's predispositions toward people, situations, and things" (264). Because the youngsters may perceive negative teacher attitudes, they may, in turn, respond to teachers and oral art criticism activities in a negative defensive spiral that fuels a self-fulfilling prophecy that they are incapable of the higher order functioning required for certain art criticism tasks.

Many African American educators viewed Judge Joiner's ruling and the equity now being sought for Black English with caution, possibly because they feared that in acknowledging and reinforcing its relevance within the African American cultural heritage, these same students will lose the incentive to master so-called "standard English" which is so essential for success in a white dominated society (Ivory, 1980; Jones, 1982; Taylor, 1980). Taylor responds in the negative to the question "Should black English be taught in elementary schools?" Yet, he concludes his answer by making the following seemingly contradictory statement: "*No*, black English need not be taught in the schools, but *Yes* it should be widely used as a medium of instruction and a basis for developing cultural pride in black children" (22). While Black English need not be taught as a separate subject, its value and use must be considered in structuring the overall curriculum.

The classroom dynamics of Black language and culture interacting with one another are not limited to the problems encountered by the attitudes of teachers and other pupils to Black English speakers. Jones (1982) addresses another roadblock on the way to open exchange amongst people. "Because of the way I talk", she says, "some of my black peers look at me sideways and ask, 'Why do you talk like you're white?' " (7).

Aponte (1989) also documents this cultural phenomena wherein the favorable reaction from teachers to his speech brought "fierce verbal attacks from my peers" outside the classroom (11). Youngsters who are verbal and articulate with so-called standard English in class discussions tend to perform better as students than their solely dialect-speaking counterparts. Teachers need to be sensitized to the adjustment problems of those on the other end of the Black language spectrum as well, and they must recognize that effusive praise of African American youngsters who are articulate in "talkin' white" carries a high personal price tag for them as well.

When Jones speaks of a "Jeckyll-and-Hyde-ish" phenomena in her description of her ability to code switch as a dialectically bilingual American, she seems to be indicating that she does not view this as positively

as one might typically expect for second language acquisition. "What hurts most," she says, "is to be stripped of my own blackness simply because I know my way around the English language" (7).

Confrontations may be manifested through differences in language patterns but can be arrayed around such commonplace sociological phenomena as social class, economic status, educational achievement, neighborhood and family relationships. Competition, rivalry and open hostility can sometimes exist among groups of African American youngsters with language use as a focal point. These factors can present a further obstacle to effective discussions about art in the classroom (Brooks, 1978).

Teachers may also find that they are fighting to get past additional communication barriers that are manifestations of aesthetic preferences in discussing works of art from different cultures. This will depend upon where students place themselves within a field that includes an Afro-centric and a Euro-centric conception of self. For many Americans of African descent, an unresolved internal struggle for identity results in "no true self-consciousness" which manifests itself as two separate and "unreconciled strivings" one African and one American (Hale, 1982, 21). Yet, it is imperative that this schism be dealt with and the roots of African heritage be allowed to nourish the cultural deprivation in which many African-Americans find themselves.

However, in a real sense, not much has changed in the perception of young African American dialect speakers who still regard calling someone "black" as a sufficient "come-back" for an insult directed toward them. Neither has there been much change in the Euro-dominated art world when it comes to "blackness." Several personal experiences and observations lead me toward this view.

One of these pivotal experiences occurred when I walked into a gallery where an environmental installation was in progress that revolved around the concept of a safe secure space surrounded by a hostile or dangerous environment. The house form covered with pastel images at the heart of design, surrounded by menacing shiny black life-sized silhouetted figures (that were the dominant visual motif in the surrounding hostile environment) suddenly communicated a very strong aesthetic statement of which the artist was not aware. Subsequent conversations revealed not only the subliminal nature of the artist's message, but also the lack of awareness of the possibility of a different interpretation of the visual elements by whites who had viewed the same scene.

The conversations took me back twenty years to the day and time when people questioned not only the existence of a Black aesthetic but also the existence of "Black culture" as a valid term. In a predominantly white environment, one almost invariably faces the challenge of educating a new generation at the same time one must continually re-educate those who ought to have learned their lessons the first time around.

African American art educators also encounter some interesting dynamics as it relates to race and ethnicity. A group of my predominantly European American university elementary education students went to see the exhibition "Romare Bearden: Origins and Progressions." They all seemed to enjoy themselves, choosing to fulfill a course requirement by participating in a special art event. In reporting on the experience to the rest of the class, several of the students quite openly said that they found the Bearden exhibit to be "really depressing." As it turned out, the source of the depression was the fact that "the people were black," and many of the students "could not relate" to the images.

Although these students were generally rather expressive in discussing art works in class and had written a critical examination of at least one of the pieces, they were not able to be more articulate about their aesthetic response to these Black images. The one Black student in the class suggested that the white students were not comfortable viewing art works where Black figures were black—that is, not rendered in naturalistic skin tones. Many of the students accepted this hypothesis, though at least one of them could find no clear-cut reason for her discomforting reaction. As for myself, the scenario served as a reminder of how tenuous is the balance point between aesthetic pluralism and personal values. Art viewers need help in confronting the racial stereotyping that has been inherited, but it is a challenge that is not for the faint-hearted or thin-skinned. Only those professionals who are keenly aware of racism as it manifests itself in deeply (and dearly) held values need apply.

Part of the special qualification for the job involves a great deal of openness to the unexpected— both in terms of the students' aesthetic responses and in terms of one's own feelings about those responses. Fortunately, the improvisational quality found throughout the artistic traditions of African peoples finds its counterpart in the visual arts as well as styles in interpersonal communication. African American youngsters value spontaneity and may find the deliberate, step-by-step formal analysis proposed by many as a model for art criticism to be very dull and boring. The African American aesthetic preference for pictorial complexity and spatially compressed compositions in visual art has its parallel in the lively interplay of simultaneous conversations.

Jones (1982) uses the term "colorful" in describing her occasional emersions into Black English. The vocabulary of Black English is as colorful as the canvases of its visual artists, often intense and vibrant. So too is the vibrancy or verve of the body language of African American youngsters. This verve is frequently found to be excessive by many teachers who respond negatively to this exuberance within the classroom.

*Some Solutions*

Unless art educators plan for it, certain kinds of learning will simply not take place. Because of the strength of the relationship between language and culture, art educators should be pluralistic in their approach to art criticism with Black youngsters. At times, the focus might well be on confronting the issues raised by negative interactions, examining works that challenge stereotypes and negative perceptions such as are found in Blackstream art. At other times, the focus may be on the positive, exploring commonalities between the art of various cultures. Some works can be selected for critical study that reflect on the literary and oral tradition and bring Black language into the discussion so that it can receive the value that it deserves.

Kossack (1980) presents one important part of the solution to the challenge of diversity in African American language, culture and art criticism in her call for teachers to be trained to recognize and respect Black language, learn the history, structural characteristics, syntactical differences and vocabulary of African American youngsters whom they teach in order to avoid "artificial barriers that impede student progress" (Kossack, 1980, 618). Berko, Wolvin and Wolvin (1977) and Baugh (1983) are but two texts which address this subject in some detail. Noting that negative attitudes of teachers can be changed, Kossack (1980) points to the work of Walter Lamberg and Joseph McCaleb, who were able to train teachers to disregard oral-reading errors stemming from dialect differences during teaching and testing.

Although many researchers have found that teacher attitude is a major contributing factor to reading difficulties of Black English speakers, it does not appear to interfere with comprehensions of materials written in standard English (Kossack, 1980). Therefore, having youngsters become acquainted with the critical commentary of critics and historians is not to be shied away from for fear that the task would be cognitively inappropriate for such youngsters. As long as the vocabulary is made comprehensible, these youngsters have a right to have access to this material as well.

For educators of European ancestry, the question of identity along the ethnic ancestry/American continuum may not have surfaced as an issue before. However, one must begin with educating oneself— starting with one's own language heritage, family customs, traditions, images, values—then widening the search to the culture and heritage of the ethnic group that seems to have the strongest influence within one's own immediate educational environment.

Educators must become cultural catalysts, revealing a heritage of cultural diversity for all of America's children of whatever ethnic ancestry. But this course, too, is not without risk.

Educators and those who work with young people at all levels must become very familiar with their students and their educational environments within and without the classroom. They must also be aware of their own limitations and be honest enough with themselves and their students to seek help from the invaluable community resources available to them.

Youngsters spend 86 percent of their productive time outside of school under the influence of parents and the societal curriculum (*World Book*, 1983). In light of these influential factors, educators need to be realistic in setting goals and objectives, recognizing the critical role of readiness in their endeavors. They must be prepared for the possibility that in this area, more than in any other, the fruits of their labor may be harvested in another season.

Yet, the harvest truly is plentiful, with relatively few artists, critics and art educators currently addressing this important area of language, culture and aesthetic values. In three of my most recent paintings and collages I have used African American

language, literature and oral tradition as major subject and theme. For example, *hurry sonrise: A Postscript for Africania* was inspired by poetry and children's literature. *We Wear the Face of John Kuner* had its genesis in the literary and oral traditions surrounding the Black folk hero, High John the Conqueror and the connotations and symbolism associated with the word "coon."

"Is you de one?" (Fig. 1) is a recent collage and has been well received by African Americans and perhaps a bit uncomfortably by European American colleagues. In the next few years, I hope to continue to take these and other new pieces into more classrooms and develop additional units of instruction to stimulate dynamic art criticism activities and discussions about African American culture. Just as Blackstream artists served as catalysts for political awareness in the 1960s, African American artists of this decade can help to focus attention on the need to explore cultural awareness of aesthetic continuities. Since Blackstream and mainstream American artists of African descent co-existed within the same historical period in the 1960s and 1970s, it should be both expected and acceptable that a wide range of visual expression and response would characterize this

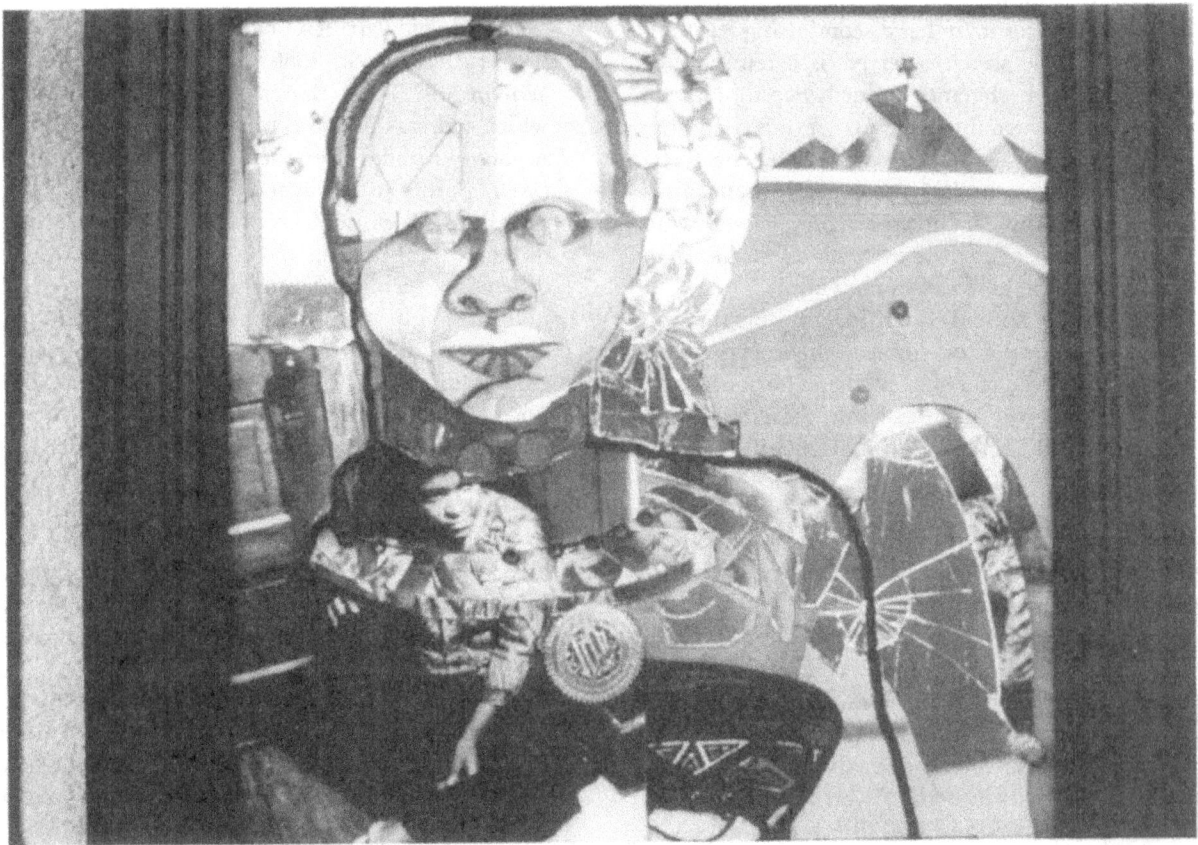

Fig. 1. *Is you de one?* 1987. Photograph courtesy of the author.

current era in the cultural history of this nation.

African American artists who do not feel drawn to express African aesthetic values should not feel compelled to do so. However, those artists who are so inclined will find a fertile field. Educating artists, critics, historians and the viewing public to the value and complexities involved in responding to this art is a challenging but worthwhile pursuit.

# Works Cited

Aponte, W. L. Talkin' white. *Essence Magazine*, January, *19*(1), (1989): 11.

Banks, J.A. *Reducing prejudice in students: Theory, research and strategies.* Paper presented in the Kamloops Spring Institute for Teacher Education Lecture Series. Burnaby, British Columbia, February 3. (ERIC Document Reproduction Service No. ED215 930). (1982).

Baugh, J. *Black street speech: Its history, structure, and survival.* Austin: U of Texas P. (1983).

Berko, R.M., Wolvin, A.D., and Wolvin, D.R. *Communication: A social and career focus.* Palo Alto, CA: Houghton Mifflin Company. (1977).

Brooks, W.C. *Speech communication.* Dubuque, IA: William C. Brown Company. (1979).

Brown, T.J. Should black English be taught in elementary schools? *Instructor*, April, *89*(9), (1980): 22.

Coleman, F. African influences on Black American art. *Black Art: An International Quarterly*, *1*(1), (1976): 4-15.

Cortes, C.E. The societal curriculum: Implications for multiethnic education. In J.A. Banks (Ed.), *Education in the 80s: Multiethnic education.* Washington, DC: National Education Association. (1981).

Fanon, F. *The wretched of the earth.* New York: Grove Press. (1968).

Fleming, P.S. Linking the Legacy: Approaches to the teaching of African and African American art. In B.A. Young (Ed.), *Art, Culture, and Ethnicity.* Reston, VA.: National Art Education Association. (1991).

Hale, J. *Black children: Their roots, culture and learning styles.* Provo, UT: Brigham Young Press. (1982).

Ivory, G.L. Judge Joiner's curious ruling. *Phi Delta Kappan*, May, *61*(9), (1980): 618.

Jacobs, J. *Since the Harlem Renaissance: 50 Years of Afro-American Art.* Exhibition catalogue. Lewisburg, PA: The Center Gallery of Bucknell University. (1985).

Jones, R.L. What's wrong with Black English. *Newsweek*, December 27, *100*(26), (1982): 7.

Kossack, S. District court's ruling on nonstandard dialect needs cautious interpretation. *Phi Delta Kappan*, May, *61*(9), (1980): 617-619.

Martin, R. The new Black aesthetic critics and their exclusion from American "mainstream criticism." *College English*, *50*(4), (1988): 373-382.

Neperud, R. and Jenkins, H.C. Ethnic aesthetics: Either/or? The meaning of paintings by Blacks for southern college students. *Studies in Art Education*, *23*(2), (1982): 14-21.

Ross, R.S. *Speech communication: Fundamentals and practice.* Englewood Cliffs, NJ: Prentice-Hall, Inc. (1980).

Spriggs, E. Michael Harris. In *Africobra. African and African American Traditions in American Culture.* Exhibition catalogue from the colloquium. Oxford, OH: Miami University. (1979).

Taylor, O. Should black English be taught in elementary schools? *Instructor*, April, *89*(9), (1980): 22.

Weaver, R.L. *Understanding interpersonal communication.* Palo Alto, CA: Scott, Foresman and Company. (1978).

*World Book.* PROS Training Manual. Chicago, IL. (1983).

# Criticizing Art With Others

## Terry Barrett

### Criticism

I have been involved with art criticism for more than fifteen years. My involvement includes writing criticism for regional journals, editing *Columbus Art* (a local bimonthly newsprint tabloid of art criticism), writing in academic journals about teaching criticism, conducting college critiques with art and photography students, and teaching undergraduate and graduate courses in art criticism, photography criticism and the teaching of criticism. In the past five years, my activities with criticism have accelerated and diversified because of an interesting new involvement. Through the suggestion and sponsorship of the Ohio Arts Council, I am functioning in a developing experimental program as a critic-in-education, parallel to an artist-in-education. As a visiting critic, I am working with different groups of people in diverse settings and leading them in the criticism of various kinds of art.

I use several different approaches to criticism. All of these approaches, however, eventually are reduced to activities of describing, interpreting and evaluating works of art—and sometimes theorizing about art. I believe that interpretation is the most important aspect of criticism and stress it over evaluation. Unless we understand it, art cannot contribute to new knowledge of the world and alternative ways of experiencing it. If people sufficiently understand a work of art, its judgment is implied or is relatively easy to derive. When people do not understand art they become intimidated by it and eventually indifferent or even hostile toward it.

Our critical discussions are guided by beliefs that art is about something: it demands interpretation, it is interpretable, and there is no one correct and definitive interpretation. The artist's interpretation of his or her own art is one interpretation among many competing interpretations. These views of interpretation aid us in resisting dogmatic interpretations and also allow that some interpretations are better grounded in evidence and more convincing than others. We challenge interpretations when they seem unfounded, too idiosyncratic or too far removed from the art object itself.

I try to establish a psychologically safe environment in which people feel comfortable to discuss art by reinforcing their comments, disallowing put-downs from others, acknowledging the role of individual histories in perceiving art, encouraging a multiplicity of understandings and drawing many people into the discussion. I especially encourage careful listening and ask members to build on each others' comments. We often begin with personal preferences for artworks and then move to interpretive or evaluative discussions of them. When we judge artworks we always ask for reasons that support evaluations and attempt to make explicit the criteria in which the reasons are embedded.

This essay relates some of my experiences in facilitating discussions about art with various groups of people. Its major points are that people of all backgrounds and ages can critically encounter artworks of all kinds. Through critical discussion of works of art, people increase their understanding and appreciation of art. They also gain self-confidence in their ability to independently enjoy experiences in artworlds they may have thought previously closed to them because of their lack of familiarity with those artworlds and a means of access to the objects they contain.

### Some Situations

My first stint as a critic-in-education was in a public elementary school in Lima, Ohio. This occurred as part of a dance residency of Stuart Pimsler Dance and Theater, a postmodern company making dances that respond to contemporary social issues. To become familiar with the Company's work, which was new to me, I studied videotapes of their pieces, watched the dancers in rehearsal and talked with them about their dance and my attitudes about criticism.

During their three-week residency, Stuart Pimsler and Suzanne Costello, principal dancer and artistic co-director, led the children in movement exercises, talked with them about contemporary dance, choreographed a core group of fifth graders into some of the Company's pieces and performed a concert for the school and the community. I arrived toward the end of the residency and after the performance. For periods of about fifty minutes I led four classes of

66

fourth and fifth grade children in critical discussions about dance and criticism.

I began the classes by asking what they understood about art criticism. We discussed how the term "criticism" has negative connotations in everyday language and that it means to find fault in people, things or events. They were familiar with film critics appearing on television shows such as "Entertainment Tonight" and "At the Movies." We added food critics, music critics and art critics. Because the critics with whom the children were familiar functioned primarily as guides to consumers, offering ratings with stars, forks or thumbs up or down, we discussed the value and limitations in society of this kind of criticism. I explained that art criticism covers much broader concepts than positive or negative evaluations. I explained that as a critic who writes about art, I am more interested in informing others about works of art and helping others to appreciate new and sometimes difficult pieces. I also explained that when I write about art, I understand it better and appreciate it more because of the focused time, careful attention and thought that writing criticism requires. For the purposes of our discussion I then asked the children to reconstruct in language one of Pimsler's pieces they saw and performed.

From the dance company they had already acquired sophisticated vocabulary to describe movement. We used this vocabulary to decipher and articulate the meaning of some of the movements in the dance. The interpretations the children had were insightful and the discussions lively. One of the dances utilized baby dolls as props and the dancers mimicked the stiff movements of toy dolls. The children readily related their knowledge of and experience with dolls and posited that sometimes people behave like dolls, passively allowing themselves to be manipulated. They enjoyed the challenge of examining their experiences and putting them into language and were pleased with their ability to intelligently discuss contemporary dance.

In a related situation, in an arts magnet school in Columbus, Ohio, elementary school students were in the culmination of a month-long residency with a visiting professional dancer, a musician and a visual artist. During this residency the artists and core groups of fourth and fifth graders built a large-scale multisensory environment. The children dramatically transformed a large room with tunnels of paper, life-size contours of their bodies cut out of diazo photosensitive paper, various textures on which to walk, dramatic lighting, original tape-recorded electronic music the children composed and child dancers in costume. School children and their parents moved through the environment throughout a Friday. I also experienced the environment that day and returned on Monday to facilitate an hour-long session

of criticism about it with a class of fourth graders who constructed and performed in the piece.

I introduced myself as a critic and the editor of *Columbus Art*, showed them a copy, said that I had experienced their environment and asked them what I should say if I were going to review it for the paper. They answered: "Say it was great!" They were very proud of their environment. I asked them to describe what *it* was but that request did not initially make much sense to them because they had seen it and I had seen it. They saw little need to describe it until I explained that the people who would read the review would not have seen the piece, and because it was a temporary piece, would not be able to see it. Now motivated to tell others what had been there, how it came about, who made it, of what and where, they had much more information to offer. I jotted their key ideas as notes on the black board, stressing that critics need to make clear and lively descriptions and praised their effective uses of language.

From this verbal reconstruction of the piece and how it came about, we next attempted to explain to our imagined readers what the piece was about and if and why it would be a valuable experience for others. The children wanted to simply declare it valuable because they had made it and because they wanted good publicity for their school. I insisted, however, that I had a conscience as a critic and could not praise things just for personal gain. I also insisted that as critics we need to offer reasons for our judgments that others could understand and believe. An enthusiastic discussion followed, with more notes written on the board.

With about ten minutes of the class period left, we organized the random scribbles on the blackboard. I told them that the editorial limitations of our review were that it was to be 750 words in length, about four or five paragraphs, with one black and white photograph. We decided how to start and how to finish the review and constructed an outline on the board that we would follow if we were to write the review. I ended the session there.

In an out-of-school situation, I accepted an invitation to conduct a critique of the work of an art club in a small rural town in Ohio. A group of about fifteen adults who, for the most part, made art for recreation brought samples of their work to the previously advertised critique on a week night. It was sponsored by the Coshocton Fine Art Guild. Most of the artists were older adults who painted scenes of barns, flowers and countrysides. One woman painted whimsical cows in eerie environments, and a recent college graduate made close-up photographs of cows in barns and photographs of herself in psychologically penetrating self-portraits which involved partial nudity. I picked a painting that we would start with and asked that the artist remain a listener and not contribute to the conversation. I led the group in an interpretive discussion, focusing the discussion on the question "What does this piece express and how?" During the two-hour session we discussed two paintings by two painters and the photographs mentioned above.

I had forewarned the group that we would not get to all of the works and had explained that the purpose of the session was to learn about art criticism itself and how art can be thoughtfully reflected upon. They were more accustomed to critiques that offered advice to artists, usually by an artist more experienced or better known than them. The discussion was lively and the speakers insightful about the artworks. Both the artists whose works we discussed and the discussants were very enthused about the evening. They had not previously participated in a critique that concentrated on interpreting their artworks rather than judging and giving advice on how to improve them; nor had they been involved in critiques that disallowed the artists' slated intentions from guiding their considerations. They were pleased with how much they could discover and articulate about an artwork and were flattered that their artworks could sustain penetrating discussions.

### Some Other Groups

My work in criticizing art with others has included a broad range of student groups. I have worked in public urban, suburban and rural elementary and secondary schools, private college-preparatory schools, Catholic schools and universities. Participants have included children considered to have mental and emotional disabilities, children "at risk" (of dropping out) and, with the help of a sign language interpreter, teenagers with hearing impairments. Outside of schools, I have had occasion to lead groups of recreational painters, museum docents, senior citizens living in a retirement home, camera clubs, classroom teachers and principals on art field trips, arts council board members, a college art history club and a large group of professional visual and performing artists serving as artists-in-the-schools.

My work with senior citizens has been very challenging and ultimately rewarding. Working with them often required some quick improvisation. For example, in one setting there were about thirty elderly people who gathered in a commons room of a Jewish retirement center. The director, expecting a lecture from me, had seated the people in rows. After an introduction he handed me a microphone with a cord so short that it allowed for no mobility. I began asking them descriptive questions about a large size reproduction of Oscar Kokoshka's painting, the *Mandril*. They quickly and angrily informed me that they could not see it because of the dim lighting in the room. They also resented the distance I was from

them. When I moved forward, I had to drop the mike and the people in the back rows could hear neither me nor those responding to my questions. The lights were as bright as they would go. The audience was increasingly annoyed and vocal. I had an hour left and resisted a very strong urge to apologize and flee. I asked the attendants to help me seat the participants in small groups. After minutes of mayhem with attendants moving people about, about six groups of five people each had their own reproduction of different twentieth century paintings and went about discussing them.

I asked that their discussions be interpretive at first, and we then moved into discussion of artistic value, attempting to identify criteria by which the artworks should be judged. I was invited to the Center to prepare them for a task at hand. This retirement center sponsors a large and progressive curated outdoor summer sculpture exhibition, and the senior citizens select a piece for a purchase award.

Their insights into the paintings, based on years and years of varied life experiences, were interesting and their enthusiasm for learning this late in their lives was inspiring. They, in turn, were enlivened by the artworks they examined and their ability to interpret and value them. They were anxious to use what they had learned about looking at art on the sculptures that they would judge. Their curiosity and desire for mental challenges compensated for any losses due to their age such as failing vision and hearing.

On another occasion I worked with teenagers with hearing impairments in an after-school photography course sponsored by the Dayton Art Institute. The teenagers learned to make photographs with Wayne Levin, a Hawaiian photographer and recipient of the National Endowment for the Arts Photographer's Fellowship. I brought several contemporary reproductions of photographs for them to critically analyze. Some of the teens read lips, some could hear with the help of microphone and amplifier, some spoke, others signed. An interpreter accompanied the group. We had a lively discussion, with all participating and all contributing insights. They compared the artworks to the images they were making. My unease due to my unfamiliarity with hearing-impaired people quickly vanished as we talked about the photographs.

One of my most personally rewarding sessions was with a group of about thirty Dayton city school fourth, fifth and sixth grade students experiencing developmental disabilities. Teachers and aides settled the children on the floor of a carpeted room. I was struck by how long it took the teachers and aides to gather and focus the children's attention. Once they were settled, I showed them several large reproductions of twentieth century paintings depicting animals of various sorts in a variety of styles. These included Picasso's *Cat and Lobster*, Macke's *Landscape with*

*Cows and Camel*, Klee's *Sinbad the Sailor* and Chagall's *I and the Village*. I elicited answers to questions based on what they could see in the paintings and had them talk about subject matter and form and the relation between the two. They had astute observations, were anxious to talk and listened to each other. The thirty minute period went very quickly for them and for me. Their teachers and I had underestimated their attention span. Our time together could have easily been extended.

### Different Kinds of Art

In addition to critically attending to dance, artworks by students and adult artists, paintings, sculptures and photographs from the twentieth century Western art tradition (including an African American collection), I have used other art shown in different settings. This has included original art of contemporary African Americans in a not-for-profit gallery, art from several cultures in a commercial ethnographic gallery of art, Islamic prayer rugs in a museum, a reel of Clio Award winning television commercials and the movie "Batman." Some of the more interesting contemporary art I have used includes the postmodern feminist pastiches by Barbara Kruger, Robert Mapplethorpe's controversial exhibition "The Perfect Moment" (*in situ* and in reproduction) and *The Deerslayers* by Les Krims.

Mapplethorpe's *Man in Polyester Suit* generated an interesting discussion among adults. A group of about a dozen classroom teachers, art teachers and principals from Lima, Ohio, sponsored by the Lima Arts Council, took a weekend trip to Chicago. The council invited a theater critic and me to engage the participants in critical dialogue about a range of contemporary arts we were to see. We viewed the now famous Mapplethorpe exhibition at the Museum of Contemporary Art. In our ensuing discussion back in our hotel suite, two Black women got into an intense but friendly interpretive dispute concerning whether or not *Man in Polyester Suit* was a racist image. The black and white photograph has great clarity of detail and depicts a Black man from below his shoulders to above his knees, wearing a three-piece suit. His face is not visible. His penis, which is uncircumcised and very large, hangs from his open fly.

One woman argued that the picture reinforced negative stereotypical constructions of Black men as sexual brutes without brains. She was offended that the image was made by a white photographer, that the man was anonymous and faceless and that he was apparently chosen for his trim body and the size of his penis. The second women argued that the image was ennobling, that it celebrated sexuality and the power of the Black man and that it was liberating in its confrontation—the white man's polyester and

all that went with it could not suppress the vitality of the Black man.

I brought slides of Krims's *The Deerslayers* to high school students in a hunting area of the state. The portfolio is a collection of grisly photographs of men, women and children with deer lashed across the hoods of their cars. About one-third to one-half of the group had hunted. Predictably, the students were divided on the issue of hunting. Several had shot deer that very season, and several thought hunting was inhumane and disgusting. Perhaps also predictably, but surprising to me, those who hunted thought that the Krims portfolio was promoting hunting; those who were opposed to hunting thought that the portfolio also opposed it. Despite my prompting questions, the students could not go beyond their own belief systems to more objectively consider what was in the photographs.

I used the imagery of Barbara Kruger with a high school class in creative writing. Kruger's work is challenging for anyone: her images can be read very simplistically and incorrectly because her denotational information is quite clear. However, the very rich connotations of her words and appropriated images are difficult to decipher. For example, *Untitled* (1981) shows a baby's plump hand reaching to grasp an adult female hand. Two strips of words declare in bold type: "Your every wish is our command." On the face of it, the image can be read as a cute and simple Hallmark greeting card message about parenting. The student critics, mostly female, were able to offer several sophisticated readings that were in keeping with Kruger's socially critical work. They considered the pronoun "your" to be referring to adult males and "our" to refer to women rather than reading either as referring to the infant. They also considered issues of unwanted pregnancy and issues of lawmakers legislating about women's bodies and their right to abort.

In Lodi, Ohio, in a junior high school in a farming community, we deconstructed award-winning television commercials, seeking to determine who was selling what to whom and by what means. I showed a thirty second or sixty second spot once, entertained answers to the general questions, then showed it again and again and asked them to count shots, look for cuts, angles of view, lighting, casting and costuming to support their interpretations of the commercial.

These students were tracked into "academic" (normal) and "challenge" (gifted and talented) classes. A Pepsi commercial, specifically targeted to their age group, baffled the academic group, leaving them unable to determine much beyond that it was Pepsi that was being sold. They were unable, without considerable help from me, to decipher that they were the intended audience and could not decipher the advertiser's means of manipulation. The challenge group was quite insightful in their psychological penetration of the ad. They also deconstructed some full-page cigarette ads we tore from magazines, adeptly considering questions about the selling of desire.

The following day we turned our attention to the movie "Batman," recorded on video tape, and critically attended to scenes I randomly selected. The students already had a general context for the scenes (all but one or two had seen the movie and several had seen it many times), so plot reconstruction was not necessary. We viewed a complete scene with sound; I then asked for general observations about how the scene was constructed and toward what effects. We viewed it again, without sound, looking for the psychological effects of the director's formal decisions such as the rhythm with which the shots were cut, and we contrasted dialogue scenes with action scenes.

The disparity between the two groups of students, however, is worrisome to me and points up the need for more education about television and advertising *somewhere* in the school curriculum. The challenge students could spend a lot of time on one ad or movie scene, seeking more and more insights without tiring; the academic students tired after two viewings, wanted to move on and be stimulated anew.

When dealing with artworks from outside of a group's culture, we seek information about that culture by which we can better understand and appreciate the work. When someone with a group has expertise, I gladly turn over the session to them. An American woman married to an Iranian and who had lived several years in Iran before the revolution led us in a very informative investigation of Middle Eastern prayer rugs on temporary loan to the Columbus Museum of Art. When the group visited the Ethnographic Gallery, a moderator was assigned to research the cultural origins of the collection and to lead our discussion. In these situations where the group needs information, we still avoid lectures and instead invent strategies by which they can more actively learn.

### Critical Activities

All of the critical sessions discussed in this essay are highly interactive among participants. I ask for answers to probing questions about the artworks and ask that the participants direct their insights to each other rather than to me. I frequently ask the group if they are able to physically hear a response and then if they agree or disagree with what has been said. Answers are based on evidence of an internal source (within the artwork) or an external source (contextual information). Some of the information I supply if I think it will further the discussion, but I keep my remarks brief and avoid lecturing. Most of the time the discussions are interpretive, understanding meaning and effect through what the art expresses. I encourage participants to challenge interpretive

assertions that are not based on evidence or which are too far removed from the work in question. I frequently and sincerely compliment insightful comments. Through the process I also learn things about works of art with which I am already quite familiar.

I often but not always begin discussions by asking for descriptions. When discussing representational work I usually start with subject matter rather than form because I think this is a more comfortable and natural place to start. When using Picasso's *Cat and Lobster*, for example, I begin by asking: "What is happening in the picture?" Once the audience deciphers this very expressionist painting to be a cat and lobster fighting, I ask: "Who is going to win?" The lobster. "How do you know?" They discover that they know because they are able to read the formal properties of the work: because of the aggressive angle of the lobster, its metallic color, the frenzied strokes Picasso used for the cat, because the cat is receding off the canvas's edge and so forth.

Occasionally we judge artworks. When we do we usually direct attention to criteria and how an artwork ought to be judged as good. I sometimes ask participants to place a colored "stickum" on the reproduction they think the best and a different color one on the work they like the most, and we discuss the reasons for their different choices. It is especially interesting when their preferences differ from their judgments of value. In a session with mostly African American high school students in Dayton, after I noted the paintings that received no votes from the students, I tried to select paintings "that they would really hate." In general they preferred representational images and realism. At first I succeeded in finding paintings they did not value by showing them works by Helen Frankenthaler, but then some students began seeing value in abstraction and minimalism and defended her paintings to the other students. Midway through the session I argued that all the paintings were good for different reasons but that the most realistic piece I had was the weakest aesthetically. I provided reasons for my views and asked for counterreasons from the students. At this point the two art teachers jumped in rather emphatically: one was a realist himself, and the other did not want her students exposed to any negative judgments about art, believing they should value it all.

Occasionally we begin and end with preferences. In Chicago I asked the group of Lima teachers and administrators to tour the many commercial galleries in the River North gallery district and to come back and tell us which one piece of art they would buy. To accomplish their assignment, they perused many galleries, talked with gallery directors and occasionally artists. In the process they learned the economics of the art market and generally became much more comfortable with and less intimidated by a gallery world.

### Conclusion

Art is powerful because of its content as well as its means of expression. The power of art is evident in the stimulation people feel in thinking and talking about it. This is particularly the case if they are given some hints as to how to proceed and a psychologically safe environment in which to talk and learn. They need ways to enter into works, a means to extend their attention and a way to proceed productively in thinking about and interacting with art. They especially need enough confidence to begin.

Choices of what artworks to present to a group is important. The more challenging the work, the more engaging the session. If the artworks are very simple and noncontroversial, then one's questions have to be stimulating. If artworks are too far removed from the viewers' experiences, however, then the viewers will have little with which they can relate. In this situation they must be funded with relevant information. Their need for too much funding can result in a spontaneous lecture by the facilitator, an action which will prevent critical discussion among the participants.

In group discussions, wonderful things can happen between and among individuals when they engage with each other about works of art. This cannot happen when viewing art individually. A group of individuals can construct a broader range of meaning than an individual can. Groups also tend to be self-correcting about interpretations that are too far removed from the work to be convincing. Groups can widen narrow, dogmatic or idiosyncratic views about both art and life.

It was an awesome experience for me to watch a group of wary adults with little prior experience with contemporary art move through the difficult exhibition of photographs by Robert Mapplethorpe. They were moved by the beauty of the exhibition and simultaneously repelled by some of its tough subject matter (mutilated testicles, a man urinating in another's mouth, anal penetration by a fist and forearm). They were willing to articulate their reactions and to talk about their responses with others. The exhibition engendered some frank and honest discussions about homosexuality, sadomasochism, black-white relationships among men and men and men and women, child nudity in erotically charged environments and rights of artistic expression.

I can imagine that these Ohioans returned to their communities and told of their experiences to family, friends and colleagues. It is likely that they articulated some understanding, honest uncertainty and a sense of excitement about being challenged and being able to adequately meet the challenges of art. Our trip took place a few months before the Mapplethorpe uproar in Washington when the Corcoran cancelled the same exhibition we had seen in Chicago, and several months before the Contemporary Arts Center of Cincinnati and its director were indicted on obscenity charges for displaying the same photographs. The Lima group beamed with pride over their ability to consider the issues passionately and reasonably.

Similar results can be obtained with less sensational work and with people of much younger age. After a full session of discussing twentieth century paintings in an elementary school in Toledo, a fourth grade girl looked up wistfully and to no one in particular sighed, "Oh, I could just do this forever!"

The experiences these persons have had with critically attending to art are not fleeting. In May of 1988, in a small rural school near Bowling Green, Ohio, I had a class of fourth graders describe and interpret twentieth century paintings for a class of kindergarteners. The kindergarteners listened for the whole forty-five minute period, and the fourth graders spoke to them in language they could understand. The attentiveness of the small children and the care of the older ones in communicating with them was very endearing. The following spring I returned to the school and met those kindergarteners who were now first graders. Before starting our session, I asked them if they remembered me from last year. I expected comments on my beard but instead got detailed recall from memory about the subject and form of every painting they had seen a year ago. They were excited to see some new paintings, but they first wanted to see again last year's with the excitement of seeing old friends.

In talking about art that is difficult to decipher, for whatever reason, people can be taught to listen respectfully to the insights of each other if they are genuinely interesting in coming to grips with the work. In a private school in Cincinnati, a fifth grader noted that Wynn Bullock's landscape photographs were "rather enigmatic." When I asked him to explain further, he did and quite accurately. More amazing to me, however, was that no one laughed or jeered him for his sophisticated language. These children listened intently to their classmate and nodded in understanding and in approval. They had already learned to respect intelligence. Works of art were just another occasion to reflectively engage in stimulating thought and talk.

In my work in schools and communities, I keep myself motivated and stimulated by seeing how far children and adults can go with art. I keep trying new works and different strategies. I began with contemporary dance, then dealt with art by children taught by adult artists, brought in the work of a variety of contemporary photographers, gathered reproductions of paintings with diverse subject matters and styles, took advantage of exhibitions from other cultures and tried the work of Mapplethorpe and Kruger, "Batman," TV commercials, ads in magazines and other artifacts from daily life.

There is a shortage of good quality, large reproductions of contemporary art and especially art made by women, people of color and other underrepresented artists. When I find such artworks on posters or show announcements, I save them. I frequent bookstores after January looking for calendar sales, hoping to find art calendars, and buy exhibition catalogues and books of contemporary art and remove the bindings to make sets of comparatively inexpensive reproductions.

There are many ways to teach people about art, but I think engaging them in the thoughtful criticism of art, the art they themselves may make, art from throughout the world and especially the art in their own communities, is a particularly good way to teach. Their acts of criticizing art get them involved in deciphering what is being shown to them and make them less dependent on the authority of artists, historians or docents and more independent in their ability to move through their visual world, which is a cacophony of competing messages both spiritual and crass.

My experiences have shown me that there are far fewer limits to what can be done with people and art, in schools and out, than we may imagine and that the activities of criticism are several and can be widely applied to a range of objects with anyone who is willing. I think the results are that some people are less afraid of art, less susceptible to visual manipulation, better equipped to enter multiple artworlds from street fairs to museums, more joyful in their encounters, more respectful of their fellow critics and artists and more tolerant of a diversity of experiences and expressions.

# Toward an Understanding of Skin Art

## John Wilton

The only difference between tattooed and non-tattooed people is tattooed people don't care if you're not tattooed.

FTW
*No Boundaries*

Understanding, writes Feldman (1967), is the chief goal of art criticism. Works of art provide information to those who understand them. Understanding comes from specific knowledge, education, training, information, involvement and exposure. It has become a practice in Western society to depend on art critics as specialists who gather this specific knowledge, formulate critical judgments and disseminate this knowing to the interested masses. Accordingly, we ask the art critic to explain mainstream art movements like Expressionism, Neo-geo and Post-modernism to those who do not have the time, motivation or facility to gain that specific knowledge. Their considered opinions, explanations and profound understanding help others see art as it was intended.

While understanding works of art becomes possible through information provided by the works themselves, related knowledge, involvement with and exposure to the works, the artists and the culture within which the works were created, lack of knowledge often breeds contempt and fear, even in art. As a rule, without knowledge there is misunderstanding. Even *with* knowledge there is often misinterpretation, again leading to fear and contempt. The 1989 events involving Robert Mapplethorpe, Andres Serrano and Jesse Helms should certainly attest to this condition.[1] While knowledge is no guarantee of acceptance, I must hope that it leads to tolerance and enlightenment.

When understanding is blocked, we are deprived of Feldman's (1967) second goal of art criticism—that of delight or pleasure. This, I believe, is the case with skin art. The lack of knowledge available to the general population has prevented understanding, which in turn has perpetuated a widespread fear and contempt of skin art, those creating skin art, and those collecting skin art. Consider the listing for "tattoo" in the *Encyclopedia Britannica*: it instructs the reader to "see Mutilations and Deformations."[2] Without the necessary critics of art gathering specific knowledge, formulating considered opinions and disseminating explanation and understanding, the general popula-

tion will most likely continue to be deprived of the potential delight and pleasure inherent in skin art.

If we are to move towards pluralism in art criticism, we must move towards an understanding of all of the "other than mainstream" forms of expression. Living near Daytona Beach, Florida, prompted me to explore the form of expression called "tattoo." Once a year Daytona Beach is a mecca for the largest group of tattoo owners in the nation. The event is Bike Week, and participants come from all over the country to ride the beaches, show off their "hogs" (Harleys, not Hondas) and display their latest art acquisitions. In the fall of 1989, I spent a weekend photographing tattoos and learning about their owners. All it took to get volunteers was a simple sign that read "got any tattoos?"

That experience left me with a desire to know more and a need for a critical base. I found that the stigma attached to skin art is perhaps one of the most unyielding; therefore, it is my intention here to provide a historical perspective, some cultural perspectives and an examination of the many functions of skin art. The following information has been compiled with the hope of moving the reader away from this stigma and toward a critical understanding of one more form of human expression.

### The Practice of Body-Marking

'Short is the pain, and long is the ornament.'

Tattoo Chant
*Modern Primitives*

Archaeologists provide us with evidence that body-marking was practiced as far back as 12,000 years before Christ (Burchette, 1958). The first markings were the result of scarifying, cutting, branding and painting. Today, skin art falls into three categories: scarification, piercing and tattooing.

Decorative scarification, or raised keloids in design patterns, are common among darker skinned populations for whom tattooing would be ineffective (Fellowes, 1971). This practice involves cutting deep marks into the skin and rubbing charcoal or a similar irritant material into the cut, thereby keeping the wound open. Eventually it is allowed to heal, leaving a deep scar. Small scars are frequently made on the

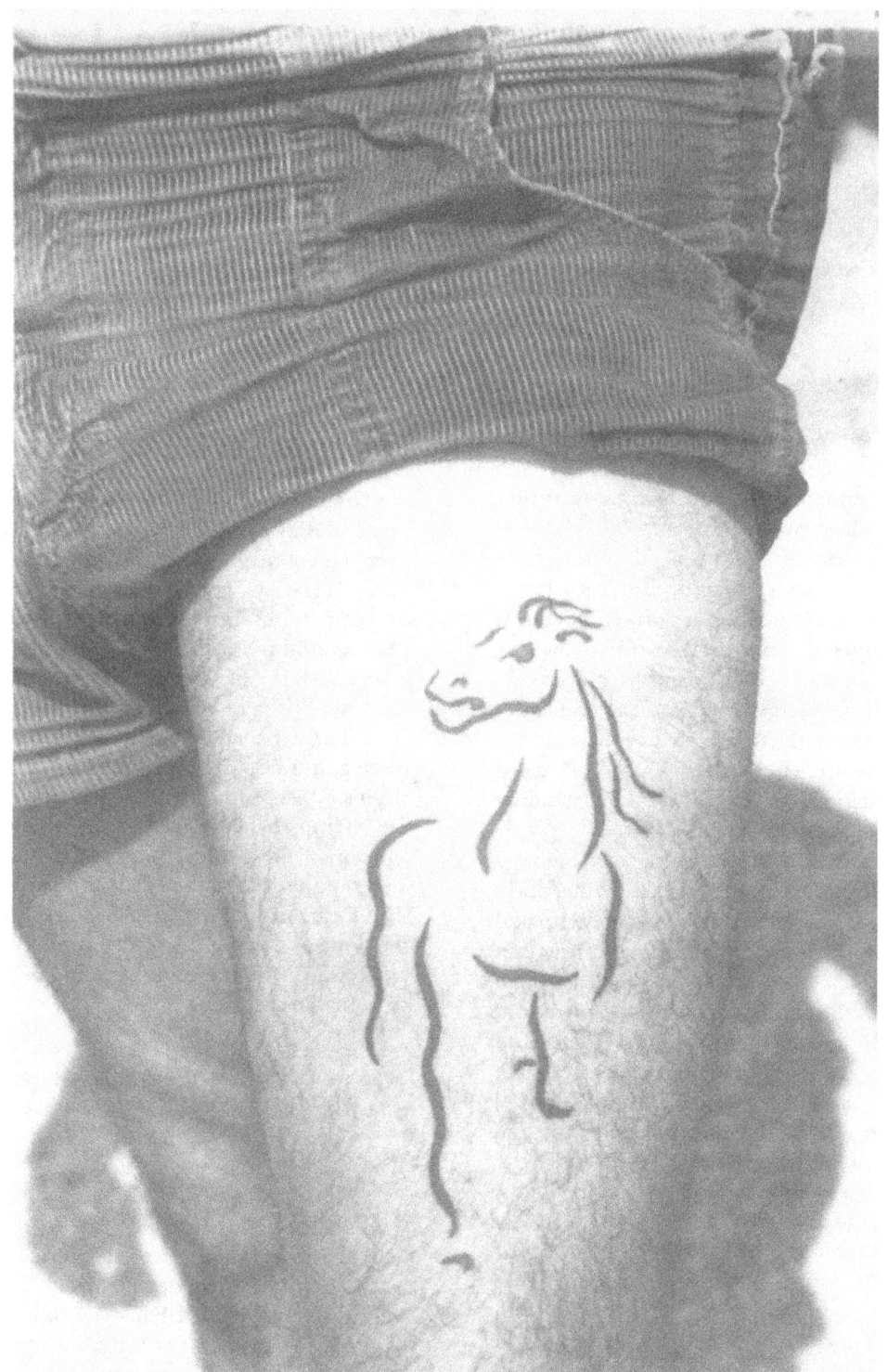

*Legend Horse.* An example of tribal style artwork using line and shape, not color or shading, to communicate the message. Owner: Geri Farmer, Daytona Beach. Artist: Wondo Loski, Daytona Beach. Photograph by J. Wilton

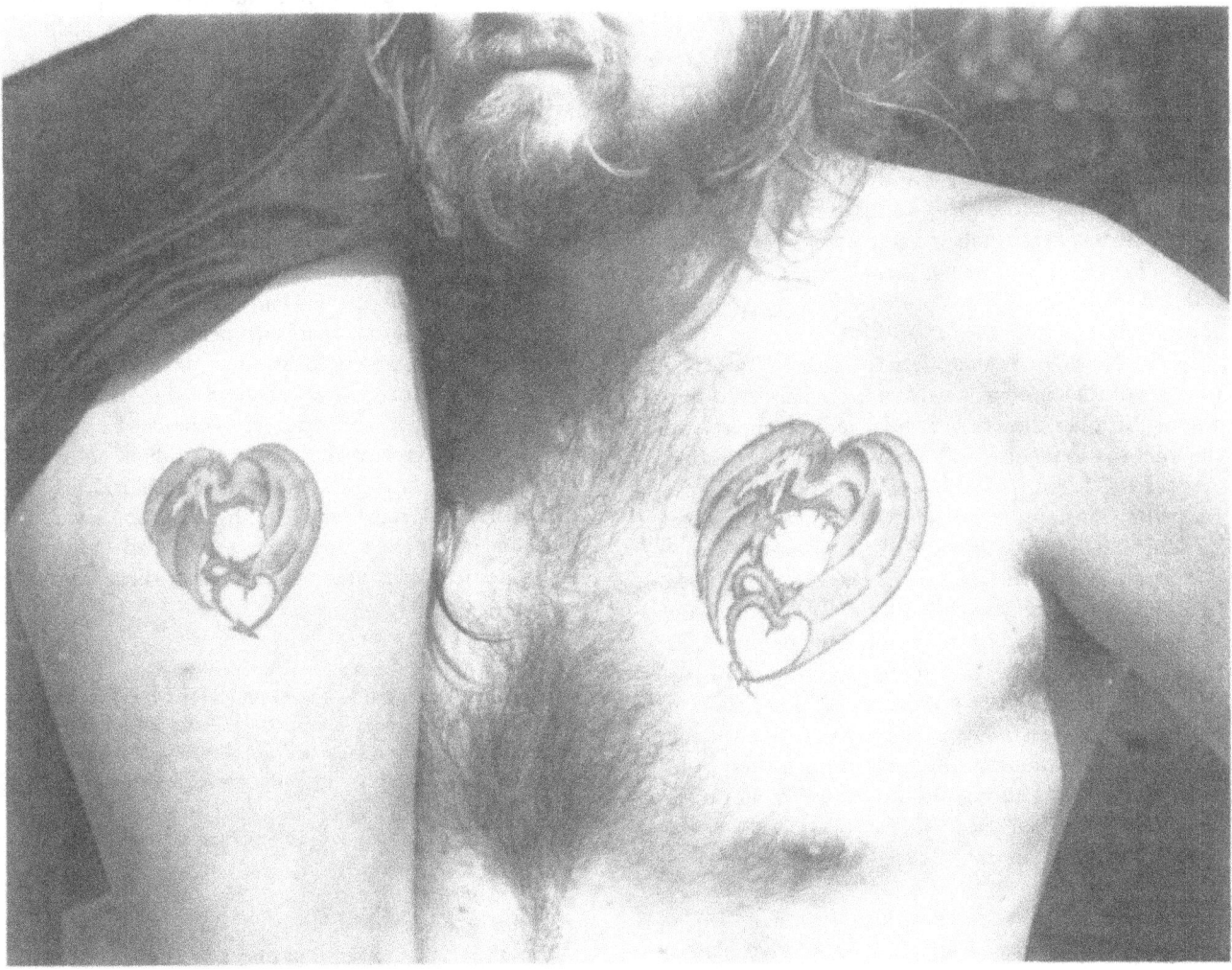

*Matching Dragon Hearts.* Owners: Norma and Geri Farmer. Created at Southern Refried Tattoos, Daytona Beach. Photograph by J. Wilton.

face as tribal or clan identification. Magic and ritual is the motivation behind the scarifying of women during pregnancy in many African tribes, while personal adornment is often the primary reason for creating elaborate patterns on the chest, arms and legs.

Piercing in the Western World is a manifestation of adornment borrowed from ancient as well as modern tribal rituals. It can indeed be classified as deformation and manipulation because, unlike the surface decorations of tattooing and scarification, piercing alters the size, shape and function of various parts and areas of the body. Although piercing and scarification are types of skin art—like body painting—these techniques are practiced by very few individuals or cultural groups. They are isolated rarities and remain outside, if you will, the "mainstream" of skin art, tattooing. To move toward an initial understanding of skin art, it would seen most beneficial to investigate the more conventional manifestations of the art form, not the rarities.

The desire to pierce myself has always been in part for political reasons—the politics of deviance. Earlier in my life as an art student, the Dada movement had a profound impact on my life. It helped me realize the ridiculous sensitivities that the 'establishment' suffered from, which in turn kept that 'establishment' from progressing. My piercings are my 'weapon' to struggle against the authoritarian/conformist tendencies of America which attempt to dissuade the populace from individual initiative and diversity.

Zapata
*Modern Primitives*

### Tattooing: A Chronology

While the practice of tattooing can be found all over the world, it seems no other art is as threatening, mysterious and seductive as the tattoo (Zucker, 1955). Although its history stretches back to the dawn of human expression, tattooing continues to fascinate and frighten societies around the world (Wroblewski, 1987).

Tattooing by puncture, using a sharp tool that

deposits pigment under the top layer of skin, was first practiced in Egypt between 4000 and 2000 B.C. (Burchett, 1958). According to Fellowes (1971), the earliest *written* evidence of tattooing appears in the Old Testament (Leviticus 19:28, 21:5 and Deuteronomy 14:1) prohibiting the practice because of its connection to a cult of the dead. Classical Greek and Roman writers refer to tattooing as a loathsome Barbarian custom. Roman criminals and slaves were marked with tattoos for identification, while the Emperor Caligula ordered Roman citizens tattooed for his own amusement.

The New Testament offers the possibility of the first use of the tattoo as a symbol for a counterculture when it implies the use of special tattooed marks on the forehead to identify followers of Jesus (Revelation 7:3, 13:16, 22:4; Galations 6:17). Conversely, the Emperor Constantine forbade tattooing of the face, viewing it as a disfigurement of that human feature made particularly in God's own image. At the Synod of Calcuth in Northumberland, 787 A.D., all forms of tattooing were forbidden, presumably because they were seen as a connection to pagan Britain during the Middle Ages. These governmental decrees along with the Old Testament passages were taken quite seriously, and tattooing disappeared for a time from most of Europe. Although forbidden by the Koran as well, tattooing survived in Moslem lands, with practitioners explaining that the soul would be purified by fire before entering paradise, thereby removing all marks of tattooing (Fellowes, 1971). Meanwhile, in Ancient China one of the Five Classic Punishments was facial tattooing (Wroblewski, 1987).

The "Age of Exploration" and the "Voyages of Discovery" in the period from the thirteenth to the sixteenth century were the cause of the European rediscovery and adaptation of the art to their own means and bodies (Webb, 1976). Before this period, European languages lacked a specific term for tattooing. It was known as "pricking," "marking" or "painting" (Fellowes, 1971). Captain Cook, upon return from his first voyage to Tahiti in 1771, introduced the word "tattoo" to Europe (Webb, 1976). The Tahitian pronunciation is actually *tatau*, meaning "the results of tapping" from the root word *ta*, "to strike, beat or tap." This maritime contact with cultures that tattooed extensively probably accounts for the initial popularity of the practice among seamen (Fellowes, 1971). Ironically, while Christian missionaries endeavored to save the souls of the "primitives" who tattooed their skin, sailors carried the custom back to Christian lands where the Bible had long ago banned the custom (Wroblewski, 1987).

Although the rediscovery of tattooing was readily accepted by the seafaring subculture, it was most likely viewed as primitive heathen debauchery by the majority in most Western cultures. While innocent in intention, researchers like Margaret Mead probably contributed considerably to the prevailing attitude towards tattoos. In reporting the connection of tattooing with puberty rituals in Tahiti and the Marquesas, mourning festivals in Hawaii, New Zealand and the Marquesas and human sacrifices in New Zealand, it would seem that Mead (and other researchers) helped reinforce the stigma which is still connected to tattooing. Admittedly, without an understanding of cultural significance, mourning marks on the tongue (Hawaii) would seem to be a barbarous act. Tattoo marks as memorials of revenge obligations, as practiced in the Marquesas, or as permanent war markings were reported to us not long after a time when we were very concerned with the "savage" behavior of the American Indian, so-called murders who only *painted* their war markings on (Mead, 1928). What were we to think of the "savages" who had their markings permanently and painfully etched into their skin while performing human sacrifices!

All my life, since I was about six or seven years old, I had this strange craving for a tattoo. I was about seven when I first asked my mother if I could have a tattoo—and she came completely unglued at the seams. After her violent reaction I have never asked her again—but I never lost the strange urge to have one."

Bill Mokry
*Tattoo: Pigments of Imagination*

The reasons for tattooing, from antiquity through the present, are many and varied. While all individual fascinations and motivations may never be fully known or understood, it is possible to move *toward* an understanding of the most personal of all art forms.

People decorate themselves in many ways. Costume is one of the earliest forms of decoration. The body was probably the first surface to receive ornamentation. In many cultures, the distinction between clothing and ornament is blurred. Just as clothing serves as mental and physical protection, the tattoo is often used as protection from evil spirits in certain cultures while its purpose is purely ornamental in others.

A great deal of tattooing is simply a matter of customary behavior for a cultural group, very often symbolic of membership in a social category of age, rank, sex, religion, ethnic group or occupation (Fellowes, 1971). The face is a prime candidate for such decorative and personal marks. The Maoris of New Zealand wore complex marks indicating bravery and status. When a warrior was killed in battle, his head, if decorated, was cut off and carefully preserved. If plain-faced, the corpse was ignored. Women of Nukurd Atoll in Micronesia have had their pubic regions tattooed for procreation while children born of untattooed women were killed at birth. The Dyak tribes of Borneo believe that in their heaven everything

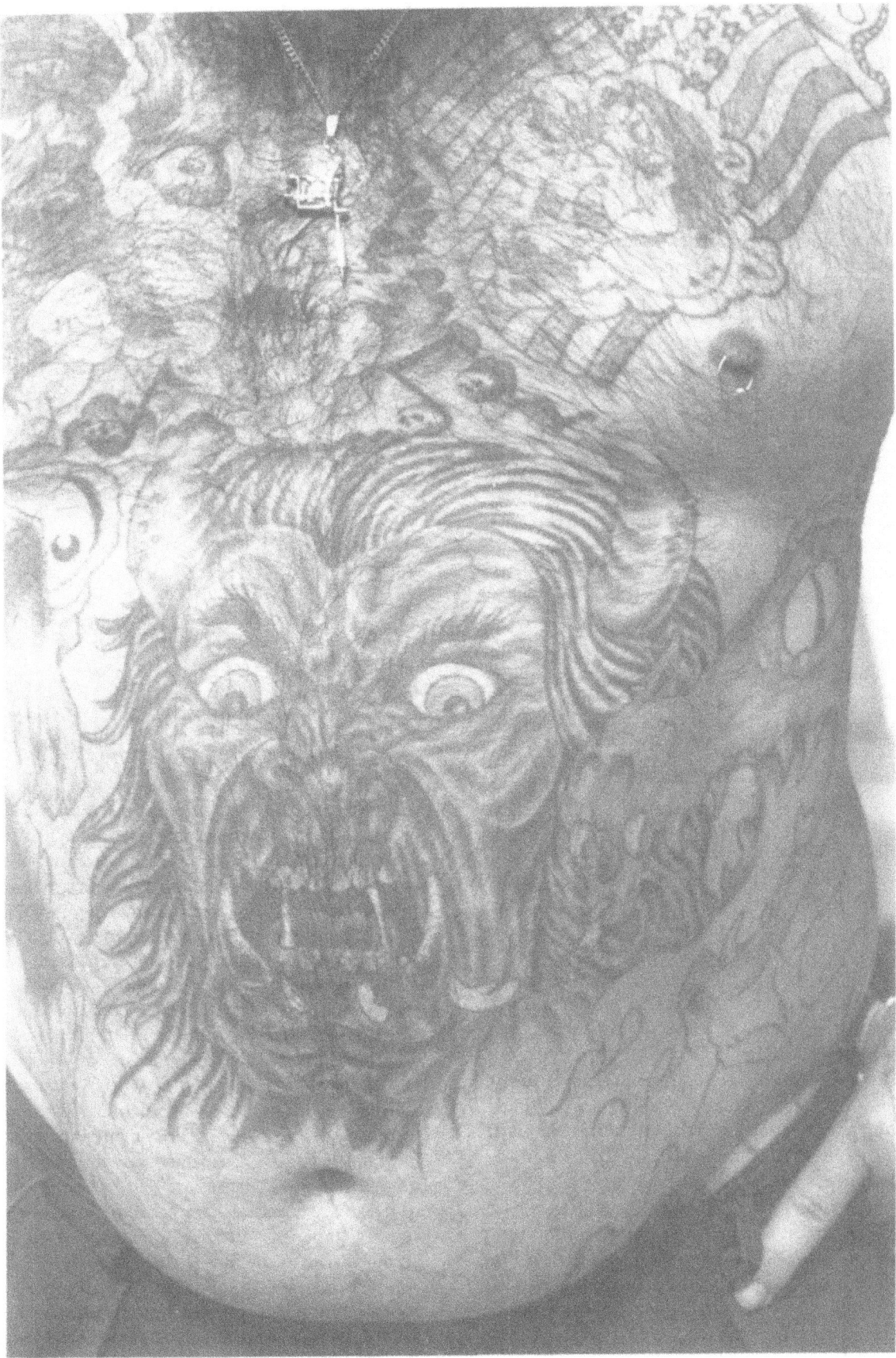

*The Purple Devil* (Wondo's Baby Picture) with pierced nipple. Owner: Wondo Loski. Artist: Randy Adams, Arlington, TX. Photograph by J. Wilton.

becomes the opposite of its terrestrial form; so among other things, light becomes dark. Women of the tribe tattoo themselves with dark pigments so that when the polarities reverse in death, the tattoos will shed enough light to guide them through the dark regions between earth and heaven (Wroblewski, 1987).

During the nineteenth century in the Deering Region of Northwest Alaska, four lines were tattooed on both checks of Buckland River Eskimo men who had killed another man in battle. These markings were believed to protect the wearer from revenge by the dead person's spirit (VanStone & Lucier, 1974). In Samoa, the elements of tattoo designs were the same for both sexes but the arrangement was considerably different (Mead, 1928). In Rangoon, the tattooing of a woman had a unique significance not recognized elsewhere: It meant that she was seeking an Englishman as a husband (Wroblewski, 1987).

Emerging from the umbrage of a lingering Puritan aesthetic, tattooing in the Western World had attained the status of a popular but highly personal art form by the 1880s. High society was shocked to learn in 1879 that the soon to be King George V and his brother had been tattooed on a cruise to the Orient (Fellowes, 1971). Czar Nicholas II of Russia also wore a tattoo (Steven, 1989). Soon other European royalty followed and many American bluebloods, according to Fellowes, forgot their righteous indignation.

As the popularity of tattooing grew, so did authoritative control. In 1909 the U.S. Navy declared that "indecent or obscene tattooing is cause for rejection." Many World War I recruits and veterans seeking reentry were suddenly requesting corsets and camisoles for the brazen ladies previously tattooed on their bodies. By the 1920s, the decoration of minors was forbidden throughout America, and soon many cities and states outlawed the practice completely (Fellowes, 1971). Today, for example, it is illegal to get a tattoo in the city of Daytona Beach, Florida, without a doctor present while cities only five miles to the north or south of Daytona Beach consider tattooing a legal activity.

In Japan, before a nineteenth century government campaign against ornate kimonos and body tattoos, the tattoo was regarded as a highly respected work of art (Zucker, 1955; Wroblewski, 1987). In Borneo, certain tattoos are still believed to have great therapeutic value (Virel, 1979). In Paris it was long the voice of protest for the lower class. To America's criminal underworld, it was and is a visible sign of contempt for regulations, conventions and authority (Zucker, 1955). Many consider it a mark of fearlessness, virility, contempt for physical suffering and the sign of a person "in the know."

Much tattooing has historically taken place in prison, the result of boredom and "Garrison fever" and was often performed by a comrade (Zucker, 1955).[3]

Incarcerated tattooists have exhibited great ingenuity in devising their tools from motors of cassette players or electric shavers, with ballpoint pen tubes serving as holders and sharpened guitar strings producing the "joint style" tattoo (Wroblewski, 1987). Although boredom is a major factor, emulation is probably the prime motivator. To appear to be the toughest, the most feared and to belong to a particular group seems to be of great import. Tattoos constitute very visible insignias of audacity, evoking feelings of fear from others. In the prison environment, this is a premium commodity. While proclaimed to be non-conformist, it simultaneously becomes an act of imitation and conformity (Zucker, 1955). Prison tattooing also serves to symbolize an idea, feeling or philosophy to which the inmate clings. Deprived of other means of self-expression, tattoos offer a way to materialize and make a banner of certain personal beliefs. Usually lacking cultivated vocabularies and commonly untrained in expressing themselves in abstract terms, members of this subculture resort primarily to the tried and proven clichés and inscriptions which have flourished over the years.

Tattoos are like a little picture of what people are and what they would like to be, it's kind of their reality and their dream...you could be next.

                                                                          Jeanne
                                                                    *No Boundaries*

### Techniques: East to West

Whereas other early cultures practiced simple pricking or shallow cuts with thorns, sharp rock flakes or knives, the Polynesians had advanced to a miniature sharp-toothed rake which was tapped into the skin with a small stick, and the introduction of pigment into the wound caused a permanent mark. For Eskimos and similar neighboring cultures, the favored method was to insert an awl or needle under the skin, drawing a soot-covered thread through the holes. This technique led the Russians in Siberia to refer to the practice as "face embroidery" (Fellowes, 1971). Traditionally, the Japanese artists all worked with groups, or a "stick," of needles. Working fast and with a light touch, reportedly no pain is felt from this technique (Zucker, 1955). Today many Japanese artists have adopted the Euroamerican electric tattooing needle that was patented in 1891. Although limited to the lower economic classes in the later nineteenth century, Japanese tattooing was the most technically accomplished at the time (Fellowes, 1971).

Tattoo prolocutor Roy Boy Cooper (1986) identifies four levels of contemporary artistic expertise: tattoo artists, master tattooists, tattoo mechanics and scratchers. A scratcher is just learning; a mechanic can stencil a stock piece and color it in; a master can create new and specialized pieces; and an artist, says Cooper, "creates whole scenarios of art utilizing body position,

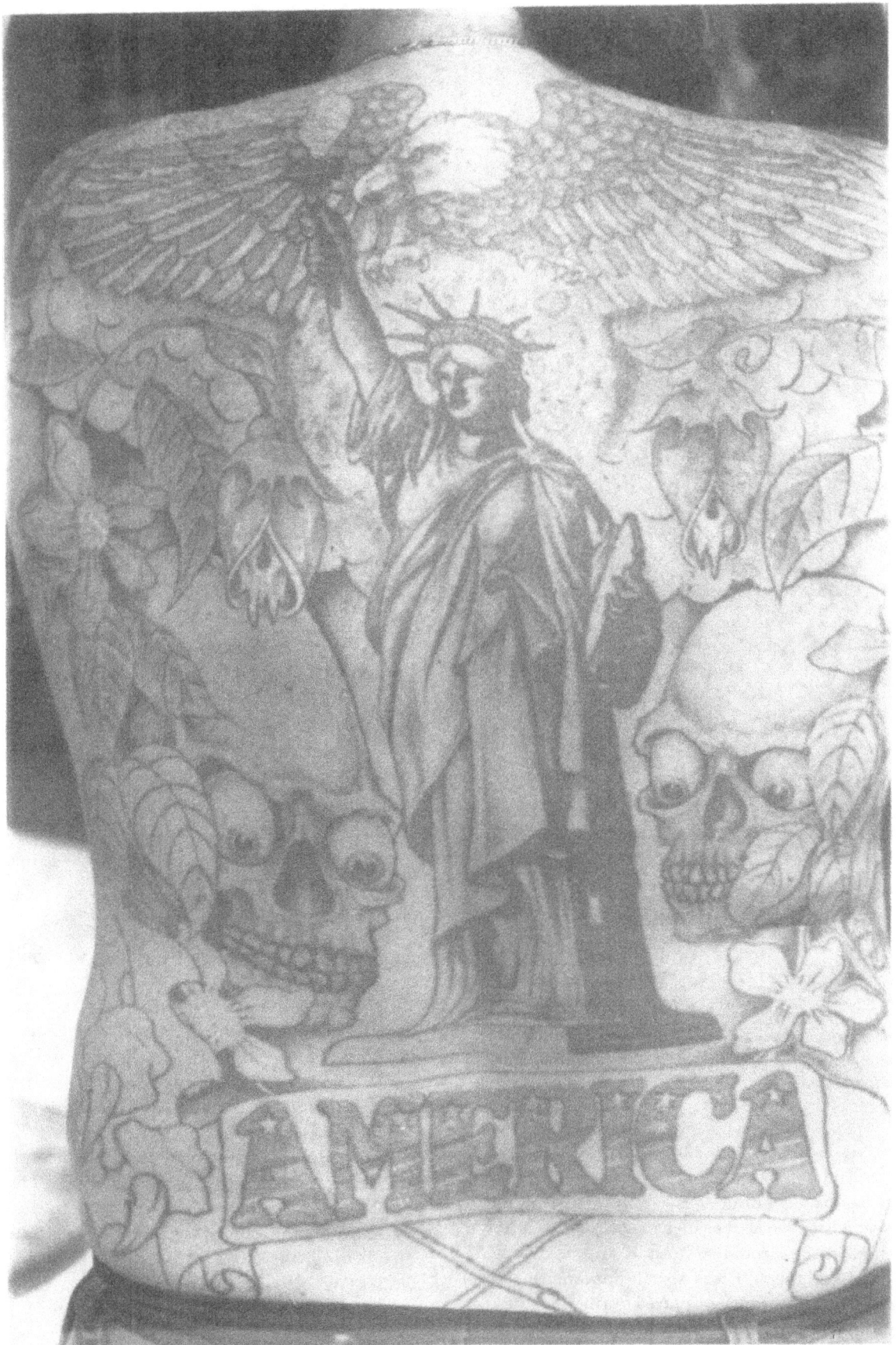

*Liberty or Death.* Owner: Wondo Loski, Daytona Beach. Artist: Gill Monte, Hollywood/San Diego. Photograph by J. Wilton.

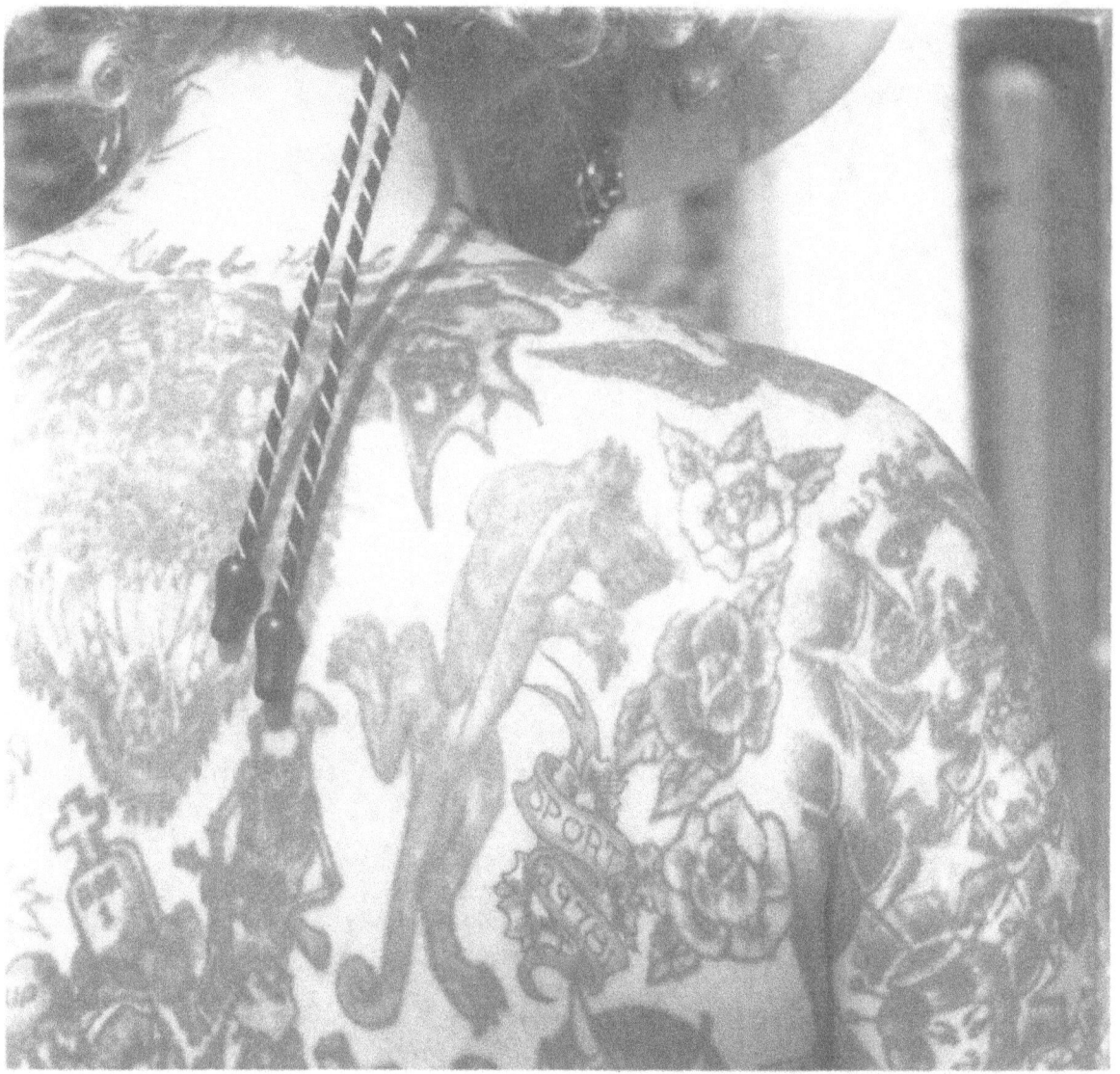

*Sport's Prison Number.* A freshly created tattoo endearing a girlfriend currently in prison in Las Vegas sits among older artworks. Owner: Asa Lee Crow III, Daytona Beach. Artist: Wondo Loski. Photograph by J. Wilton.

size and shape, creating a one of a kind artwork on a skin canvas.''

I give them a handful of money and tell them to go to work. I give 'em all the freedom in the world—free skin! That's how you get the best work.

A Collector
Daytona Beach, 1986

### Style, Design and Expression

In Samoa, certain designs were at one time the exclusive possession of the chiefly class. By the 1900s, those same designs could be worn by anyone capable of paying for them. Great social importance was connected to the fortitude displayed during the tattoo operation. The amount of tattooing possessed by an individual was also a matter of social significance and judgment. A father who did not make it possible for both sons and daughters to follow the fashion of tattooing, by their eighteenth birthday, was considered ignoble (Handy, 1924).

The extensive masterpieces of abstract art worn by inhabitants of Tahiti and the Marquesas, while taking years to complete, indicate rank and lineage, recall various feats and unusual events in that person's life, specify rank of initiation and the rights to which the wearer is entitled. The rules governing composition of such specimens are as well defined as those governing status and lineage (Virel, 1979). The pain involved in tattooing is an integral part of its ritualistic significance: the bigger the tattoo, the greater the bloodletting, the more respect must be accorded the wearer (Wroblewski, 1987).

Not just anybody can sit down and get tattooed.

Tattoo Artist
Daytona Beach, 1986

In Japan, tattoos are designed to be discretely hidden under clothing, as a private and personal possession. This practice probably stems from tattoos being outlawed in Japan from early 1900 until the 1950s. Contrary to Western practices, the Japanese tattoo is conceptionalized as one unified piece, with the *total* design being as important as the elements of which it consists (Steven, 1989). The Japanese "body suit" originated around 1700 as a reaction by the middle and lower classes to laws regulating conspicuous consumption—an indulgence apparently reserved for royalty (Webb, 1976). Only they were allowed to wear elaborate ornate clothing, leaving the commoners with no form of decorative expression. Later the body suit came to be associated with the Yakuza, the gangster subculture of Japan (Steven, 1989).

Many Japanese tattoos are adaptations of traditional images symbolizing Japanese ideals of strength, steadfastness and fidelity and based on the styles of famous artists such as Hokusai, Kuniyoshi and Utamaro (Steven, 1989; Webb, 1976). One popular style is traced back 180 years to the illustrations from a popular novel featuring a band of tattooed Robin Hood-type outlaws. Laboring class men began getting tattoos emulating these heroes and their anti-authoritarian values, and tattoos in this style were seen as the mark of a rebel (Steven, 1989). Today, according to Geoff Steven (1989), there are barely a dozen tattoo artists in Japan with approximately one thousand Japanese people wearing tattoos, all rarely seen by the public, as tattooing is currently considered an anti-social act strongly connoting the Japanese underground. In his recent documentary film on Japanese tattooing, Steven identified three reasons for acquiring a tattoo: to show initiation or commitment to a group, a desire to display images of virtues to which the wearer relates or pure aesthetical enhancement of the body.

Whereas Polynesian and Japanese designs stress symmetry, continuity and conformity to body contours, Western styles usually consist of many individual pictures acquired from different artists over a period of years. Western tattoos are often acquired as a kind of memento while Japanese tattoos tell a complete story. The acquisition of such extensive Japanese designs involves a great deal of thought, planning, time, money and discomfort. Japanese and Euroamerican tattoos share the characteristic of being mostly figurative while Polynesian examples are totally abstract in design (Webb, 1976).

Sailors, miners and other such groups who have used the tattoo as a mark of fraternity, thereby keeping the tradition alive over the years, have, at the same time, been put at blame by some critics for the stagnation of imagery and symbolism in Western tattooing over the past two centuries. In *Tattoo, Pigments of Imagination*, Chris Wroblewski (1987) states that "a dreadful poverty of imagination led to a limited repertoire of moribund images and banal aphorisms which celebrated the virtues of home and hearth, filial piety and patriotism in a style that was visually dreary, discouraged creativity in the tattooist and failed to exploit the body's natural perspectives" (3).

No form of tattoo design, says master tattooer C.H. Fellowes (1971), is more distinctly American in expression and origin than the patriotic. These "tribal" signs of loyalty were worn with special awareness during and immediately following times of war. The bold spread eagle and "death before dishonor" decorated many a seaman's chest, but only sweethearts and winsome women could claim as much epidermal space as symbols expressing love of country. The most basic of tattoo designs are those of religious concern. For sailors, says Fellowes, they are magic talismans for warding off the evils of the devil and the mishaps of the deep blue sea. Near the end of the nineteenth century, it is estimated that eighty percent of the U.S. Navy wore some sort of tattoo marking (Fellowes, 1971). The most common marks are relatively inconspicuous and include initials, crucifixes, fraternal symbols, flowers and good luck symbols.

By the 1920s American tattooists were actually supplied with sheets of simple mass produced designs, generically known as "flash," from which the client could choose the image considered most suitable (Wroblewski, 1987). Wroblewski cites improved technology as the factor which lead to the emergence of a new breed of artistically ambitious tattooists. They found their subjects in the youth cultures of the 1950s and 1960s and produced fine line and shaded work of exceptional artistic quality. As styles and icons of other cultures were borrowed and modified, new hybrid designs began to evolve, and by the 1970s a new school of super-realists emerged in California producing work rendered with an almost photographic tendency. Symbols of modern Western culture were dominant: Hendrix, Bowie, Monroe, Bogart and the Starship *Enterprise* all became tattoos. Even Disney characters and other cartoon personages were brought in for the tattooists to work from. Experts on the history of tattooing agree that it was the customers, not the masters, who were really responsible for the new fashions in design (Fellowes, 1971). In the 1970s New York artists introduced conceptual tattoos—abstract, complex, non-specific images which took the art form full circle back to its Polynesian roots (Wroblewski, 1987).

### Stimulation and Inspiration

Most of us have tattoos on our wrists—not like the tattoos of your sailors—daggers, hearts and nude girls—but just a name, a few letters or designs. The Owl Woman who guards the road to the spirit lodges looks at these tattoos and lets us pass. They are like a passport. Many Indians believe that if you don't have these designs on your body, that 'Ghost Woman' won't let you through but will throw you over a cliff. In that case you have to roam the earth endlessly as a ghost. Maybe it's not so bad being a ghost. But as you see, I have my arms tattooed.

Lame Deer, Seeker of Visions
*Modern Primatives*

In *Modern Primatives* (1989, 203), Edger and Dingman identify three answers to the question "why?"

First, tattoos have distinct anti-authority appeal. The origin of this appeal might be traced to the early Christian proscription of tattooing and the resulting European laws against the practice. Whatever the source, tattooing today has an aura of the forbidden about it. Second, tattooing may have inherent appeal due to the pain involved in the operation and the permanency of the design; thus tattooing is restricted to the brave and dedicated. Third, and most important: in some circumstances, people are deprived of the opportunity to acquire and display the ordinary means of identifying and presenting the self. Although all three factors are obviously related it is the final one, that of deprivation of the opportunity to acquire and display the usual and desirable means of self-identification, that we see as most basic to an understanding of tattooing.

Whereas the tattoo has been widely used as enhancement, it has also been used as punishment. Samoa is one Polynesian culture where it has been included as a community-enforced punishment (Mead, 1928). In the Western World, the British tattooed "D" on deserters in the First World War; the Germans tattooed numbers on concentration camp victims; and the Russians have tattooed dissidents being held by the government (Wroblewski, 1987). This tyrannical usage is one reason (among many) why tattooing continues to maintain a negative image. However, if we are to move toward an understanding of the tattoo as art, we must first comprehend the difference between tattoos applied against one's will and those applied for the mutual pleasure of the wearer and the viewer. One could liken it to the difference between the act of rape and the desire of two people to mutually achieve an act of love.

There is also a noticeable gender difference among skin art collectors. Zucker (1955) proposes that in terms of psychological motivation feminine tattooing has differed greatly from masculine. For the female, it is a mark which flatters the male's vanity—imposed, suggested or advised by him. Zucker further suggests that women are usually not as copiously tattooed as men are, hesitating possibly because of a greater epidermic sensitivity or less resistance to physical suffering. Yet many wearers report the process to be mostly painless.

To many (and quite possibly most) people in Western societies, a tattoo means a skull and crossbones on a biker's arm; a heart, a flower, or a girl's name on a sailor's hand; the words love, hate or Mom on a convict's knuckles. Tattooing is viewed as macho and sentimental, indulged in by indigents, servicemen and society's misfits (Wroblewski, 1987). Sleazy, sinister and dirty could be synonyms for the practice and for the wearers, an art form seen as disfigurement rather than decoration. And the disapproval of all three major religions—Christianity, Judaism and Islam—ensures its position as a sub-culture art form. However, as we continue to develop theories of egalitarian pluralism, perhaps it is time to aesthetically acknowledge this other-than-mainstream art form which has fascinated anthropologists and psychologists for so long.

One might ask, "why would anyone want to permanently stain their skin?" Possible answers would be: to shock, to scare, to peacock and preen, to attract, to distinguish (Wroblewski, 1987). Some diverse reasons for tattooing are listed by R.W.B. Scutt and C. Gotch in *Modern Primatives* (1987). They include:

1) To camouflage an unclothed body when hunting.
2) To secure a place in heaven.
3) To ensure an easy passage through difficult phases in life, such as puberty and pregnancy.
4) To prevent disease and injury and acquire fertility.
5) To propitiate malignant spirits at time of death.
6) To acquire special characteristics through totemism and ancestor worship.
7) To acquire the special respect of the community; to allow the individual to climb the social ladder....
8) To terrorize the enemy on the field of battle.
9) To make the body sexually interesting.
10) To express sentiment (patriotism, love, friendship, anti-authoritarianism).
11) To register incidents of personal interest, places visited, etc.
12) To achieve personal or group identity (primitive tribes, gangs, sailors).
13) To make money (circus, sideshows).
14) To register important medical data, e.g. blood group.

Amid an almost universal feeling of powerlessness to "change" the world, it gives individuals the opportunity to change the one thing they totally control—their bodies (Vale & Juno, 1989). Through artificial means such as tattooing, scarification and body painting, writes Andre Virel (1979), naked skin becomes a living ornament. In a society that puts ever greater value on conformity, being tattooed is a way of declaring one's difference, demonstrating membership in another club. The 1970s saw the establishment of a series of international tattoo conventions, providing for the first time the opportunity for artists and wearers to exchange ideas, admire handiwork, discuss techniques and developments (Wroblewski, 1987).

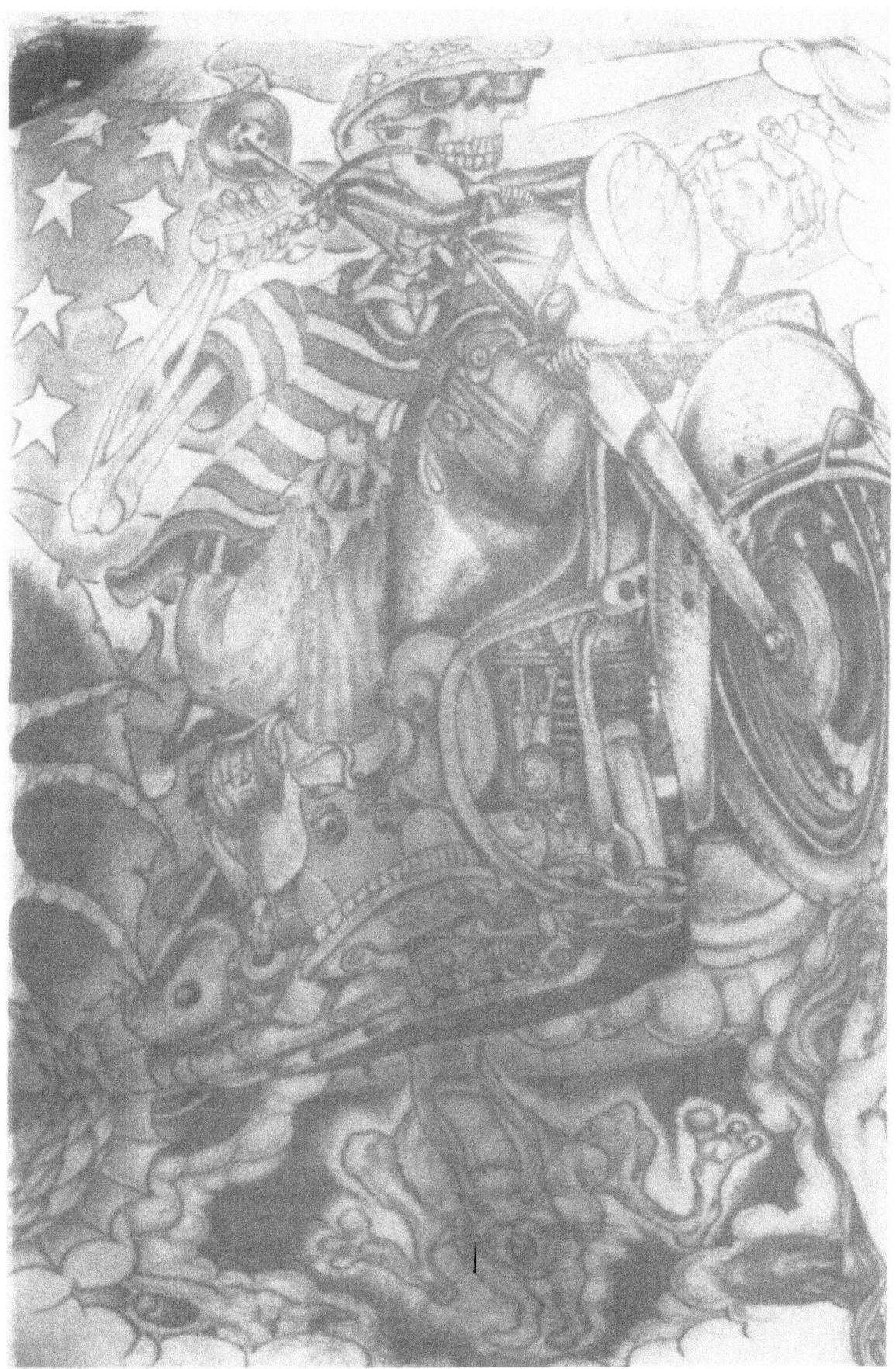

*Clay's Motorcycle.* Owner: Clay Basket, Daytona Beach. Artist: Gill Monte, Hollywood/San Diego. Photograph by J. Wilton.

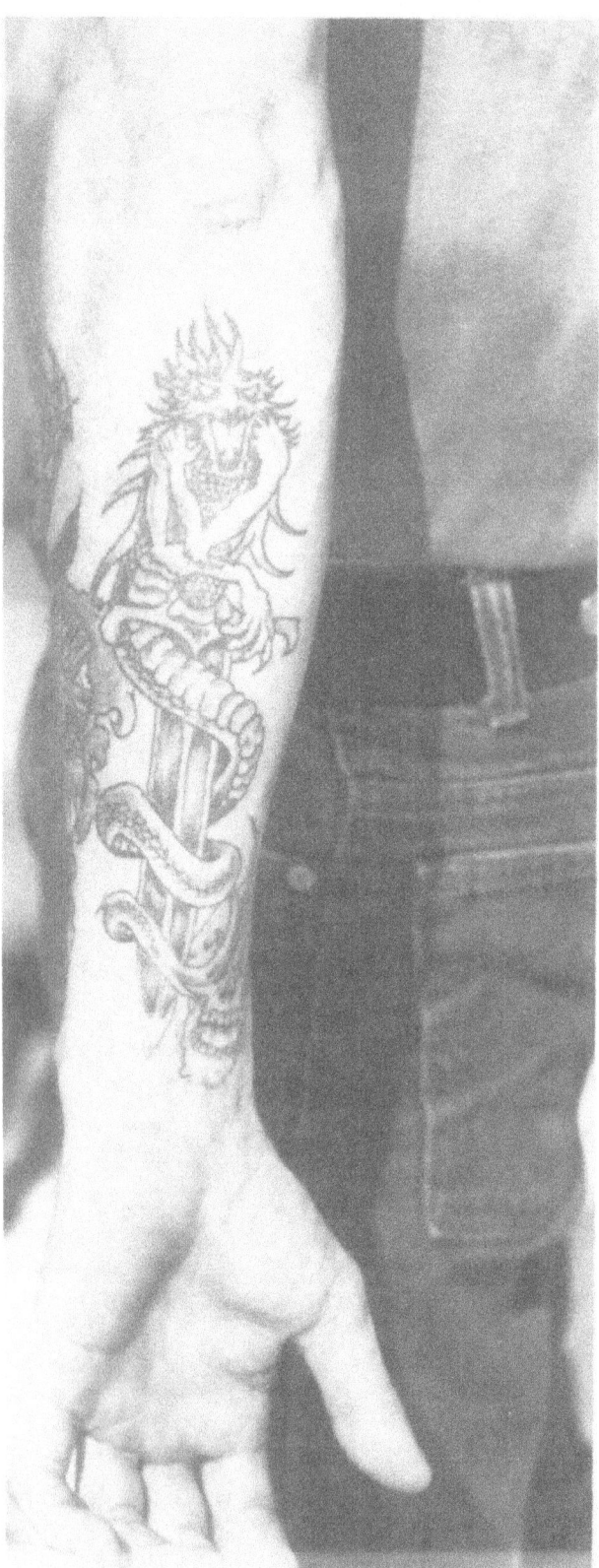

*Dragon on a Sword.* Owner: M.D. Rueske, Daytona Beach. Artist: Moses, Biloxi, MI. Photograph by J. Wilton.

To those skin art critics and collectors, the tattoo convention has all the significance of a new fashion line from Paris, jewelry from an ancient tomb or a Van Gogh retrospective. Yet it is a most mortal art form, not to be left behind by the collector—preserved only by the camera, often hidden in its own subculture. An apparent sexual connection removes tattooing even further from the mainstream.

*Tattoo* and *taboo* are the only Polynesian words in the English language, providing a possible mystical fascination and romantic undertone since its introduction into Euroamerican cultures (Zucker, 1955). The piercing of the skin, the insertion of the needle, the leaving of a liquid in the skin, according to Zucker, constitutes a sexual act. Some people of masochistic propensity find sexual gratification in the "thrill" of the needle. More commonly, it is a form of exhibitionism. The tattoo beautifies; it works magic; it gets a woman a lover; it gets a man a woman. Small designs worn by women are often acquired for sexual enhancement or as a mark of liberation, since tattooing is traditionally seen as an aspect of masculine strength and aggression (Webb, 1976). Zucker reports that many adolescents receive their first tattoo about the same time of their first sexual experience. So-called primitive societies also use the tattoo as a means of ritual initiation at the time of puberty. Zucker further states that there is often a sexual relationship between the tattooer and the tattooed wherein the act of tattooing becomes a method of sexual excitement and/or satisfaction.

Strong influence today from rock and roll musicians and artists such as Mick Jagger, Ozzie Ozborn and Cher has brought acceptance by millions of young people who over the last ten years, have grown to become today's leaders (Cooper, 1986). Actor Peter Fonda wears three small red stars on his left arm, explaining that there are many levels of personal meaning involved (Steven, 1989). The star is the oldest of nautical symbols, and red is the color of port (the left side of a ship, and Fonda is left-handed); three is his life number, as well as a representation of the trinity; three is a balanced entity, and he has three children. Cher's 1989 music video, featuring tattoos on her buttocks, shows her performing in concert, proudly displaying her body art to a very receptive crowd, validating its effect as highly sensual decoration. In his video *No Boundaries*, Roy Boy Cooper (1986) claims that fifty percent of the tattoos today are done on women, yet the stigma attached causes some of the best tattoo artists in the world to be located in parts of town the "better" people do not want to go.[4] Some artists, however, prefer it this way. When it is an illegal art, underground and unlicensed, each tattoo done is like committing a crime. Perhaps this explains the vast use by the largest subculture (bikers) in the nation.

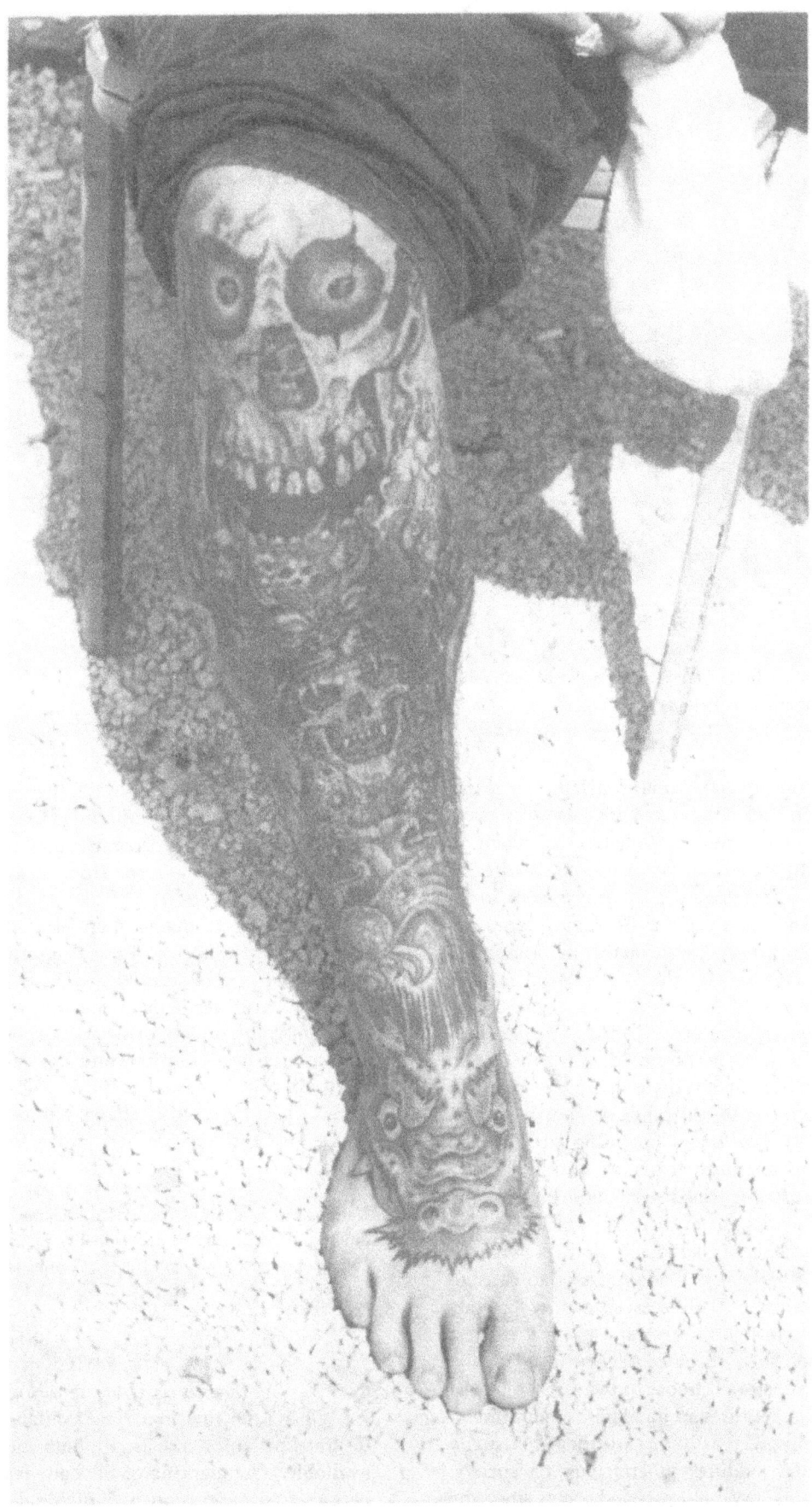

*A Leg Full of Art.* Owner: Wondo Loski. Artist: Clay Basket. Photograph by J. Wilton.

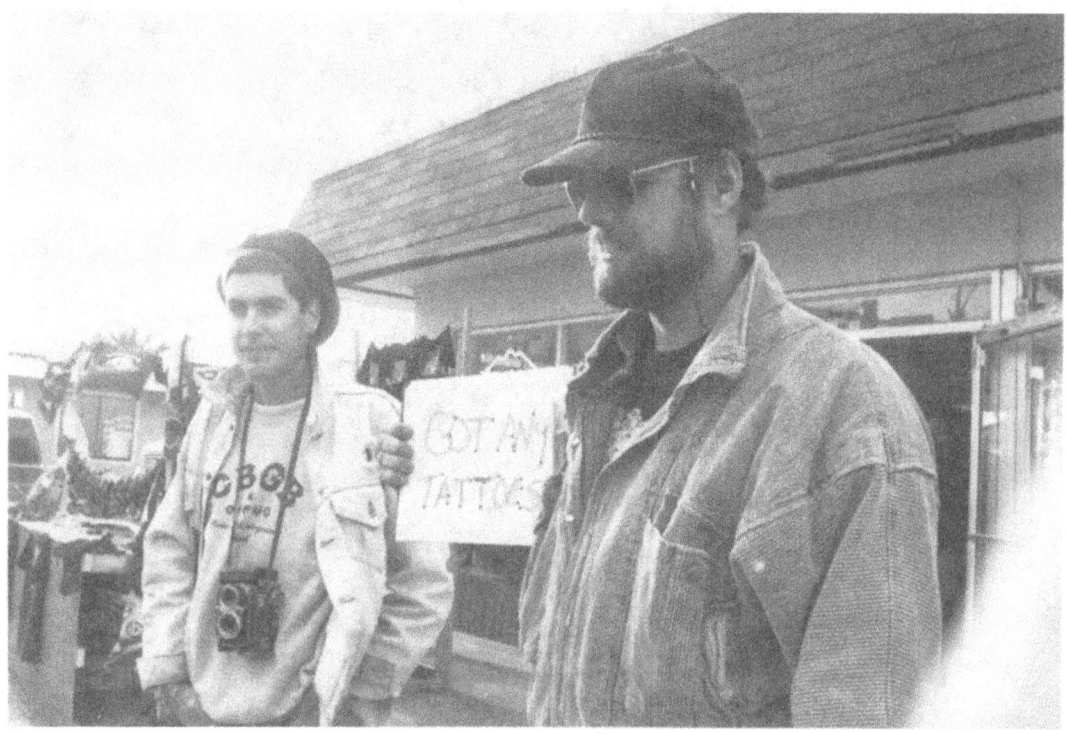

Witton (right) and an associate collecting data; Bike Week, Daytona Beach.
Photograph by Delinda Karnehn.

One underground Daytona Beach tattoo artist, now working in California, explains tattoos as signs of honor to bikers. They are "medals" of rebellion and fantasy, an extension of one's personality, a personal diary, a travelogue. Tattoos represent social statements and a way to fit in. Collecting tattoos is seen as collecting art, an "externalization of fantasy," wearing one's fantasies on the skin. "Women," the tattoo artist once told me, "won't leave you alone. We become tattooed love gods." A lot of people who are criminally intent, he disclosed in 1986, like to document their life but it is done in a code—only the collector and the artist really know what it means. They are considered *collectors*, not billboards, "human canvases who document their history on their arms." This particular artist specializes in "doom and gloom" biker tattoos—skulls, grim reapers, Harley David-sons—"any symbol of defiance" and prefers the underground life where he "doesn't have to cater to everyone off the street." He sees tattoos as "a body art—just another form of expression—a way to express your feelings and show them to other people."

Tattoo collectors choose a means of self-expression which requires an incredible commitment. Rather than being seen as living art, they are usually viewed as social oddities—aberrations of society. Articles by doctors, psychologists and others stress the antisocial, eccentric and bizarre aspects of tattooing, reporting it as an activity fraught with strong sexual

overtones (Webb, 1976). Rarely, says art critic Marcia Tucker, has Western tattooing been treated as a genuine variant of the decorative arts, with a venerable artistic heritage derived from Asia, Africa and Polynesia (Webb, 1987).

Clearly more than a manifestation of antisocial sentiment, allegiance to a social group or exhibition-istic sexual expression, tattooing is a profoundly serious form of aesthetic expression, with its inherent personal value underscoring its purpose. Tattoos can and should be recognized and appreciated not only for their role in visual communication but for the artist's mastery of line, shape, value color, etc. just as we do with any other visual form of artistic expression.

Tattoos can be a lot of things...a social statement, rebellion, fantasy, an extension of a personality that's inside of you, a collection of art, a way to fit in...it can be anything you want it to be!

A Collector
Daytona Beach, 1986

### Towards an Understanding...

Of all the raw materials available to humanity for transformation into art, the body is the most readily available. The marking of the body is often a human being's first expression of individuality, the putting of something of the inner self on the outer skin. The body art of tattooing is a personal means of immediate self-expression, a permanent visible statement of self. It is clearly a decorative art, one of embellishment and ornament, the external manifestation of vanity, the need to adorn and to attract attention. There is no question that tattooing shares many of the criteria we assign to the other pictorial arts, yet these living works of art remain excluded and misunderstood, artistic territory thus far untapped by the ubiquitous Museum/Gallery apparatus of the twentieth century.

# Notes

[1]In 1989, Senator Jesse Helms introduced a bill in Congress which would prohibit federal grants to support what he considered "indecent or obscene" art. Helms objected to a National Endowment of the Arts grant to Andres Serrano (whose photographs include a crucifix in a jar of urine) and an NEA grant to the Corcoran Gallery which provided funding for a retrospective exhibit of Robert Mapplethorpe's photographs portraying homosexual erotica and sadomasochism.

[2]This directive was included in the fourteenth edition of the Encyclopedia Britannica, printed in 1973. The fifteenth edition, printed in 1987, does not contain the phrase "see mutilations and deformations."

[3]"Garrison fever" is a term used to explain the behavior of people in confinement, specifically men who have been in military service too long without recreational distractions. It is a condition similar to cabin fever or "stir crazy."

[4]Roy Boy's 1986 claim that fifty percent of the tattoos today are done on women seems to indicate a change in behavior since Zucker's 1955 statements indicating decidedly more male than female tattoo activity.

# Works Cited

Burchette, G. *Memoirs of a tattooist.* New York: Crown. (1958).

Cooper, R.B. *No boundaries.* [Video]. Badlands Productions: Roy Boy's Place. (1986).

*Encyclopedia Britannica. 16.* Chicago: William Benton. (1960).

Feldman, E. *Art as image and idea.* Englewood Cliffs, NJ: Prentice-Hall. (1967).

Fellowes, C.H. *The tattoo book.* Princeton, NJ: Pyne. (1971).

Handy, W.C. *Samoan house building, cooking, and tattooing.* (Bulletin 15). Honolulu: Bernice P. Bishop Museum. (1924).

Mead, M. *An inquiry into the question of cultural stability in Polynesia.* New York: Columbia University. (1928).

Steven, G. (Producer). *Signatures of the soul.* [Film]. Broadcast Corp of New Zealand: Seehear Films. (1989).

Vale, V. & Juno, A. (Eds.). *Modern primitives: An investigation of contemporary adornment and ritual.* London: Re/Search. (1989).

VanStone, J.W. & Lucier, C.V. An early archaeological example of tattooing from northwestern Alaska. *Fieldiana Anthropology, 66*(1), (1974): 1-9.

Virel, A. *Decorated man: The human body as art.* New York: Harry N. Abrams. (1979).

Webb, S. (Ed.). *Heavily tattooed men and women.* New York: McGraw Hill. (1976).

Wroblewski, C. *Tattoo: Pigments of imagination.* New York: Alfred van der Marck Editions. (1987).

Zucker, H. (Ed.). *Tattooed women and their mates.* World folk art series, No. 1. Philadelphia: Andre Levy. (1955).

# Women Artists and Their Critics
## in American Literature

## Kathryn Lee Seidel

For the last ten years, contemporary literary critics have begun the process of examining the metaphors which writers use to describe the creative process as it applies to women. The publication of Sandra Gilbert and Susan Gubar's brilliant analysis of nineteenth century fiction, *The Madwoman in the Attic: The Woman Writer and the Literary Imagination* (1979), inaugurated a decade of critical studies in which the female protagonist in works of fiction was seen as an artist figure who often represented the author herself. In this paradigm, the novel's female heroine is often silenced by the men who try to define her. More recently, Marianne Hirsch writes in the *Mother/ Daughter Plot: Narrative, Psychoanalysis, Feminism* (1989), the female protagonist with "artistic ambitions" often must differentiate herself from her mother, who speaks with the voice of patriarchal society, in order to assert her individual identify (10). The parallel of the main character's problems to the plight of the women writer becomes the focus of much of this criticism. Anne Goodwin Jones's *Tomorrow is Another Day: The Woman Writer in the South, 1859-1936* (1981) examines several novels of the American South written by women whose main character is a "mask" for the writer. Jones sees Scarlett O'Hara in *Gone With the Wind* (1936), for example, as having the freedom to fight convention that Margaret Mitchell herself enjoyed briefly early in her life but then abandoned after she married.

In the same way art historians have often commented on the creative process in women by noting instances of women writers who describe the difficulties of creativity in a patriarchal culture. Lisa Vogel writes succinctly in "Fine Arts and Feminism: The Awakening Consciousness" (1988) that "the art world's exceptionally elite social basis" excludes those outsiders who are often women, often poor, and who create art in genres that are not deemed to be "fine arts" (23). As Valerie Jaudon and Joyce Kozloff explain in "Art Hysterical Notions of Progress and Culture" (1978), art criticism has a double list of the way traditional art critics select good versus bad art: they prefer "fine art above decorative art, Western art above non-Western art, men's art above women's art" (38).

"High art" is art which concerns man, the Greeks, the Romans, the Renaissance, religion, science, logic, war, virility, violence and power; "low art" refers to the art of "Africans, Orientals, Persians, Slovaks, peasants, the lower classes, women, children, pagans...chaos, anarchy, exotic...ornaments, decoration...weaving...patterns...fabrics and furniture" (41-42). Gisela Ecker's *Feminist Aesthetics* (1986) is one of a number of collections of essays analyzing this problem.

This chapter will add to this discussion by showing how writers of fiction openly present women artists themselves. By this I mean that many authors overtly portray women actively at work as artists— musicians, painters and artists who create what has been called folk art, fine arts and what can be called the art of the everyday. In all of the fiction I will present, the woman artist faces limitations of time, accessibility of materials and training. She often must create her art without "models," as Alice Walker writes in *In Search of Our Mothers' Gardens* (1984), and without awareness of the tradition of female creativity. In fiction, the woman artist is most hampered by her family, friends and mentors who attempt to limit and discourage her. These people can be likened to patriarchal art critics, for in the fiction they speak with great authority and are embued with traditional patriarchal values. They support the conventional notion that art is exclusive and unique, that its value is determined often by its being kept apart from the people; it is a commodity to be hung in a museum, not used or made accessible to the populace except as an object of awe (Berger, 1972). These attitudes work against the women artists in many nineteenth and twentieth century novels and short stories. Those selected for this chapter are Toni Morrison's *Sula*, Harriet Arnow's *The Dollmaker*, Alice Walker's "Everyday Use" and *The Color Purple*, Kate Chopin's *The Awakening*, Ellen Glasgow's "The Difference" and Gail Godwin's *Violet Clay*.

As a way of understanding the strategies of the art critics in this fiction, the work of Joanna Russ, *How to Suppress Women's Writing* (1983), can be adapted. Russ summarizes the intricate process by which women artists are devalued and suppressed:

—informal prohibitions (including discouragement and the inaccessibility of materials and training)..., 
—belittlement of the work in various ways, 
—isolation of the work from the tradition to which it belongs..., 
—assertions that the work indicates the author's bad character and hence is primarily of scandalous interest, 
—and simple ignoring the works, the workers, and the whole tradition. (5)

When we apply these categories to fiction, we are able to observe a systematic pattern of suppression of the work of women artists recorded in fiction. This paper will group the writers works by the type of art its women characters produce (i.e., folk artists and painters) and within each category proceed chronologically so as to create a brief survey of fiction from the most recent one hundred years, from 1899 when Kate Chopin's *The Awakening* appeared to the publication in 1982 of *The Color Purple* by Alice Walker.

I have chosen the term "folk artist" because the artists draw their inspiration from their cultural group and use readily available materials as the medium for their art. The painters, on the other hand, use the oil paint especially manufactured for the making of two-dimensional oil paintings. This latter group is more economically privileged than the folk artists, and one painter is academically trained. The differences in these groups, however, are far less important than one might think.

### Folk Artists in Fiction

When Toni Morrison (1972) writes of her title character Sula that she was "an artist with no art form," she is cogently summarizing the criticism of centuries of artists who create but whose creations are not defined as art (121). These folk artists suffered from the problem which Joanna Russ sardonically describes as: "She made it, but she isn't really an artist and it isn't really...art" (76). In fact, these artists challenge traditional assumptions of who is an artist and what is art. An important novel that explores this problem is Harriet Arnow's *The Dollmaker* (1954). Gertie Nevels is a strong, large, working class woman whose husband moves the family from rural Kentucky to the automotive boomtown of 1940s Detroit. In this naturalistic novel, the forces of capitalism do not improve the family's lot but instead slowly erode their common roots, their warm feelings for one another and eventually take one of their lives. Throughout, Gertie's habit of woodcarving, her "whittlen foolishness" as she calls it, sustains her and articulates her attempt to preserve her sense of autonomy, to maintain contact with her cultural origins in Kentucky and to make sense out of an increasingly desperate situation.

Gertie's carvings are unique and individual carvings of people, animals and religious figures. These "dolls," as her husband Clovis calls them, are actually Gertie's way of defining herself even though she is otherwise an inarticulate stoical person. They are also her medium for original experimentation and interaction with her environment. Gertie knows her material well; she grew up with the feeling of wood under her hands and feet. She chopped down trees to make her house and furniture. She walked in the forest as a girl to observe the beauty of the trees; there she learned their differences in texture, color and smell. A self-taught artist indeed, she learned with all her senses open to the beauty of and uniqueness of each type of wood. Gertie's work as a carver is thus an expression of her "values, aesthetic preferences, and...sense of identity" (144), as Kristin Congdon (1986) writes of folk artists.

When Gertie moves to Detroit, her husband begins to sell her carvings. Her hesitation to begin a cottage industry is supplanted by the necessity of helping to support the family. Nonetheless, she works carefully on each figure; her concern is to select the wood according to its weight, strength, grain and color. Her philosophy of art, as she explains to her daughter, is that in each piece of wood a man or animal is inside waiting to emerge (55). This account of the origins of artistic inspiration reflects Gertie's belief that her task is to release the figure in the wood and, by so doing, give reverence to the importance of the wood which is God's creation. For this reason her work emphasizes religious elements, a choice which reflects her faith and places her in the long tradition of wood carving in Christianity. The Cross of Christ as a tangible legacy led to the many exquisitely carved crucifixes and altars in the European tradition. For these countless artists, working with wood was a symbolically reverent activity reflecting faith in Christ. This faith is certainly true of Gertie.

Although at one point a female art teacher praises Gertie's work, the art critics in this novel are for the most part men, and they are close to home. Clovis, Gertie's husband, becomes increasingly hostile to her work even though accounts for a substantial portion of the family's income. His surprise at learning she had sold a piece causes him to evaluate her work for the first time. His evaluation is devoid of aesthetic or personal appreciation; he criticizes the figures because they are unpainted. His inability to understand her reverence for the intrinsic beauty of the wood is joined by virulent capitalism. For him, her art is a commodity, not a private or creative expression; all of his subsequent acts emerge from his wish to commercialize and exploit her efforts, to mass produce her art. He increasingly pressures Gertie to work faster, make more figures and spend less time on their individual features. He brings home increasingly inferior woods, thus exerting control over her materials. He reinforces his demands with physical violence. Bowing to this pressure and to her family's increasing poverty—the automotive industry is slowly dehumanizing Clovis in the ways he is degrading Gertie—Gertie concedes and creates quick shoddy pieces.

All the while, however, Gertie also proceeds with a project she hides from Clovis, a master sculpture from a piece of cherry wood she has cherished. The choice of cherry wood, a strong healthy wood, represents a self that Gertie sees being literally chopped away. At first the emerging figure seems to be the Christ, symbolically the savior of this tormented family, but as Kathleen Walsh (1984) points out, the emerging figure is that of Judas the Betrayer. The figure is, thus, the metaphorical expression of Gertie carving her own strong self but reflecting her despair at compromising her other art works and her inability to be the savior of her family. Feeling that she has betrayed her art, she compares herself to the arch betrayer. Harriet Arnow's novel thus starkly reveals that in poverty and with art a slave to material concerns, the woman artist can only endure nobly but cannot prevail.

Alice Walker's short story "Everyday Use" (1973) directly discusses the derogatory criticisms of folk arts previously defined by Russ. This complaint, aimed at folk artists in the visual arts and so-called regionalists in literature, accounts for the central tension of the story. A quilt made by Maggie and Dee's grandmother from pieces of the dresses worn by family members becomes the source of conflict. Their mother, a strong sensible African-American, must decide which of her daughters should inherit the quilt. The quilt takes on symbolic meaning that radiates from its literalness. It is the heritage of this community; it represents the birthright in a Biblical sense of the cultural and artistic legacy passed from generations of gifted Black women.

The mother herself, although not a quilter, is described as having created her house and garden as an ordered harmonious oasis, a domestic Eden. The mother can be considered a creator of what can be called the art of the everyday. As Russ points out, because women's art often is not big, not painted in oils, is useful and is domestic, it is not recognized as art (114). Small though it is, the mother's garden is her garden of Versailles, no less ordered and harmonious. As Walker writes in *In Search of Our Mothers' Gardens*, the mothers and grandmothers of the rural South kept alive the "creativity of black women" through their beautiful gardens, their vigorous stories and their waiting for a day when their

identities as artists could find a medium for expression (232).

Like the mother in "Everyday Use," Maggie is ostensibly a shy homebody, silent and uneducated. Her older sister, on the other hand, has a college education, lives away from home and has changed her name from Dee to Wangero, a name which she considers to be a more politically correct. When Dee/Wangero visits her mother, she is outraged to hear that Maggie plans to use the quilt:" "Maggie can't appreciate the quilts...she'd probably be backward enough to put them to everyday use" (2372). Dee's outburst results from her conviction that the quilts are indeed art but that her sister does not regard them as anything more than blankets; she believes that Maggie is incapable of seeing the quilts from any perspective other than a utilitarian one. Dee proposes to hang the quilts on the walls of her up-scale apartment; the quilts are "priceless," she claims. Dee's response reveals that she seems to take a pluralistic approach to art criticism, to use Kristin Congdon's terminology (1989); Dee acknowledges the artistic merit of the quilt, and she is not bound by a Western ethnocentic vision. Yet Dee regards the quilts as commodities to be evaluated only in terms of their static monetary value as elite works of art. She wants to hang them, as if in a museum. These attitudes reveal her to be what can be called the elite art critic in the story.

Maggie plans to use the quilts on her bed, to which Dee objects that the quilts would be "in rags" in a few years. The mother points out that if this is so, Maggie "can always make some more. Maggie knows how to quilt" (2373). The statement, tossed politely at Dee, is a key one, for it reveals that while Dee believes herself to be the true *critic* of what art is and where it belongs, Maggie is the true *artist*. She can quilt; it is she who has inherited the genius of her family, she who can produce art, and not merely consume it as Dee does. Maggie responds, "I can 'member Grandma Dee without the quilts" (2372). To her the quilts embody the collective memory of her family; thus she is not the ignorant girl her critic-sister believes her to be. Maggie, the artist, possesses the memory of her foremothers; thus she has already claimed her birthright. The mother's decision is not merely who should receive the quilts, but she must also decide whose definition of the quilt is valid, as Marianne Hirsch (1989) points out. When the mother hears Maggie say she can remember "Grandma with the quilts," the mother says, "something hit me in the top of my head and ran down to the soles of my feet....Just like when I'm in church and the spirit of God touches me and I get happy and shout. I...snatched the quilts out of Miss Wangero's hands and dumped them into Maggie lap" (2373). Thus she acts as an art critic who chooses to honor the traditions of her community rather than the commodity value of the quilts.

The importance of art as a connection to one's traditions and one's cultures is underscored in Toni Morrison's *Sula* (1973) in which the title character is isolated because of her desire to elude the conventional expectations of her community. Bound to it by her friendship with Nel, Sula is dissatisfied with the roles of wife and mother that the townspeople prefer for her. Possessed of "tremendous curiosity and her gift for metaphor," she becomes restless because she has no outlet for these gifts and no community of like-minded people (121). Sula is described as possessing the qualities of an artist who has no community to help develop her traits. "Had she paints, or clay, or knew the discipline of dance, or strings," she may have developed into an artist (121). Isolated and lonely, she has no medium of expression; she is an "artist with no art form" (121). The isolation of the artist without community defies the myth that the artist requires a romantic isolation without models and supporters. As Russ writes: "deprived of tradition," a tradition of a supportive cultural milieu that welcomes her art and of other women artists, women artists can be discouraged and silenced (96). On the contrary, connections with one's family and one's culture, as both Arnow and Walker show, produce art of beauty and meaning. Without these connections, artists such as Gertie feel they have "sold out," artists such as Maggie would continue to be devalued by the Dee-critics, and female artists as represented by Sula would be silenced. Thus, to these three writers the folk arts are not mere local anomolies; they are the representatives of the unique yet universal spirit of creativity.

### Painters in Fiction

The folk arts challenge traditional assumptions regarding who an artist is and what art is. What is remarkable is that in fiction, even when these categories are not in question, when the woman artist is producing oil paintings, she faces a variety of impediments from her critics. She must contend with the lack of privacy, space, materials and education, as Virginia Woolf points out in *A Room of One's Own* (1929): women writers must "have five hundred a year...and rooms of our own...the great women writers live in you and in me, and in many other women writers who are not here tonight, for they are washing up the dishes and putting the children to bed...the great women poets live and need only the opportunity to walk among us" (1383). Three contemporary writers who explore this premise among three painters are Kate Chopin in *The Awakening* (1899), Ellen Glasgow in "The Difference"(1923) and Gail Godwin in *Violet Clay* (1978). All three authors begin at least with the premise that their artists require a room of their own but as each acquires that room,

a set of new obstacles intervenes. Each finds that there is what Russ calls "a double standard of content": she may have painted it, but is the subject matter abnormal for a woman, ask these critics (40). In fact, given the subject—often female sexuality—should the woman have written about it at all?

When reading *The Awakening*, one is so struck by Edna Pontellier's overwhelming discovery of her own sexuality, critics have often overlooked her artistic awakening and her attempts to nurture her creative ability. Edna appears to have the economic prerequisites that Woolf defines as essential to the artist: as the wife of a wealthy man she had income, servants to cook and provide child care, and she has ample education. She has time, space and money. However, her sketches and paintings are of subjects such as a portrait of her friend, Adelle Ratignolle, conventional sketches of landscapes and an occasional vague female figure. However, as her sexual awakening proceeds, the subjects of her paintings change and reflect the larger themes of the novel. The narrator reports that Edna had thought of her friend Adele, Edna becomes more ambitious as an artist in her attempt to capture Adele's look as a "sensuous Madonna" (13). Although her friend Robert is impressed and says she has talent, Edna is disappointed with the work: "After surveying the sketch critically she drew a bored smudge of paint across its surface, and crumpled the paper between her hands" (13). Edna is not content to be complemented for mere verisimilitude; she wants to capture a spiritual quality of her subject. At this point, she is a perfectionist and her own harshest critic. Her dissatisfaction causes her to spend increasing amounts of time painting in the attic of her house, to the dismay of her husband who begins to object as her pastime becomes her occupation: "I feel like painting," says Edna, to which Pontellier replies, "Then in God's name paint! But don't let the family go to the devil" (56). Edna chooses to continue to paint.

Unlike Gertie in *The Dollmaker* whose husband is similarly disapproving, Edna has the good fortune to have a role model for the artist, Mademoiselle Reisz. Reisz is herself an artist; she is a pianist who is respected for her passionate playing. Much in demand among the upperclass for after-dinner entertainments, Reisz can never play in concert or make much money as a musician, however, because such public performances were considered unseemly for a woman. Although Reisz knows the limitations of her society upon the woman artist, she encourages Edna to continue to paint. The choice of art or family, however, is one with which Reisz cannot help Edna; Reisz has already chosen to be forever single just as Edna, in a way, has also already made that choice since her marriage and children are irreversible. In this society, a woman must choose. When Edna tells Mademoiselle that she wants to be a painter, Reisz laughs and says that an artist must "possess a courageous soul, one that dares and defies" (63).

While Edna's actions with her lover Arobin are certainly daring, Edna also becomes more experimental with her painting. No longer interested in the safe content for women's art—scenery, portraits of friends—she attempts to sketch her dour Calvinistic father. Chopin gives an original account of the female artist with the male model: under Edna's gaze, her father sits "rigid and unflinching, as he had faced the cannon's mouth in days gone by" (68). The comparison of his facing Edna as if facing a cannon reveals that metaphorically she has a good deal of power and control over him, a situation much changed from her meekness with him when she was a child. Now she has the ability to define him, to control his image before the world. Perhaps because they are at last on an equal footing, the sessions allow Edna to feel warmly toward her father for the first time in her life. Her art begins a process of healing the rift between father and daughter.

When Edna moves out of her husband's house into the small house she calls her pigeon house, she appears to have the freedom to paint as she desires. We are not told much about what she paints, only that she is far more satisfied with her efforts than she was before. The one work of art about which we learn, however, is significant. She chooses a subject that is entirely new for her, a sketch of the head of her lover, Alcee Arobin. She had asked him for a photograph so that she might study it when he could not sit for her. This innocuous request leads to an incident that greatly influences her relationship with Robert LeBrun, the man she loves. Robert discovers the photograph and realizes that in polite Creole society, a wife and mother ought not to be painting the head of a man who is not her husband or father. Chopin does not need to have Robert find out about Edna's affair with Arobin in an overt manner; rather the conventions of what women of that time were allowed to paint reveal Edna's indiscretion.

Chopin herself was certainly using Edna's art as a metaphor for her own situation as a writer; her previous stories had focused on discrete exposés of the mores of New Orleans. Even the subjects of miscengenation and flawed marriages were tactfully handled. With *The Awakening*, Chopin, like Edna, leaped out of the safe topics into the murky and forbidden waters of women's sexuality. In so doing Chopin incurred the hostility of critics far worse than those of Edna; the critical reception of *The Awakening* is itself a tale of the female writer/artist struck down for her use of "unnatural" topics. These reviews, reprinted in the Norton critical edition of *The Awakening* and discussed by Anne Goodwin Jones (1981), show the dismay of Chopin's contemporaries

at what they called her "sick" and "unholy and unclean" book (Culley, 1976, 147, 150). As a reviewer for the *Providence Sunday Journal* (1899) says, "Miss Kate Chopin is another clever woman, but she has put her cleverness to a very bad use...the story can hardly be described in language fit for publication" (Culley, 1976, 149). Surprised and discouraged by these reviews, Chopin published very little thereafter.

Ellen Glasgow, a writer whose setting was Virginia in the early part of this century, moves the argument regarding the immorality of the woman artist a step beyond Chopin. In Glasgow's story "The Difference" (1923) Rose Morrison is a painter already with a room of her own, a small apartment, an artist's studio. Writing only twenty years after Chopin, Glasgow does not have to give the readers the account of how Rose managed to establish herself as independent of her family in order to adopt the bohemian life; by the 1920s, society had made a small bit of space for the female artist. Glasgow is not, however, entirely pleased with this space. Rose Morrison is the mistress of a married man whose wife discovers the affair. Rose invites the wife, Margaret, to her apartment to tell her that she and Margaret's husband are in love; Rose asks the astonished Margaret to step aside and allow this magnificent love affair to flourish. Rose is part artist and part flapper; her audacity certainly qualifies as a spirit which dares and defies in a way Edna in *The Awakening* could not. Rose conforms to the image of the artist as immoral; she wears Oriental kimonos, has wild red hair and has an air of what the narrator calls "glittering hardness" (900). Her nails are dirty and her flat is in the same state of disarray, Glasgow implies, as her morality. We are not told what she paints; rather her painting appears to be a pastime meant to justify her behavior. Thus it is not always the case that a woman novelist is free from the conventional expectations regarding the correct demeanor of a woman who is an artist. Glasgow harshly condemns Rose's tawdry and naive misunderstanding of the situation; in fact, Margaret's husband, in the typical double standard of the day, regards Rose as no more than "recreation" (908).

As our society altered its mores regarding female sexuality, the female artist slowly shed the image of immorality. In her novel *Violet Clay* (1978), Gail Godwin creates a painter who has had many advantages: she has her family's support and appreciation of her talent, a sound education in art and the ambition of becoming a famous painter by the time she is thirty. With all these advantages, however, the contemporary artist encounters obstacles more subtle than poverty and lack of education. As a young woman who works hard at her painting, Violet must contend with the subtle criticism of her grandmother. The grandmother urges Violet to marry rather than paint, citing her own situation when she gave up a career in music by pretending to a suitor that it was not important to her. Violet refuses to heed this advice; she marries and continues to paint but finds paradoxically that marriage and art are still at odds. Her well-educated, liberated husband begins to erode her self-confidence; his need to be in control, to be powerful, leads to physical abuse. Without her sense of integrity she becomes depressed, begins to sleep more and paint less. Her recovery can be traced to one scene in which Violet, like Edna in *The Awakening*, chooses to paint a man; in Violet's case, it is her husband. She asks to paint him in the nude; he is at first cowed and ashamed to be naked, even under the gaze of his wife. John Berger (1972) points out that it is often the case when the painter is male and the model female that the model becomes an object of sexual desire. Because Violet sees him not as a nude but as a naked man, she can also see him as flawed; he is not powerful unless she allows it. Through the relationship of artist and model, Violet is able to control him. To keep him silent and still, ironically the wish of centuries of men for women, Violet tells him jokes to amuse him as she paints. Like Sheherazade, Violet wards off the man's potential violence; while he is immobile, he cannot hurt her. As with Edna Pontellier, painting a man allows Violet to begin to grow away from her victimizer.

As this flawed marriage dissolves, Violet begins to support herself with a job as an illustrator of the covers of Gothic romances. Violet regards this cul-de-sac in the art world as temporary, but she remains at it for nine years. Most of her acquaintances believe that she is not really creating art because the genre is not right. As Joanna Russ (1983) points out, when women paint portraits, elite critics would label that genre as art, but if they paint in a different genre, their work is called craft or decoration or, as in Violet's case, illustration (61). Violet has one friend, a male writer who regards her drawings as splendid emotional renditions of the novels he writes—he is a male romance writer. But art, even a subgenre of it, is not prized; the romance editor eventually prefers as covers the photographs of actual women being raped or murdered. This horrifying exploitation of the actual misery of women as a commodity to replace art is clearly Godwin's comment on the art scene of New York.

Violet's courage in returning to painting rather than looking for another position serves as a hopeful credo for contemporary women artists. Violet moves to a room of her own, a cabin in Vermont. Far from being isolated, she makes acquaintance again with the materials of painting, the hues and tints she has had to avoid as a cover illustrator. Violet also finds in Vermont a supportive, woman-centered community that nurtures her as well. She becomes friends with

Samantha, a tall and physically strong woman who inspires Violet to paint what becomes Violet's finest work. The joy of this awakening of her ability, even without the security of financial success, restores Violet to her vision of herself as a creator of meaning. Violet attempts to capture Samantha's luminous inner strength by placing her with arms raised amidst a wash of translucent light. The quality of light in the finished portrait entitled "Suspended Woman" provides an image of what Violet calls the situation of today's women, being "suspended in...her own possibilities" (322). Godwin's novel is an optimistic presentation of the woman artist.

### Two Contemporary Artists

This optimism permeates the final novel of this chapter, Alice Walker's *The Color Purple* (1982) which describes two contemporary women artists, Shug and Celie. I will close the chapter with it to show that by the 1980s a writer can create a novel in which her artists enjoy the acceptance of their art from the very beginning by the groups that might have been expected to be its critics. While we recall the ways in which Shug is a mentor to Celie in terms of her self-esteem, her removal from her crippling marriage and her sexuality, Walker's novel is also an eloquent plea for the release of women's creativity. Shug is a musician, a singer of blues songs in nightclubs. Although her profession might make her a victim of the criticism that woman artists focus on prurient material, Shug has the good fortune to be loyally appreciated by an audience of local people who revere the tradition of the blues song. Thus her private behavior, although a question in the minds of her audience, is considered a separate issue from her talent as a singer and the content of the songs she sings. Her confidence in her talent never wavers; as society changes and the blues song becomes a genre that is no longer marginalized, Shug's ability is recognized and acclaimed by both white and Black audiences. Shug becomes wealthy. In fact, she is one of the few female artist in a prominent novel who receives the critical and material rewards of her creativity without being called upon to compromise her art, make a commodity from it, mass produce it or become a pariah to make it. Walker manages to convince the jaded reader that our society has changed, or at least is changing, so that the woman artist can hope to achieve this balance of fortune and creativity.

As a mentor to Celie, Shug has a challenging task indeed. Raped by the man whom she believes to be her father and sold to her husband who beats her daily, Celie appears at first to be too degraded to lead even a normal life. She does, however, have several important advantages that Joanna Russ (1983) and Alice Walker (1984) have pointed out are essential to the woman artist: Celie has a role model for what the woman artist can do—she has Shug. Although first an ostensible rival for her husband, Shug becomes a friend to Celie. Shug's generous nature affords Celie the nurturing and affection she has never experienced; her own warmth begins to be released after years of suppression. Responding like a flower to the sun, Celie blossoms late but fully. She begins to be surrounded by a warm supportive group of women; no longer an isolated victim, she begins to create. At first the pants she makes are for herself and her friends, but as she develops more confidence she begins to sell them. Unlike Gertie, Celie is not so poor that she is tempted to mass produce these pants. She retains her integrity by concentrating on the richness of the materials, the meticulousness of her technique, and when possible, the individuality of the wearer. She is a true artist of the everyday, creating an object that is not only useful but beautiful. Like Maggie in Walker's story "Everyday Use," Celie is an artist whose work connects her with her friends and with her culture. It is a means of private expression in a public context. Her art is not meant to be hung on walls or sold in auctions although it could be. It is meant to clothe, to delight, to allow art to be part of the daily existence of ordinary people, not to be hidden in the mansions of the rich.

This vision of art and artists has been one hundred years in the making. Women artists have been accused of prurience, their art has been marginalized, their critics have been vituperative. Yet for all that women have created; as we discover their courage at creating against the odds, these artists, poor like Gertie and despairing as Edna, become the guardians of female creativity. Their failures warn us and their successes inspire and lead us from our own cul-de-sacs, help us to recognize the strategies of our unhelpful critics, and nurture the artists about us and within ourselves. These authors invite us to join with Celie and Maggie, with Violet Clay and with Shug to recreate reality in our image and with our images.

# Works Cited

Arnow, H. *The dollmaker.* New York: Avon. (1954; rpt. 1973).

Berger, J. *Ways of seeing.* London: British Broadcasting Corporation and Penguin Books. (1972).

Chopin, K. *The awakening.* Ed. M. Culley. New York: Norton. (1899; rpt. 1976).

Congdon, K.G. The meaning and use of folk speech in art criticism. *Studies in Art Education, 27* (3), (1986): 140-148.

Congdon, K.G. Multicultural approaches to art criticism. *Studies in Art Education, 30* (3), (1989): 176-184.

Ecker, G. (Ed.). *Feminist aesthetics.* Boston: Beacon Press. (1986).

Gilbert, S. and S. Gubar. *The madwoman in the attic: The woman writer and the nineteenth-century literary imagination.* New Haven: Yale UP. (1979).

Glasgow, E. The difference. In N. Baym and R. Gottesman (Eds.), *The Norton anthology of American literature,* 2nd Ed. New York: Norton. (1923; rpt. 1975): 891-908.

Godwin, G. *Violet clay.* New York: Penguin. (1978).

Hirsch, M. *The mother/daughter plot: Narrative, psychoanalysis, feminism.* Bloomington: Indiana UP. (1989).

Jaudon, V. and J. Kozloff. Art hysterical notions of progress and culture. *Heresies, 4,* (1978): 38-42.

Jones, A.G. *Tomorrow is another day: The woman writer in the South, 1859-1936.* Baton Rouge: Louisiana State UP. (1981).

Mitchell, M. *Gone with the Wind.* New York: Macmillan. (1936).

Morrison, T. *Sula.* New York: Signet. (1973).

Russ, J. *How to suppress women's writing.* Austin: U of Texas P. (1983).

Vogel, L. Fine arts and feminism. In A. Raven & J. Frueh (Eds.),*Feminist art criticism: An anthology.* Ann Arbor: UMI Research P. (1988): 20-58.

Walker, A. Everyday use. In S. Gilbert and S. Gubar (Eds.), *The Norton anthology of literature by women.* New York: Norton. (1973): 2366-2374.

Walker, A. *The color purple.* New York: Washington Square Press. (1982).

Walker, A. *In search of our mothers' gardens.* New York: Harcourt Brace Jovanovich. (1984).

Walsh, K. Free will and determination in Harriet Arnow's *The Dollmaker. South Atlantic Review, 49*(4), (1984): 91-106.

Woolf, V. A room of one's own. (excerpt) In S. Gilbert and S. Gubar (Eds.), *The Norton anthology of literature by women* New York: Norton. (1376-1383). (1929; rpt. 1985).

# Part III
# Criticism That Asserts
# Life, History and Human Rights

# The Handmade Books of Dennis Bye:
# Self-Documentation as Aesthetic-Expressive Criticism

## Doug Blandy

A democratic society will be concerned with the critical discourse of all of its citizens. One form of critical discourse should not take precedence over another. If this should occur a society will become unbalanced in its distribution of power and limited in its ability to be collectively self critical. Habermas (1983) suggests that aesthetic-expressive elements along with the cognitive and the moral-practical should be considered in this communication process.

Critical discourse which is primarily aesthetic-expressive is most commonly recognized in the work of academically trained artists who engage in social criticism through the public presentation of objects and images which address issues of public concern. Notable examples include the work of the Political Art Documentation Distribution Group (PADD), the Art Workers' Coalition (AWC) and the Guerrilla Girls.

Congdon (1986) has argued that people have the right and responsibility to be critical in the language that is most familiar to them. In her opinion, talk about art and artifacts should not, and does not, have to be modeled on the discursive methodologies of professionals. Congdon makes a very persuasive argument for the need of additional research in this area by demonstrating its neglect in the literature of art education and related fields.

The neglect of some types of verbal critical discourse that Congdon discovered can also be said to exist in relation to aesthetic-expressive discourse. Many examples of aesthetic-expressive criticism emanating from the so-called fine arts are routinely cited in the art literature. This is the realm in which PADD, AWC and the Guerrilla Girls operate. Very few examples of aesthetic-expressive discourse have been documented which come from citizens who are not connected to the so-called fine arts. Those examples that are documented are largely derived from third and fourth world countries (Brett, 1986). However, Lippard (1984) can be credited with including several so-called non-fine art examples of aesthetic-expressive criticism in her critical writings on art and social change in the United States.

This chapter will respond to this neglect of aesthetic-expressive criticism originating in the lives of people who are not academically trained as artists by focusing on the example set by Dennis Bye in his hand-made books. Our examination of these books and the context in which they are made will provide answers to questions about the influence of social context on aesthetic-expressive criticism, the structure of such discourse, its relationship to life problems and the implications of aesthetic-expressive criticism for social change.

### Dennis Bye's Handmade Books

Dennis Bye documents his life in self-crafted books. Each book of the seven that I know to exist measures approximately 9" x 12" (Fig. 1). All are non-case bound western codex style along the left-hand edge with minute pieces of masking tape interwoven within the pages to hold the pages together. The soft covers of Dennis Bye's books are made from the most inexpensive of craft paper. Turning back these covers reveals a profusion of opaque and translucent pages constructed of myriad materials. The source of these materials is the debris of Dennis Bye's daily life and what he finds of interest in the waste collections of others. This material includes previously used cellophane tape, newspaper circulars, glossy magazine illustrations, mail advertisement catalog pictures, past calendars, Polaroid film packages, Polaroid photographs, mattress tags, bumper stickers, school report cards, work reports, shopping bags and political buttons. These materials are combined, collaged and drawn on to form books of approximately 100 pages. Frequently, half or quarter-sized pages are grouped to form a book within the larger book. Fold-out pages of approximately 18" x 12" are also included. The Polaroid photographs that appear in the books were taken by Dennis Bye. He is also responsible for the drawings that appear. These photographs and drawings include self-portraits, portraits of his friends and neighbors, landscapes, interiors, everyday still-lifes and assorted other unrecognizable images. Self-portraits predominate. They were taken by Dennis Bye while he held the camera at arm's length.

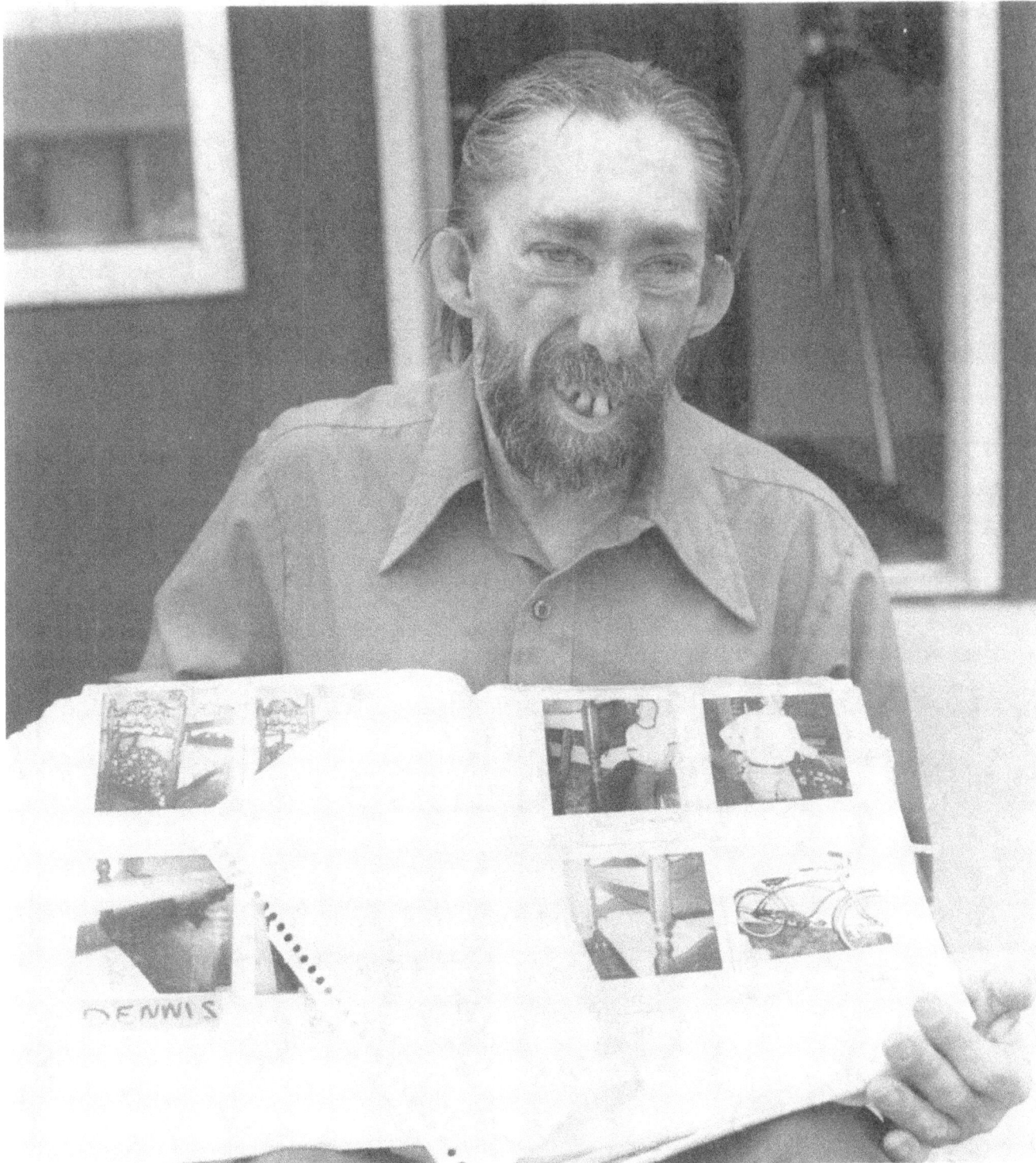

Fig. 1. Dennis Bye with one of his books. (photograph by Russ McKnight)

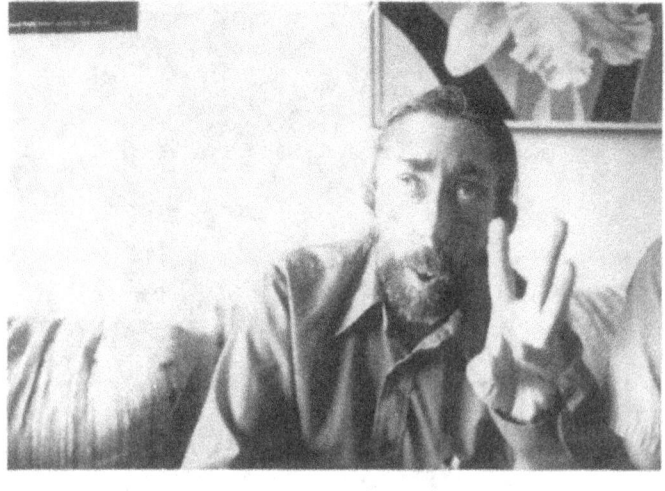 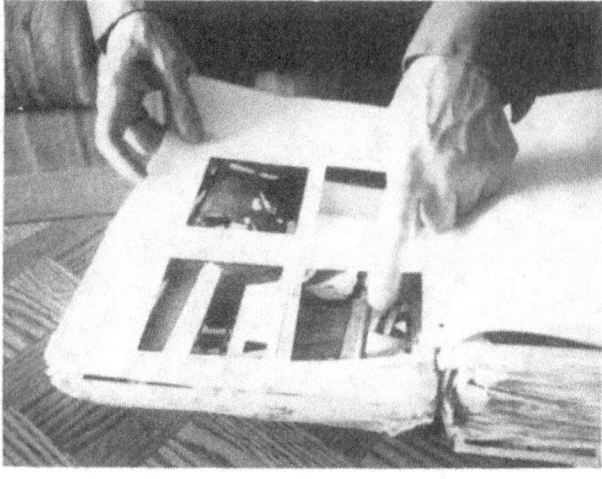

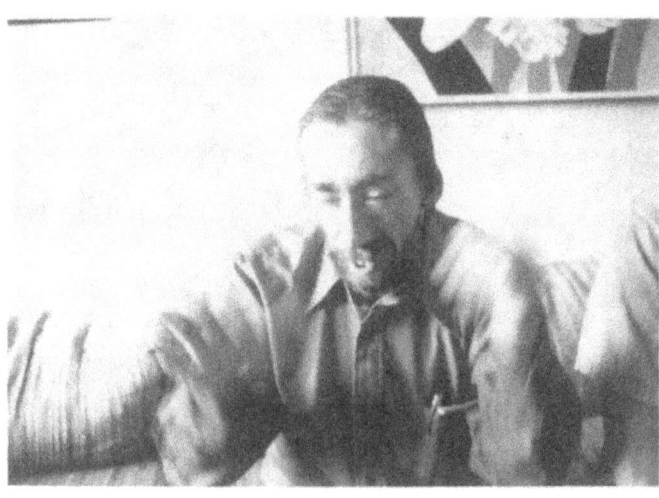 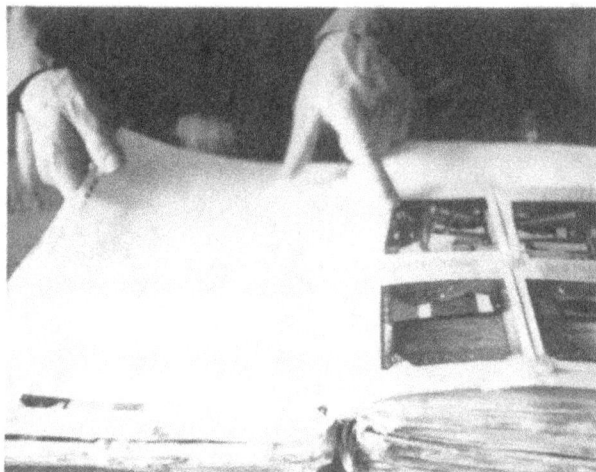

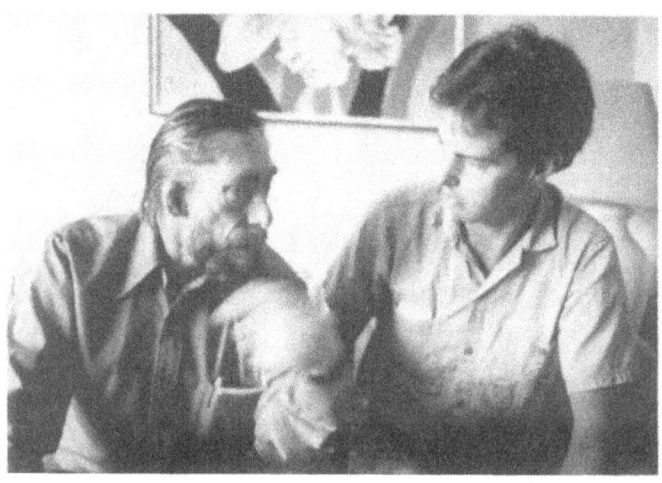 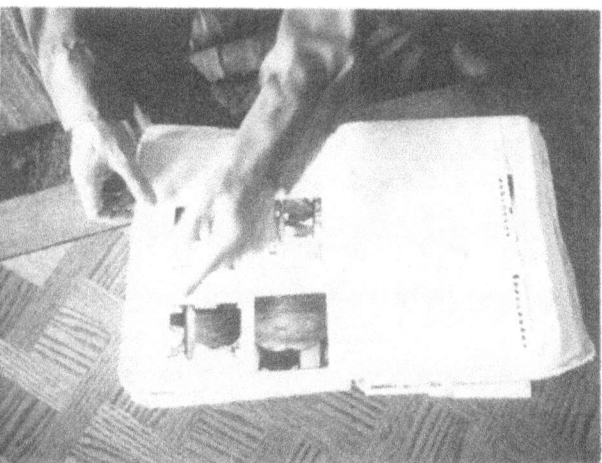

Fig. 2. Dennis Bye shares one of his books with the author. (photograph by Russ McKnight)

Dennis Bye's speech is very difficult to understand and he primarily communicates through a few sign language gestures, pantomime and his books (Fig. 2). His books are meant to be experienced with their maker at your side turning pages, signing and pantomiming as you leaf your way through them. Dennis Bye makes his books at home during his leisure time in the evening and on weekends. He currently lives semi-independently in Bowling Green, Ohio, in an apartment complex for people labeled mentally retarded. He makes his living through the Wood County Board of Mental Retardation and Developmental Disabilities Community Supported Employment Program. Prior to his current residence, Dennis Bye lived in a group home for ten to twelve adult men experiencing mental retardation. However, Dennis Bye has spent the greatest portion of his life living in Ohio's state administered total institutions for children, youth and adults with mental retardation.[1]

Dennis Bye is now middle-aged. Those years that experts in human development acknowledge as formative were lived in a total institution. During the summers of 1973 and 1974 I worked in one of the total institutions in which Dennis Bye lived. One summer I worked as an activity therapist assistant and the next summer as a ward attendant trainee. Although I did not know Dennis Bye at the time, my experience there convinces me that he was living in a setting in which values, attitudes and beliefs were markedly dissimilar from what I was experiencing during my non-working hours "off grounds." Imagine locked wards, barred windows, imposed nakedness, solitary confinement, gender segregation, physical abuse and incessant boredom. These conditions were commonly experienced by those who lived in this institution. Patti Burt's oral history of life in a total institution for people with mental retardation as recorded in Bogdan and Taylor (1982) confirms what I was experiencing in the privileged position of a staff member and suggests what Dennis Bye was more directly experiencing as a resident. The horror possible in the total institution is apparent when Patti Burt states:

When I first arrived there and saw all the people, I thought, "Oh, no. What am I getting into now? What's going to happen?" There were all these people just sitting around and rocking back and forth and back and forth. Some of them were pulling their hair and eating it. One was in a strait jacket. They had to keep her in it because she hurt other people. They were just sitting there looking at their hands and twirling them around. I knew that it was a place for punishments and I told myself that I wasn't going to stay there and live there. (133)

Goffman, in a series of essays published as *Asylums* (1961), characterizes total institutions for people experiencing mental illness or mental retardation as sites dedicated to the forced concentration of like-situated persons who are segregated from their communities and whose lifestyle is authoritatively designed and scrutinized by others as an outcome of official cultural policy. Such settings are rooted in pre-Renaissance western European social fabrications modeled on the leprosorium (Foucault, 1973). Foucault argues that as leprosy vanished in Western Europe the stigma associated with leprosy was transferred in the minds of the general population to the person experiencing mental and physical disabilities.

The conditions allowable in the total institution were and are equal to the perceived social standing of those incarcerated. Life in the total institution is described by Goffman as a life of mortification and deculturation. Residents are possessionless, under constant surveillance, unable to feel personally safe, are allowed no environmental control and are often forced to speak to their overseers in humiliating ways. These conditions work together to influence a culture transmitted through self-concern and self-pity, institutional rituals, time devastation and time destruction through staff prescribed activities such as watching television and playing games (Goffman, 1961).

Gene Minnich, Dennis Bye's former group home house manager, reports that it was in the total institution that Dennis Bye first began to make his books.[2] This was an environment that provided him with little or no training in art, little or no money with which to work on his books or store the materials from which they were made, no personally guaranteeable place for safe keeping his books and little or no access to the culture existing outside of the institution. The expectations held of him by others were shaped by popular perceptions of medical etiology rather than the ability of the person so labeled and the failure of the society to accommodate the disability. Bogdan and Taylor (1977) have acknowledged that to be called mentally retarded will result in psychological, social and educational penalties. This was certainly Dennis Bye's experience.

It is surprising that such extremely adverse and dehumanizing conditions would have empowered Dennis Bye to begin to construct his books from the salvable debris available to him in the total institution. We could speculate on the reasons for this ability on the part of Dennis Bye; however, more importantly we can recognize that he was acting uniquely, possibly heroically, but also very normally under the circumstances in which he lived. There is cross-cultural evidence that suggests that there is a tradition of crafting objects that respond to social and cultural conditions that are potentially personally oppressive and debilitating. For example, Brett (1986) argues that people of all ages when involved in social situations that are precarious and overwhelming will use aesthetic-expressive processes to communicate to others about their life situation. In these situations, according to Brett, crafted objects act as a means of communicating facts/feelings, provide therapy for the trauma, and the making of such objects becomes a method for retaining humanity. Materials will be chosen from what is at hand and stylistically the work demonstrates displacement from a traditional cultural context. Dennis Bye's bookmaking conforms to these circumstances. His books were first crafted during a very precarious and life threatening period in his life. Dennis Bye's books clearly embody facts about his life as well as his emotional connection with certain people, events, places and objects. The materials from which they reportedly were, and are made, are taken from what is at hand. Their only connection with the tradition of artists' books or book making in general is the fact that they are of the western codex variety.

Object making, under the circumstances described by Brett, assumes an audience who can be persuaded through the work to experience as the artist is experiencing. Hopefully, social change will result. Exemplary of this type of aesthetic-expressive criticism are the arpilleras, or patchwork pictures, produced by working class women in Chile. Brett duly acknowledges the significance of these images as being "a complete and detailed chronicle...of the Chilean working class since the brutal military coup of 1973" (29). Under the circumstances described by Brett, makers of images act unselfconsciously and critically to initiate fresh viewpoints, suggest possibilities and depict constructions of social reality which are just. Other examples of this type of aesthetic-expressive discourse include the popular painting movement in Africa, the eyewitness paintings from Hiroshima and the work of the spare-time worker artists of China (Brett, 1987).

### The green book

At this point it will be instructive to examine one of Dennis Bye's books more closely for the purpose of discovering the ways in which he constructs his aesthetic-expressive criticism and the content of his visual text. In doing this we will gain insight into what he is persuading us to do. Unfortunately, none of the books currently in Dennis Bye's possession date to the time of his confinement in a total institution. It is likely that they have been lost, destroyed or stolen during his many moves. We will have to make do with a fairly recent example. Our examination of Dennis Bye's book will be based on the structure of visual books identified by Smith (1984). Smith is well known among book artists and collectors for his one-of-a-kind visual books. Many of Smith's books use the western codex format. Dennis Bye is not in any way associated with the fine arts context in which the visual books of Smith are made and appreciated.

However, Dennis Bye in choosing to use the western codex form for his books does confront the structural problems associated with this format. Smith, who has articulated these problems, will be helpful in illuminating Dennis Bye's approach to the structural problems of display, picture relationships, movement and composition integral to this form.

The *green book* dates to Dennis Bye's placement in the group home for men with mental retardation in Bowling Green, Ohio. Its designation in this chapter as the *green book* is for ease of discussion as it is unclear to me if the book has been formally titled by Dennis Bye. The majority of it was probably crafted no later than 1983 and no earlier than 1978. However, it is important to acknowledge that Dennis Bye periodically returns to seemingly completed books and adds to them. The *green book* is covered with green craft paper. Its cover bears an approximately 3/4'' x 3'' irregular strip of orange craft paper on which Dennis Bye has printed his name. This strip of paper is placed where one would expect to find the title, but it may also be there simply for the identification of the book's owner and maker. The size of this book conforms to the dimensions of Dennis Bye's books given elsewhere in this chapter. The *green book* contains twenty-five to thirty Polaroid photographs of Dennis Bye, other residents of the group home, interiors of the home (dining room, bedrooms, kitchen, office, living area, basement) and photographs of other homes in the neighborhood in which the group home is located. The majority of the photographs are self-portraits of Dennis Bye. Sections of some have been cut away and replaced with images of people and objects from mail order catalogs, magazines as well as line drawings of people and objects in felt marker. These drawings were rendered by Dennis Bye.

As mentioned previously, Dennis Bye's design is similar to all western style codex books. He is concerned with the uses of the page, the relationships between the images on the page, movement within the book and the composition of singular and multiple imaged pages.

The recto and verso sides of each page in the *green book* are used to contain images and collaged materials. Some of this material bears an alphabetic text. However, the *green book*, like all of Dennis Bye's books, does not rely on an alphabetic text. Pre-printed text is used to form visual patterns. Pictures and drawings, photographed or collected by Dennis Bye, are the primary source of information. Each page of the *green book* contains many such pictures. Pages are not bordered and margins do not seem to be of importance. Frequently Dennis Bye groups pictures by a common theme such as self-portraits, domestic spaces or neighborhood. Less frequently pictures will be grouped in sequences. Examples include multiple views of a dining room or sleeping room. However, these sequences are non-narrative in a conventional and linear start to finish sense.

Timing and pacing within the *green book* is implied in the complexity of the picture composition as it is revealed on the turn of each page. Timing and pacing of the book is also revealed as Dennis Bye personally leads a viewer through each book. Some pages will be skimmed while others receive prolonged study.

The *green book* is structurally dependent upon Dennis Bye's variations on an autobiographical theme. This theme is explored through self-portraiture, the portraits of his group home family members, the symbolic representation of other personally important persons through collected images and the pictorial documentation of the material world surrounding him in his home and as suggested in clippings from mail order catalogs and advertising circulars. Dennis Bye's autobiography is celebratory of self as explored through photography, drawing and collected pictures. In Dennis Bye's autobiography the viewer experiences an affirmation of the self as an active, expressive and reflective participant in the world. Dennis Bye is persuasive through his own example.

The *green book* is a document which proposes and demands social action from its viewers while simultaneously suggesting the proposed course of action. Because the *green book* celebrates the pleasure that Dennis Bye derives from his personal relationships, his material surroundings and his community, it persuades the viewer that its maker is acutely interested and involved with people, places and things in a way that demands a recognition of that commitment. Dennis Bye does not permit the viewer of the *green book* to consider him as detached, dispassionate or unintelligent. In not permitting us to view him in this way, he confronts the prejudices of a society which has a long and brutal history of seeing him and others experiencing mental retardation as not being completely human and equal. Dennis Bye's *green book* is in some ways similar to the family scrap book and photo album. The *green book*, like those familial mementos, clearly connects him with what many of us hold to be important: friends, community, work, home. His response to our prejudice is to simply communicate to us what he sees in himself. Our response, in turn, can be to keep company with him as we join him in constructing our own self-image and life history. In doing this he reminds us that the label with which he lives is not of his making. He affirms Bogdan and Taylor's (1977) position that the concept of mental retardation has more to communicate about those who devised it than about those to whom it is applied.

## Conclusion

Dennis Bye is, of course, not the first person to visually document the life or lives of people labeled mentally retarded. During the 1965 Christmas season, Blatt and Kaplan (1966) walked through several total institutions for children, youth and adults experiencing mental retardation. Attached to Kaplan's belt was a hidden camera which photographically documented what he was viewing. These photographs, with an accompanying text by Blatt, were published as *Christmas in Purgatory*. Kaplan's photographs revealed living conditions that could not be defended, tolerated or excused under any circumstances. Persons are shown naked and tied to wooden benches. Faces peer from miniscule windows in the doors of solitary confinement rooms. Rooms are devoid of material which makes a space personal and home-like. People roam and sit in idleness. Children are shown on the floor, heads to wall with hands covering their faces.

There is no doubt that Kaplan's photographs have made a significant contribution to the aesthetic-expressive discourse on the misguidedness of society's treatment of people experiencing disabilities. It stands with those other documents that were influential in advocating for normalization and de-institutionalization. However, as significant as Kaplan's aesthetic-expressive criticism is, it is limited by the fact that its portrayal of people experiencing mental retardation is such that it makes them only appear as hopeless and worthy of our pity. He fails to persuade us that these people can also be strong and self-reliant in the face of dire circumstances. Kaplan's portrayal of people experiencing mental retardation is in keeping with a tradition of reform photographers who wish to reveal the failures of social systems but only do so through a "paternal bourgeois benevolence" which replaces one form of objectification for another (Westbrook, 1987).

Blatt, Ozolins and McNally (1979) present a more multi-dimensional view of persons experiencing mental retardation in *The Family Papers: A Return to Purgatory*. In this photo/text essay there is a view of living as a mentally retarded person that includes active domestic participation in a home-like environment.

However well-meaning these publications are, they are still extremely limited by the fact that their authors and photographers can never completely understand what it means to live as a person labeled mentally retarded. As Bogdan and Taylor (1977) have reminded us: "People who are labeled retarded have their own understanding about themselves, their situation, and their experiences. These understandings are often different from those of professionals" (230).

Dennis Bye's aesthetic-expressive discourse is revolutionary criticism in that he has taken the initiative to advocate on behalf of himself. In doing this he makes the most significant contribution to that body of aesthetic-expressive discourse which demands an equal place for him and others so labeled in the society. He is also denying the observation made by Bogdan and Taylor that "to be labeled retarded is to have wide range of imperfections imputed to you. One imperfection is the inability to analyze your life and your current situation. Another is the inability to express yourself—to know and say who you are and what you wish to be" (218). Dennis Bye is refusing to be shown as victimized, helpless or an object of pity. Instead he portrays himself as an active, expressive and contributive member of his community. He assumes a critical position on social constructions that would have him be otherwise and suggests alternatives for the transformation of those constructions.

# Notes

The author wishes to thank Russ McKnight for the photographs that he contributed to this chapter. Russ McKnight is an internationally exhibited photographer. He is currently on staff at The Logan Elm Press at The Ohio State University.

[1] I am using the term "total institution" as it has been defined by Goffman (1961): "as a place of residence and work where a large number of like-situated individuals, cut off from the wider society for an appreciable period of time, together lead an enclosed, formally administered round of life" (xiii).

[2] My interviews with Dennis Bye's friends and rehabilitation supervisors have failed to confirm when and where Dennis Bye first began to use a Polaroid camera and how it came into his possession. Total institutions often forbid the use of cameras within their confines unless that use is supervised by the administration. For this reason it would be of interest to know if Dennis Bye did obtain his camera while living in a total institution, and if so, what restrictions were put on its use. To the best of my knowledge, I do not believe that Dennis Bye currently holds any photographs from this period in his life.

# Works Cited

Blatt, B. & Kaplan, F. *Christmas in purgatory: A photographic essay on mental retardation.* Boston: Allyn and Bacon. (1966).

Blatt, B., Ozolins, A. and McNally, J. *The family papers: A return to purgatory.* New York: Longman, Inc. (1979).

Bogdan, R. & Taylor, S.J. *Inside out: Two first-person accounts of what it means to be labeled "mentally retarded".* Toronto: U of Toronto P. (1982).

Bogdan, R. & Taylor, S.J. The judged, not the judges: An insider's view of mental retardation. In B. Blatt, D. Biklen, & R. Bogdan (Eds.), *An alternative textbook in special education: People, schools and other institutions.* Denver: Love Publishing. (1977): 217-232.

Brett, G. *Through our own eyes: Popular art and modern history.* Philadelphia: New Society Publishers. (1986).

Congdon, K.G. The meaning and use of folk speech in art criticism. *Studies in Art Education,* 27(3), (1986): 140-148.

Foucault, M. *Madness and civilization* (R. Howard, Trans.). New York: Vintage Books. (1973).

Goffman, I. *Asylums: Essays on the social situation of mental patients and other inmates.* Garden City, NY: Anchor Books. (1961).

Habermas, J. Modernity: An incomplete project. (S. Ben-Habib, Trans.). In H. Foster (Ed.), *The Anti-aesthetic: Essays on postmodern culture* (3-15). Port Townsend, WA: Bay Press. (1983).

Lippard, L.R. *Get the message? A decade of art for social change.* New York: E.P. Dutton. (1984).

Smith, K. *Structure of the visual book.* Rochester, NY: Visual Studies Workshop Press. (1984).

Westbrook, R. Lewis Hine and the ethics of progressive camerawork. *Tikkun,* 2(2), (1984): 24-29.

# Art Criticism as Social Change

## Mario Asaro

Yet in retrospect we see how the artist's fidelity has strengthened the fiber of our national life. If sometimes our great artists have been the most critical of our society it is because their sensitivity and their concern for justice, which must motivate any true artist, make [them] aware that our nation falls short of its highest potential.

I see little importance to the future of this country and our civilization than the full recognition of the place of the artist. If art is to nourish the roots of our culture, society must set artists free to follow [their] visions wherever it takes [them]. We must not forget that art is not a form of propaganda: it is a form of truth.

John Fitzgerald Kennedy*

Former President Kennedy's remarks are particularly relevant today for artists and art educators alike. His observations emphasize the need for the artist's proper role in a free society, the artist as social critic. However, Kennedy's vision of the artist is one which is neglected. Art is often looked upon as purely decorative or neutral by the general public. In affairs of the state and in the education of our children, art is frequently assigned a secondary position, taking a back seat to academic subjects such as math or science.

Ironically, art educator's own attitudes may lay at the root of the public's misconception of the importance of art for our students and our society. As Feldman (1983) pointed out in his presidential statement of the National Art Educators Association on the errors of art education

> We taught students that art is made by recipe, like baking a cake; that art consists essentially of agreeable combinations of colors and shapes, like choosing which tie or blouse to wear with which shirt or skirt; that art is nothing but the forms one sees on a canvas or in a sculpture, as if forms and colors and textures have no meaning once they are recognized. This was incredibly stupid as a professional strategy, since it guaranteed that art would have less educational value than recess. (8)

Teachers who are reducing art to a simplistic exploratory search or a primer course in technique are giving the public a justification for believing that the arts are frivolous. Art could and should be fun; more importantly, it should also be meaningful to students. Art educators must demonstrate that the arts are valid, needed and integral to our schools and communities. Feldman (1983) supports this position:

> If thirty thousand years of art history prove anything, it is that art has always been a major source of meanings, meanings connected to vital human concerns. We must promise ourselves out of professional self respect to stop teaching art as if it were divorced from every significant dimension of personal and social existence. (8)

It is apparent that the reason art has been devalued in schools is at least partially due to the way teachers have approached and presented it. Art education, when portrayed as a meaningless appendage to the school curriculum, leads to budget and program cuts. Art educators should instead reflect on Kennedy's words anew and implement art programs that link art with social criticism. My purpose in this chapter will be to give examples of my own attempts to make such linkages through my association with Artists/Teachers Concerned (ATC).

### Social Education Through Art

In the Fall of 1985, I was introduced to ATC. At that time, ATC was a newly formed grassroots organization dedicated to the implementation and dissemination of socially motivated artwork in New York City Public School classrooms. While finishing my graduate internship in a local city intermediate school and working on my master's thesis on incorporating social education into art, I became interested in the group's proposal for "Seen and Heard," an exhibition of socially concerned student art (Fig. 1).[1] This exhibit received its title from the old adage that children should be "seen and not heard." The exhibition contained a variety of socially conscious art projects that included found object collages on the homeless, redesigned newspapers and dollar bills; of special significance were the early works of KOS, Tim Rollins' South Bronx students.[2] "Seen and Heard" provided a public forum for my class to perform "The Last Flower," a multimedia anti-war piece we had created for our school's spring assembly. Based on James Thurber's poem of the same title, it deals with the historical cycles of war and peace, emphasizing the need to learn from the errors of previous generations. The children used choral speaking, music, poetry, art, dance and theater to illustrate the profound message in Thurber's verse.

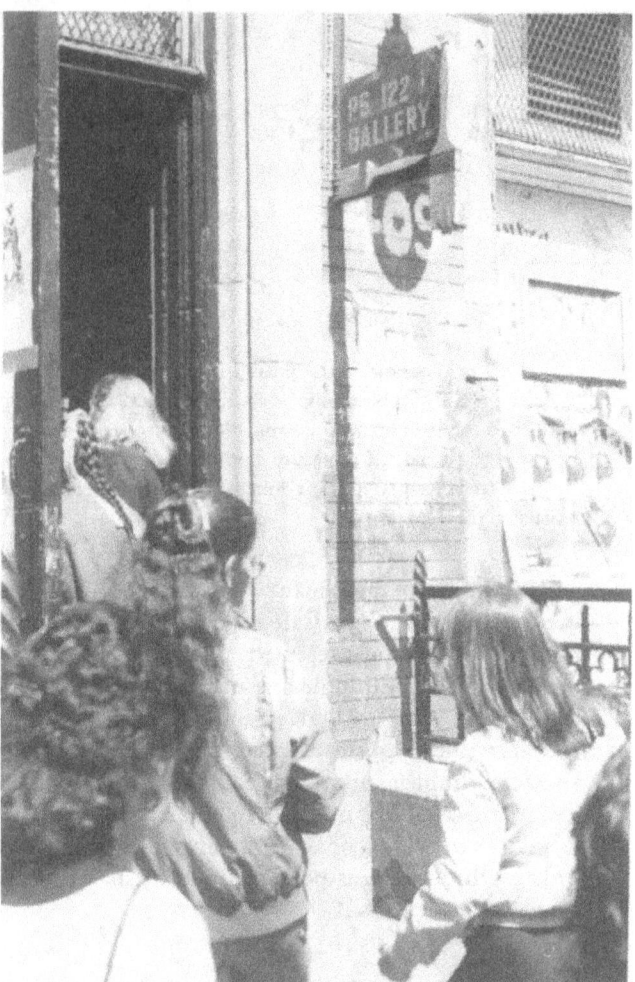

Fig. 1. Students file into the PS 122 Gallery to view an exhibit of their socially critical art work. (photograph courtesy of Mario Asaro)

After "Seen and Heard," ATC continues to sponsor meetings for socially motivated artists and educators. We present our work at city, state and national art education conferences and collaborate with various arts, educational and community organizations. Most importantly, we continue our primary function of organizing additional student exhibitions. These exhibits help the children in two ways. First, they give students a chance to analyze and critique the issues which are directly influencing and shaping their lives. These issues include, but are not limited to, housing, education, environment, drugs, crime, race relations, health and child welfare. Second, they serve to remind children that they are able to contribute to and better their community. Through these exhibits, the openings/awards ceremonies and subsequent press coverages, students are acknowledged as important participants in serious art exhibitions.

Since our first exhibit, we have collaborated on two major professional art exhibits at the DIA Art Foundation in New York: Group Material's "Democracy and Education" and Martha Rosler's "Homeless: The Streets and Other Venues."[3] Both of

these exhibitions included children's artwork with those of professional artists and laypeople to give a more balanced representation of the issues addressed by the shows. ATC has also organized two of its own exhibitions, "Out of the Classroom" and "Kids Speak Out" (Fig. 2).

"Out of the Classroom: Social Education Through Art," was held from March 3 to April 2, 1989, at the Minor Injury Gallery in Greenpoint, Brooklyn. This gallery exhibition featured over one hundred thirty issue-oriented artworks from over four hundred students. Along with the exhibit, we produced a catalog/teaching guide which not only documented the exhibit but also outlined the participating teachers' motivation and goals in working with their students. "Kids Speak Out," our next exhibit, was held from March 10 to June 30, 1990, at the Red Spot Outdoor Slide Theater in New York City. It was a unique environmental piece in which over six hundred socially motivated black and white drawings by students were transferred onto two-and-a-quarter-inch acetate slides that were projected nightly on the side of the building in New York City's Soho District. Exhibitions such as these give artists, teachers, students and community members the chance to meet and exchange concerns, methods and strategies. In addition, these exhibits and the media attention they receive play a crucial role in demonstrating to the public the severe impact our current social problems have on young people and how all community members can share in the responsibility of responding to—and correcting—our social ills.

*Correcting the Situation*

Never before has the need for organizations such as ATC been greater. The majority of teachers who collaborate with us work in inner-city urban environments. Many of us are frustrated with the lack of constructive input teachers have in the large bureaucratic settings we call public schools. Of equal frustration is the realization that for many of our students, as is the case for their parents today, there are few real economic, social and political choices. My experience indicates that there is little sense of hope for many urban youngsters who see themselves caught in a system of welfare, unemployment and poverty.

It is evident to the caring eye that art education must concern itself with culture, meaning and content as they relate to our students' social needs. Unfortunately, many educators are not prepared for this task. Through the ATC network, I have encountered many teachers whose artistic training is seemingly flawless but who feel uneasy or unsure of how to connect this training with important issues in their students' lives. Our training as art educators often detaches art and learning from life. We are trained

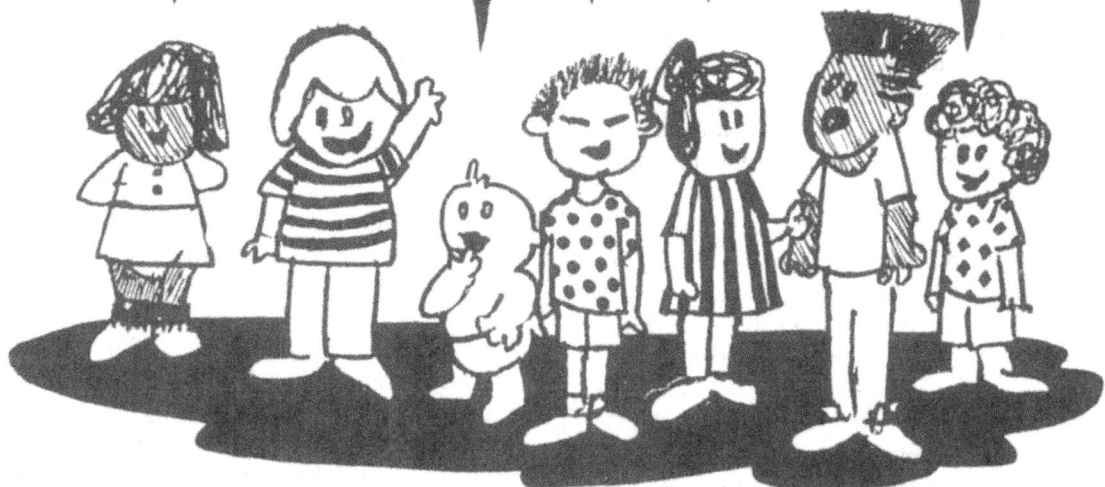

OPENING: MAY 12TH 9PM RAINDATE: MAY 19TH AT THE INTERSECTION OF BROADWAY AND SPRING

A SHOW OF STUDENT SOCIALLY MOTIVATED DRAWINGS PROJECTED ON AN OUTSIDE WALL

SHOWS CAN BE SEEN EVERY NIGHT TUESDAY THRU SATURDAY AT 9 PM UNTIL JUNE 30 TH, 1990 CURATED BY ATC AND RED SPOT

RED SPOT

Artists/Teachers Concerned SOCIAL EDUCATION THROUGH ART

KIDS SPEAK OUT!

THIS SHOW IS FUNDED IN PART BY VICTOR HASSELBLAD, INC. N.Y.C.A.T.A./UFT, THE NEW MUSEUM AND SUPPORT FROM MATERIALS FOR THE ARTS, DCA. PRINTED AT THE LOWER EAST SIDE PRINT SHOP

THE RED SPOT OUTDOOR SLIDE THEATER

Fig. 2. A Flyer for "Kids Speak Out." (courtesy of Mario Asaro)

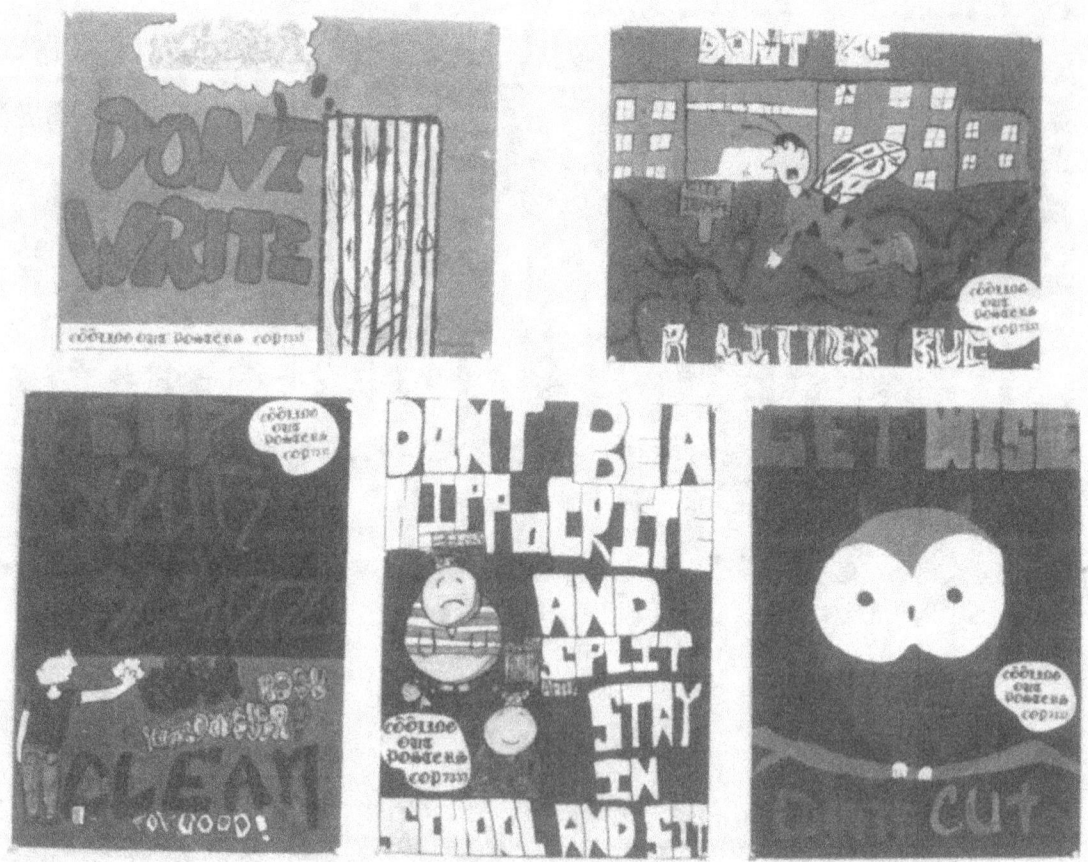

Fig. 3. Posters by the "Cooling Out Poster Crew" of Junior High School III. District 32, in Brooklyn, NY. (photograph courtesy of Mario Asaro)

to recognize and utilize artistic principles but are often left with an inferior knowledge of human conditions. ATC bridges that gap by documenting and sharing successful socially relevant art projects with interested educators.

My own situation at a Chapter One Junior High School in one of the poorest neighborhoods in Brooklyn serves as a very good example.[4] The majority of my students are from single-parent families, usually headed by the mother, or if the mother is unable to care for the children, the grandmother or an aunt. The father may have abandoned the family, is incarcerated or is unable to live at home for fear of losing city aid to the family. A frightening eighty percent of my students will not finish high school. As such, they will be unable to compete in the job market. This explains the large number of people in my school district drawn to alternative sources of income; the top three being car theft, drug trafficking and prostitution. This cycle of unstable family life, poor education and limited productive opportunities gradually eats away at the moral fiber of the community until it seems that change is impossible. As educators in the middle of these destructive chains, we must re-address not only what we teach but question

education as a whole if we are to become part of the solution.

In my own case, I quickly realized that training my students to differentiate between a Picasso and a Braque would make very little sense in this unstable environment. As an art educator, I am fully aware of the importance of art in a culture and of the refinement and totality of the human experience that the exposure to and the creating of art offers, but I must ask whose art and for what reasons? The answer is certainly not, as some mainstream educators suggest, to train students to be supporters rather than producers of the arts. By often focusing on the experiences of predominantly Western European artists and art, these educators reduce art to a subject whose content can be taught and systematically measured. There are serious ramifications to this approach in today's multicultural society. The arts should be used to support and enlighten people rather than alienate them further. This is especially true for the teacher of the economically disadvantaged student. Is it reasonable to expect people to support the arts over their own families?[5]

The values associated with traditional Western fine art—or for that matter much of today's contemporary art—function within the elite world of artists, gallery/museum, critic and collector. This work is often unattainable, incomprehensible and irrelevant to most citizens and most of my students. Art educators should strive to make a connection between traditional and non-traditional art forms and their relevance, positive or negative, to the students we are teaching. Criticism of art is also an important skill for students to master, but it is social criticism that is vital to the progress of the student "at risk."[6] Students need to be able to decipher the enormous amount of visual and nonverbal messages that they are bombarded with daily through the electronic and print media. They have to be able to decipher the obvious and subtle agenda behind such messages in order to develop their own sense of values and self-identity. It is important for our students to be critical about art, but it is crucial that students be given the opportunity to be social critics through their artmaking.

A variety of projects have been realized by my students during my five years. as an art teacher of special education and mainstream populations in Brooklyn. Through these projects, I have taught numerous artistic principles and concepts. My students and I have studied many different artists, art movements and styles. Much of what we have covered could not be accomplished successfully if not tied into actual and vital student concerns. Certainly, there were times when we used art merely as escapism, fantasy and therapy. However, it was of greater significance to give my students a chance to actively voice their opinions about their concerns and be positively recognized for caring about themselves and their futures.

These projects have included a multimedia rap performance based on a song by a local singer named Larry B. Students created art works, songs and dramas around the personal anti-drug theme in Larry's song, "Crack is Wack." Larry took the time to lecture and work with my students. His residency culminated in a special school assembly in which the school's auditorium was transformed by the students into a typical drug infested corner complete with burnt-out buildings, gangsters, police and other assorted neighborhood characters. In another project, we illustrated and mass-produced a booklet of essays and black-and-white pen and ink illustrations describing students' feeling on school learning. Entitled *Why We Do and Don't Learn*, the book served as a vehicle for the students to make a critical statement about themselves and the quality of instruction at their school. Another project which grew out of the *Why We Do and Don't Learn* booklet centered on the students' responsibility for assisting in finding solutions to recognized problems in the school. Posters that could be exhibited around the school were a logical medium for these ideas. Students focused on

school problems such as "cutting," trash, drugs and graffiti. Collaborative peer posters addressing these problems were created and dedicated to the school. They were later exhibited at "ArtWorks," the New York City Art Teachers Association's annual conference, as well as in an ATC exhibit. Students also participate every March in "Our New York," a unique art event coordinated by the Transit Authority and the United Federation of Teachers in conjunction with Youth Art Month. For this event, students create "car cards" depicting a positive message about New York City for subway and bus riders. These cards, displayed in place of the normal transit advertisements, provide an excellent opportunity for students to communicate their visions and feelings to a large audience. Students have also designed collaborative murals around themes based on their different cultural backgrounds. These murals are displayed at various school functions. Analyzing print and television messages and creating our own advertisements and magazine covers has worked well in facilitating students' understanding of ways they are made to want material things or sold on ideas which may not be best for them. Analyzing popular culture through music, videos, films and television has also intrigued my students and served as excellent motivation for various projects. Students have created anti-drug posters which were hung in local store windows to the dismay of street corner drug dealers. This effort was applauded by the shop owners, who not only supported the students but appreciated the school's willingness to help the community.

The subtle and ongoing message communicated through participation in socially critical art activities is that youth can make changes and contribute positively to society through their art. For many of my students, participating in this form of art criticism was the first time they had been officially recognized as contributing members of the school/community. Students who had gone through school being ignored—or at worst, had only been recognized for doing wrong or poorly in school—were arousing the interest and consciousness of their peers, parents, teachers and the public. Teachers, parents and other community members who were unsuccessful with these students in conventional ways were surprised at the amount of work and dedication they exhibited. The students became aware of the power in their collective voices by sharing their concerns, hopes and fears and working together as a group. As their teacher, I am proud, but I am also concerned about how these experiences will manifest themselves in my students' futures. Will the sense of personal and political empowerment associated with these events be shortlived? Will these efforts be exceptions in the students' lives rather than the rule?

If I am going to honestly tell my students that they have the power to criticize and change their situation and society, then I have to believe that the educational and governmental systems will reinforce those objectives and facilitate the atmosphere in which such changes can occur. However, the evidence of inner city drop-out rates, juvenile crime statistics, documented cases of illiteracy, drug addiction, unplanned pregnancies, broken families and runaways suggest that the opposite occurs more often than not. This is how a group such as ATC can be most effective. By exposing students' critical art to the public, ATC not only gives students a positive social and creative experience but also makes adults aware of current social and educational problems from the perspective of our youth. ATC creates an environment in which social problems cannot be ignored. By forming a strong alliance of progressive visual educators, ATC is in the position to legitimize itself and our youth to educational and legislative decision-makers. Influencing curriculum, Board of Education policy and city/state law to be more inclusive of all our students is how the stage for social change can be set. For inner city schools, it *must* be set.

I wrote earlier of making students aware of why the cycle of poverty is so difficult to break. This includes a recognition of the role of such institutions as our boards of education, city and state government and the federal government in the perpetuation of poverty. Students can investigate how, at times, these institutions are often guided by archaic and outdated concepts that contribute to social inequity. It is up to all of us to encourage such institutions to make a commitment to an equalization process in this country with education for the potentially impoverished its highest priority.

Reaching this goal will mean that inner city schools have to be made smaller and granted more personnel to allow for more interpersonal relationships between staff and students. Teachers should be given real incentives and a voice in decision-making. Although larger salaries are a healthy incentive, they will not solve the problems alone. Teachers must be seen as and be allowed to act as true professionals. When we teach, what we teach and how we teach must be addressed by the whole school. School staffs must work cooperatively to address the needs of their communities. School-based options, shared decisions-making, cooperative learning, team teaching, core groups and schools within a school should be more than just buzzwords. Students, like teachers, should also play a more active role in learning. Education must be revitalized and arts educators must make it clear that they are to play a vital and crucial role in that process. Art educators must work to create schools that are places where all students function and excel, where they are given the confidence, skills and opportunity to do the same in society.

# Notes

*Kennedy is cited in Adelaide, 1963, p. i.

[1]"Seen and Heard," an exhibit of socially motivated artwork from students in the New York City school system was held from May 3 to May 25, 1985, at PS122 Gallery at First Avenue and Ninth Street in New York City.

[2]Tim Rollins (1986) describes himself as "an artist and a teacher who has made his teaching his art" (3). What began as teaching art to special education students in the South Bronx grew into KOS, Kids of Survival. Tim's students found bricks in abandoned South Bronx lots and painted the stories of the buildings onto the bricks. They later started painting on pages of books, giving new meaning to the classics. Since their early start, they have opened up their own workspace, independent from the Board of Education. The Arts and Knowledge Workshop is producing critically acclaimed artwork for display at some of the most prestigious galleries and museums around the world. Tim Rollins, Herb Perr (professor of art education at Hunter College) and Elana Amity (art educator at Laguardia High School) were instrumental in the formation of ATC.

[3]ATC collaborated with Group Material in a four-part exhibition titled "Democracy." "Democracy and Education," the first installation, was held from September 1 to October 8, 1988. ATC also collaborated with Martha Rosler in her four-part exhibition titled, "Homeless: The Street and Other Venues. If You Lived Here" was held from April 1 to April 29, 1989. Both exhibitions were held at the DIA Art Foundation, 77 Wooster Street, Soho, New York.

[4]Chapter One is a definition used to classify city schools which fall under certain educational and economic guidelines. A determining factor for Chapter One status is the number of free lunches a school distributes.

[5]See also Moorman (1989).

[6]See also USA Research (1983).

# Works Cited

Adelaide, S. *With a free hand.* New York: Reinhold Book Corporation. (1968).

Feldman, E.B. Art in the mainstream: Ideology and hope. *Art Education, 36*(4), (1983): 5-9.

Moorman, M. The great art education debate. *ArtNews, 88,* (1989): 124-131.

Rollins, T. Seen and heard exhibit catalog. New York: Artists/Teachers Concerned, Ragged Edge Press. (1986).

USA Research. A nation at risk/The National Commission on Excellence in Education. Cambridge, MA: USA Research. (1983).

# Women Portray Women:
# African Roots and Cross-Cultural Comparison

## Betty LaDuke

My interest in contemporary women artists of African heritage is an outgrowth of the research for my first book *Companeras: Women, Art, and Social Change in Latin America* (1985). This book brings together the personal stories and art of women in the Caribbean and Central and South America. In the process of interviewing artists of indigenous, mestizo and Hispanic descent, I also met professional artists of African heritage working in Haiti and Brazil. These women had been able to resist French and Portuguese colonial assimilation to maintain a spiritual and artistic link with Africa during 300 years of the diaspora. I then initiated further exploration in Jamaica, Nicaragua and the United States before visiting Nigeria, Senegal, Ivory Coast, Kenya, Egypt, Mali and Morocco in 1986-1989. After interviewing select women artists from these African nations I was able to speculate on their work in relationship to the women artists of the diaspora.[1]

This chapter will detail some of my speculations. The women I interviewed taught me that their art is a reflection of an individual's deepest emotions and cultural heritage. Because art encouraged these women to be more aware of common bonds among all peoples and cultures, it can serve as a catalyst for broadening understanding and appreciation of diverse world views. The creative works of these women offer us a vision of their reality and frequently their resistance to all forms of oppression. It reflects a strong relationship to their environment and cultural roots and is not created solely for an "art for art's sake" function. Another common factor shared by these artists is their reliance on the female form as a dominant aspect of their creative expressions. As a result, new archetypical images of the feminine are emerging that contradict many of the stereotypical views projected by male artists. Rather than solely approaching these artists works in terms of formalism, their work can be seen also as social criticism.

Women artists of African heritage vary from each other in their educational experiences and levels of professional achievement and recognition. However, all the artists I met have been affected by the worldwide development of Black nationalism and feminism. The

significance and achievement of African women can be better appreciated when we recognize that their art exists as it does despite a history of colonialism. Tihemba (1986) states that:

Colonialism directly and brutally weakened the African women's economic position. It also imposed a culture of subjection through Christianity, which saw women as moral inferiors; and racism, which proclaimed that black people were inferior. It suppressed African history and claimed that African culture did not exist. In fact, the colonialists deliberately set about to try and change African culture. This included...the notion that African hair and skin were not beautiful and that African women must change in order to be acceptable to the white people. But African culture lived on. (37)

In this chapter the following artists are considered for their ability to motivate social change through their form of artistic social criticism: a) Edna Manley from Jamaica, b) June Beer from Nicaragua, c) Lois Mailou Jones from the United States, d) Princess Elizabeth Olowu from Nigeria and e) Theresa Musoke from Uganda-Kenya. All of these artists emphasize the female capacity for providing leadership to social continuity and social change.

### Artists of the Diaspora

Artists of the diaspora are survivors of a colonial slave legacy that separated them from their country of origin, family, language and culture. They had the burden of reasserting pride in their African roots within the context of a dominate white or mestizo culture. This strong and determined pride is exemplified in the work of Edna Manley of Jamaica, June Beer of Nicaragua and Lois Mailou Jones of the United States.

Edna Manley is known as the "Mother of Modern Jamaican Art." Surprisingly, she was born in rural England where her father, Harvey Swithenbank, was an English Methodist minister. At seventeen she managed to study art in London. There, her friendship with Norman Manley blossomed. He was a distant cousin from Jamaica who had come to England on a Rotary Fellowship to study law at Cambridge. He supported and encouraged Manley in her career

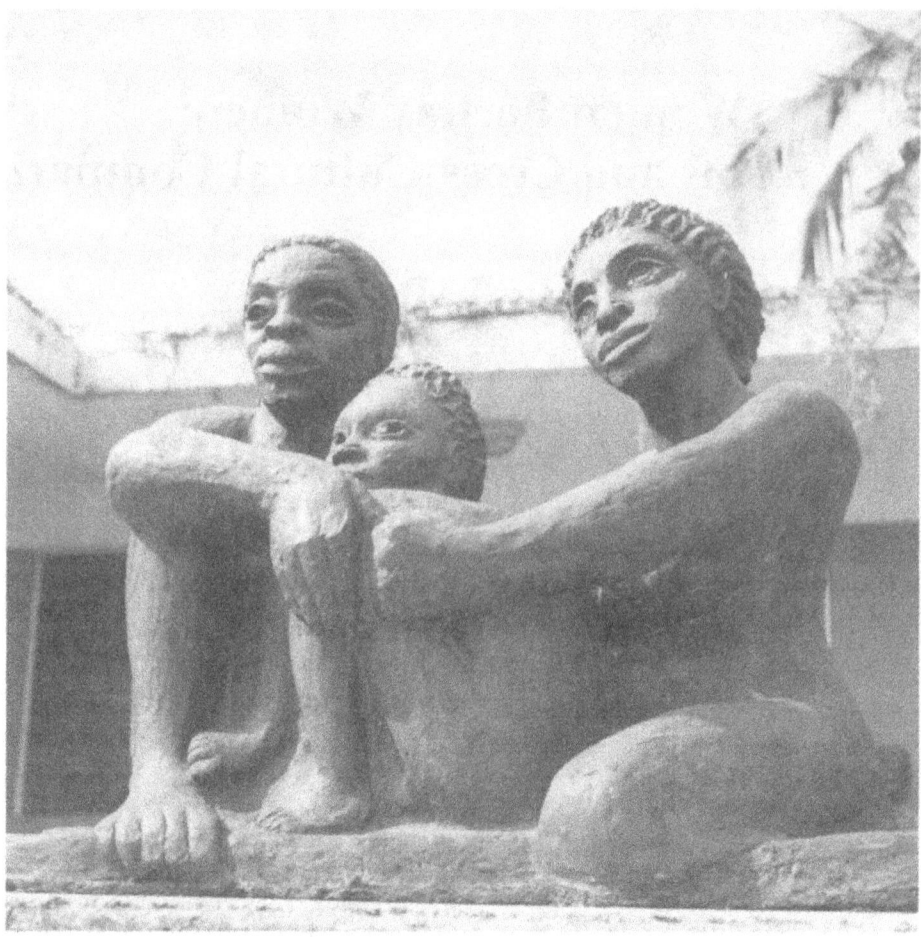

Fig. 1. Edna Manley (1900-1987), *Man-Child*. Bronze, 40" tall, 1976. Reproduced by permission of Edna Manley. In the collection of Olympic Art Center, Kingston, Jamaica. (photograph by Betty LaDuke)

aspirations. In 1922 they married and set sail for Jamaica.

Throughout Manley's long life (1900-1987) she used her art to raise the consciousness of Black Jamaicans in their struggle for fair and equal treatment. She revolutionized and revitalized the art and culture of this nation which had been economically exploited and culturally negated under English colonial rule. During the 1960s, Manley, as the wife of Jamaica's first Prime Minister, used her political power to broaden the accessibility of art for all Jamaicans. The establishment of the Jamaica Art Institute and the National Gallery are largely due to her efforts.

Exemplary of Manley's art is her 1935 wood carving, *Negro Aroused*. This work still invokes an expression of elegant defiance as it captures the spirit of Jamaicans aroused and ready for a new social order. Manley's sculptures are profound reflections upon Jamaican life and are explicitly critical of the patriarchy imposed by British colonialism. For example, *Ancestor* (1978) features a tall, elderly woman with a diminutive male figure reaching up to her. This woman "ancestor" is the guardian of the culture

whose wisdom provides continuity between the generations.

The three seated figures of life-size *Man-Child*, constructed from cement in 1976, are set in the courtyard of Kingston's Olympia International Art Center (Fig. 1). In this work a child clings to his mother and is embraced by both his mother and his grandmother. Approaching the figures, one feels as if one is coming upon an intimate family scene. Manley described how this work reflects the Jamaican family structure: "It is a matriarchal society—I am speaking about the masses—it is only recently that the father is making his presence felt—this is one of the positive things about the Rastafarian culture—but the grandmother is usually the person who rears the children; the mother is usually out making a living. The father has for centuries been absent" (Brown, 1975, 20).

Attesting to her continued strength is *Ghetto Mother* (1983), a pyramid-shaped grouping. Like the mothers in Kollwitz's post-World War I protective mother series, Manley's anguished mother rises upward like a desperate mother bird from a nest to reflect upon a barren landscape or the economic and social despair afflicting Jamaica. Her strong, wing-like arms shelter her many small, hungry children as they huddle close by.

Nicaragua is a predominantly indigenous and Hispanic nation. The artist June Beer is representative of a minority African population brought to Nicaragua as slaves in the 1600s. She lived in Bluefields, a remote town on the Atlantic Coast that was first colonized by the English. June Beer's development as a self-taught artist is somewhat miraculous in the face of economic impoverishment and emotional hardship.

Beer's life story and art are strongly connected to the Nicaraguan people's revolutionary overthrow by the Sandinistas of the Somoza dictatorship in 1979. At that time a Ministry of Culture under the leadership of Ernesto Cardenal was created to provide a supportive network for all the arts. Legislation which prohibited the sexist use of female images for promoting commercial products was passed. Nicaragua's cultural life rapidly changed from emulating Miami, Florida, to reestablishing pride in the indigenous cultural heritage. This included expressions of the African Nicaraguan community. Beer's paintings are a personal documentation of the daily life of this community. Her *Fruit Vendors* (1984) is a vivacious portrayal of two women who, in addition to selling fruit, seem to enjoying each other's company. Their broad smiles are captivating, and warm tones dominate as one woman is silhouetted against an orange-painted wall while the other holds a basket of ripe red mangoes. *The Funeral of Machismo*, or *The Funeral of Male Domination* (c. 1970), is particularly expressive of the evolving position of women in Nicaraguan society. It contradicts and critiques a stereotypical view of Latin women's subservience to men. The form of a proud and beautiful rooster or male symbol dominates the canvas. Painted above this creature is a horizon line upon which four women are standing. They are a child, a young woman, a pregnant woman and a grandmother. All are shaking their fists at the rooster. In an interview I had with Beer in 1985 she commented on the common plight of most women: "Even if you're a doctor, lawyer, or teacher, you come home from your job, you work at home while your husband sits down. He sits and watches you work." *The Funeral of Machismo* is Beer's critique of this social order and expresses her anger about the double workload that most women worldwide experience. She referred to her artistic recognition since the revolution by stating that "I never expected some of the good things that have happened...the achievement of painting something when I have the idea to do it...and to be free to paint what I want."

Manley and Beer are just two examples of women artists who are reflective of the many African Americans working out of the diaspora. We must not forget that such women have worked and are continuing to work in the United States today. Lois Mailou Jones is one such artist. She was the first African-American artist to graduate from the Boston Museum of Fine Arts. She then took a position as a Professor of Art at Howard University which she held for 47 years. She traveled widely, created and exhibited her multi-media paintings that forged creative links with North America, Europe, Latin America and Africa. Though her paintings won awards in competitive museum exhibitions in the 1950s, Jones was denied entry through the front doors of these institutions to receive her prizes.

Jones' early images of women, painted in the United States and Haiti, express her empathy with and criticism of the exploitive living conditions of their lives. This criticism can be seen in *Jenny, Domestic Worker* (1943) and *Haiti, Peasant Girl* (1954). Jenny's head is bowed as she stands in an orderly kitchen, concentrating on her task of cleaning fish. The bowed head position is repeated in Haiti by the peasant girl seated with her produce in the intense Haitian sun awaiting customers.

After her first trip to Africa in 1970, a new stage in the evolution of Jones' art began. She returned to Africa in 1972 and visited fourteen countries. In West Africa she was particularly inspired by the textiles of Ghana and Mali and the masks of Nigeria. In my interview with Lois Mailou Jones in 1986, she acknowledged her debt to Africa by stating that "I made a study of African designs and motifs and found them so inspiring that I've had to use them in part or in combination to create a work." This debt is exemplified in *Ubi Girl from the Tai Region* (1972) (Fig. 2). About *Ubi Girl*, which contains a harmony of bold fabric patterns, faces and masks, artist Faith Ringgold (1986) commented,

*Ubi Girl* combines the old with the new; Africa with Black America; painting with design; realism with symbolism. It reveals a new woman....*Ubi Girl from the Tai Region* has the face of determination. She is painted realistically, a portrait of us: Africa and Black America. Her partially masked face is strong but sweet as the flower of Black expression. (7-8)

From the work of these three women artists of the diaspora, it is evident that they have maintained a link of pride with their ancestral past. Their art expression frequently reflects national contemporary issues as well as women's roles within their patriarchal societies. Manley, Beer and Jones also offer us, in their aesthetically powerful compositions, a sense of their personal experiences and resistance to oppression that is coupled with individual strength and hope.

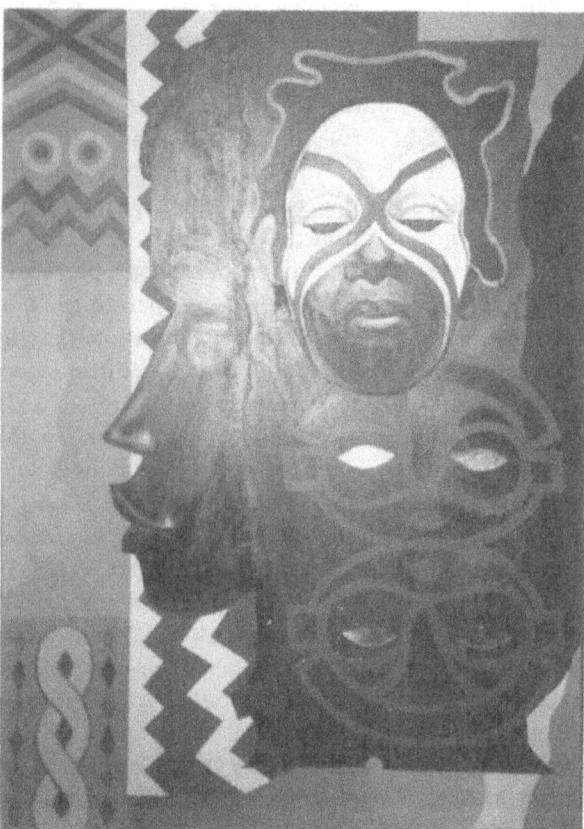

Fig. 2. Lois Mailou Jones (1905- ). *Ubi Girl from the Tai Region.*
Oil on acrylic, 110 x 150 cm, 1974. Reproduced by permission
of Lois Mailou Jones. In the collection of Museum of Fine Arts,
Boston, MA. (photograph by Betty LaDuke)

### African Artists

West African culture matured anew during the
struggles of Nigeria, Kenya and Mali for national
liberation from colonial dominance during the 1950s
and 1960s. This maturation was partially fostered by
the growth of public education which included the
establishment of national universities in Nigeria and
Kenya. Despite the fact that school tuition is free and
elementary education relatively accessible to most
women, only middle and upper-class women have
benefited. Basic survival activities that include child
care, domestic work and agricultural labor dominate
most women's lives. At school their studies are
generally directed toward business and service careers.
Therefore, the development of professional African
women artists trained within African universities, art
centers or abroad is still a rare phenomenon.

While African women artists are fewer than men,
they do compete with them for the limited teaching
jobs as well as for professional recognition. Museums
for the popularization and collection of contemporary
art are gradually emerging. Exemplary are Nigeria's
National Theatre and Art Museum and the Museum
of Art in Nairobi, Kenya. Hopefully, due to the
growing organization of women's art groups, the work
of women artists will be more visible in these national
collections in the near future.

Theresa Musoke of Uganda-Kenya and Princess
Elizabeth Olowu of Nigeria are among the first women
to graduate with bachelor's degrees in art education
as well as master's degrees in painting and sculpture.
Another achievement is that both of these women now
teach or have taught at the university level. At present,
Musoke teaches at an International School and Olowu
at Benin University.

Both women have been influenced by Western
styles and media. Musoke utilizes aniline dyes and
acrylics to create paintings and murals for private
collections and public spaces. Olowu casts bronze
sculptures. She has transgressed taboos prohibiting
women from creating sculptures in the traditional
technique of bronze casting. She also produces
monumental works cast in cement. Musoke and Olowu
have used their cultural heritages as a source of
inspiration for their work. They have also brought
forth a vision of African women's changing reality
that is dramatically personal and critical of current
male interpretations. These interpretations often
pander to romantic or exotic views of women that
appeal to tourists from Europe and the United States
or upper-class nationals whose tastes have been
influenced by the Western aesthetic.

Princess Elizabeth Olowu's life-size cement
sculpture *Acada* or *Bookworm*, (1979) portrays a young
girl intent upon reading her book. This portrayal is
a new role model or power image for Nigerian women
undergoing the stress of post-colonial transition,
urbanization and industrialization. On the other hand,
fertility is a common theme in traditional Nigerian
sculpture. Olowu's *Zero Hour* (1983), another life-size
cement sculpture, is an intimate and emotional
reflection on the dangers of childbirth from a woman's
viewpoint. A woman when giving birth "hovers
between life and death." Protective amulets filled with
medicinal herbs are worn around her neck, arm and
belly to assure her safety through this rite of passage.

Olowu has also artistically explored the theme
of power from ancient and contemporary perspectives
in *Oba* (1982), *Eshu Recreated* (1982) and *Christ* (1982).
*Oba* departs from the traditional stylized and
impersonal portraits of *obas*, kings dressed in
ceremonial regalia with many strands of coral beads
that cover the neck and chin. Olowu's expressionistic
life-size portrait of her father, Oba Akenzua, is personal
and more realistic. Seated upon his large throne as
he looks out at us through eyeglasses, he appears
humble and diminutive. His ceremonial robe is
roughly textured with a pattern composed from
Olowu's own handprint. In Benin culture the hand
is a symbol of success and is intimately linked with
an individual's destiny.

*Eshu Recreated* is a fearful image of a potent Benin

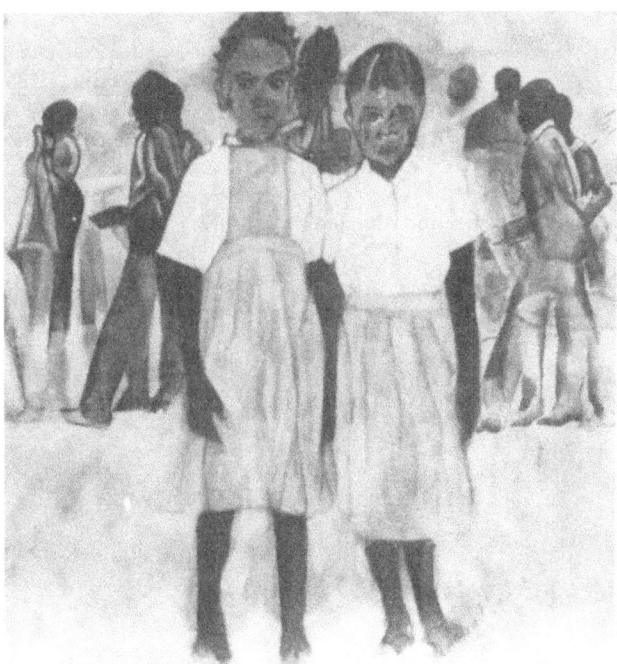

Fig. 3. Theresa Musoke (1945- ), *Market Women*. Mixed media, 30" x 36", 1986. Reproduced by permission of Theresa Musoke. In the collection of Theresa Musoke, Nairobi, Kenya. (photograph by Betty LaDuke).

underworld god that controls sickness and disease. Eshu's three cement-carved faces represent passiveness, satisfaction and discontent. These faces are embedded within a maze of large curved buffalo horns that jut out in all directions. Since Eshu can control sickness and disease, he is placated with offerings at little altars constructed in most Benin homes. In contrast to Eshu's mysterious powers, Olowu's fourteen-foot horizontal representation of Christ, bent and weighted by the cross, a symbol of humanity's sins, is a powerful and less complex form. For many Nigerians, Christianity and traditional beliefs and practices seemingly coexist without contradiction.

In a bronze sculpture *Biafra War* (1964-1967), Olowu depicts the tragic expression of two soldiers supporting each other beside a fallen comrade. This piece is a solemn, universal commentary on the tragedy of war, especially a civil war in which ethnic factions within a country fight for political dominance. The war suffering has been resolved with a solution of peaceful co-existence.

Theresa Musoke's themes are also politically potent and personal. She is the only Black woman artist from East Africa to receive widespread international recognition. Musoke is best known for her use of animal themes. She expresses their rhythmic movements in harmony with nature. She considers animals synonymous with the human quest for freedom. In *Market Women* (1986) Musoke represents

diverse Kenyan women, especially in her market scenes which emphasize not only their activities of buying and selling but also the fact that many vendors are the creators of the products they sell (Fig. 3).

Musoke has responded to issues of national and worldwide importance, such as Planned Parenthood. Her series of sensitive, mixed-media paintings on this subject are especially aimed at engaging the attention of young people in Kenya. In some canvases a young girl is portrayed playing with a doll, suggesting that this is better solution than the responsibility of young motherhood. Another canvas portrays girls clustered in a schoolyard during recess as they are being scrutinized by boys, the painting caption encourages young people to stay in school and become informed.

A recent and significant theme for Musoke is a series of introspective self-portraits. One painting which is particularly interesting features multiple views of her face. This portrait symbolically reveals usoke's multifaceted character and interests and may lead to further self-exploration in future works. As Musoke expresses her reality and her aspirations, she contributes a new role model of personal feminine energy absent in the stylized portraits of the past. Since she has not been influenced by the standards of feminine beauty emphasized by Kenya's colonial legacy or Western influences experienced during her studies in England and the United States, Musoke's work represents a significant pathway for other African women artists to consider.

## Conclusion

In this brief comparison of selected African women's art from three continents, it becomes evident that their imagery confirms their ethnic identity, femininity and cultural sensibility. If allowed mainstream visibility, they can enrich us with their personal and archetypical images of Black women's strengths, achievements and active involvement within the process of social criticism and change. They can also inspire us by their resistance to conform to our perspective of the world. They represent female strength.

It is important to realize that the aesthetic content of each artists' work is a form of social criticism when they portray images from their diverse cultural realities that contradict the mass media stereotypical portrayal of women or people of color. In addition, the artists' insistence upon imagery related to their personal experiences and their cultural heritages frequently offers us a vision of resistance to political, economic or social oppression. In their celebration of ordinary people's survival, they portray struggles that also reflect our human capacity for love and compassion.

# Note

[1]An indepth description of these interviews will be published in *Africa Through the Eyes of Women Artists* by Africa World Press in 1991.

# Works Cited

Brown, W. *Edna Manley: The private years.* London: Andre

Ceutsch. (1957).

LaDuke, B. *Companeras: Women, art, and social change in Latin America.* San Francisco: City Lights. (1985).

Ringgold, F. Lois Mailou Jones. *Women's Caucus for Art Conference Honors Awards*, 1986, Women's Caucus for Art, Philadelphia, PA. (1986).

Tihemba, A. *Focus on African women.* London: African Center and Akina Mara wa Afrika. (1986).

# There's More to Being Chinese in America than Chop Suey: Narrative Drawing as Criticism in Oakland Chinatown

## Florence Wong

When, in 1983, I started the on-going autobiographical body of photo-realistic graphite pencil drawings titled the *Oakland Chinatown Series*, I intended to make it an art statement exclusively. I had no intention of supporting it with written text because I was solely interested in resolving my visual struggle to depict the human form. After much exploration in drawing nudes from live models I came upon photographs of my family in an old album. Realizing that my parents and siblings represented human forms I started drawing from the photos, exploring with pencil and hoping to find my inner voice. Motivated, I finished the first piece titled "On Webster Street" which depicted the front of our restaurant, Great China, in a moody, mysterious way. The *Oakland Chinatown Series* was born.

Born of an unarticulated need to see myself portrayed in a non-stereotypical way, the body of art grew. As I created from an insider's point-of-view I decided not to hide my family behind other symbols. For the first time in my life I employed a directness that was out-of-character for me because, as a female and a Chinese American, I had learned to sublimate myself and my feelings. The family photographs acted as a vehicle to provide access to myself as a late-developing community-based artist.

The *Oakland Chinatown Series* visually captures a specific historical time—1940s to the 1960s—and place—Great China Restaurant in Oakland, California's Chinatown. In the drawings, neither my family nor our community are presented in exotic and mysterious ways, as I portrayed our immigrant family as ordinary working class people who struggled internally and externally during the time-frame of Chinese resettlement in America. I created my art, using my family's photographically captured moments-in-time as restaurateurs to address the viability of Chinese Americans in the United States. This personal sense makes me unique as a Chinese American contemporary artist who openly acknowledges my ethnicity which affects the declaration of my visual statements.

I credit African Americans, the Women's Movement and other contemporary Asian American artists and writers who gave me courage to explore. This essay will reveal in an intensely personal way my reasons for drawing the *Oakland Chinatown Series*, art works that meet the formalist criteria of line, shape, size, color, texture, patterns and composition. As an artist-of-color, I have exceeded the contextual traditional art forms to aesthetically authenticate, from my point of view, the considerations of community issues to include the politics of racism that necessitated the creation of Chinatowns in America, the autobiographical nature of my work, the historical framework in which I set the drawings and the sense of personal place that I strongly claim as an artist.

Through these drawings I subconsciously explored the dualities of inclusion/exclusion, individual/group, male/female, intimacy/distance and visibility/invisibility. All of the previously mentioned issues, realities in American life, thread through and are paralleled in the *Oakland Chinatown Series* because of the infrastructure of my family, in this case, both China-born and American-born. Prescribed traditional Chinese parent/offspring and sibling roles and subsequent human behavior, reinforced by a history of root country rigidity, prevailed. As a result, while my Chinese American family dealt with outside societal acceptance or the lack thereof, we also implemented those same dynamics within our primary socializing unit. Visually, I empowered myself to narrate my story for I stake my claim to be recognized, to be included and to be institutionalized in the contemporary American arts scene. By touching upon the private truths in my family as Chinese Americans then could I come to understand myself and deal with these interactive elements of human dynamics faced by others. I also share from personal observations how my self-reflecting art impacts my peer generation of Chinese Americans and others when they view my work.

Historically, the Chinatowns in America allowed the Chinese who worked in laundries, restaurants or as domestics to survive in a hostile land. When the Chinatowns in America originated during the 1890s and early 1900s the communities were influenced by the Cantonese, the first wave of immigrants from the south of China (Association, 1982). That influence molded the character of American Chinatowns until 1975 when the Vietnamese refugees, along with other Asian immigrants, settled in Oakland and changed the face of the Cantonese-flavored Chinatown (Association, 1985). With that change, my drawings— visual exploration into the physical and emotional spaces of my childhood—took on an historical aspect because the Cantonese Chinatown I loved now existed only as memory.

The Chinese arrived in America soon after the declaration of independence in the United States. In 1785 three Chinese seamen landed in Baltimore, and from that time on the Chinese presence in America was established. Throughout the years, the population grew. Following the California Gold Rush in 1849, the Chinese population in San Francisco expanded from 787 people to 4,018 by 1850. Two years later, there were 20,025 Chinese in America. Two other industries attracted the Chinese migration to America in the latter half of the 1800s. Mining and railroad labor was needed; the Chinese met that labor demand. From the 1880s to the 1900s the Chinese American population was confined to Chinatowns which developed as a result of anti-Chinese violence (Association, 1982). My art is a legacy of that Chinatown confinement; for it was our establishment, Great China Restaurant, located in the heart of the then four-block community, that provided a haven within my life.

When I first began training as an artist I timidly traced a traditional Chinese mythological design for a class assignment which the instructor rejected because of the tracing. Once on my own, I searched for a creative focus. Exploring color and women's issues, I drew colorful and bold flowers in pastels influenced by Kathe Kollwitz, Georgia O'Keeffe and Judy Chicago. The flowers, symbolizing my family's struggles as human beings, were the first images to unlock my visual expression.

At the same time being fascinated with the human body, I sketched nudes using pastels as a tool. The results were awkward, self-conscious, hesitatingly drawn. While the flowers blossomed I was unable to make statements about the human body. The soul that I wanted to bring forth did not surface. I used an eery palette, bringing together a pained attempt to say something about the human condition and focusing on thoughts of life and death, a reality at that time.

I continually searched for visibility of myself in America. I was not reflected very often anywhere. When I was, the reflection revealed a condescending lack of understanding of myself and those like me as complete human beings. Racism dictated the cartoon-type Asian characters depicted in films, literature and plays. Raised in Chinatown, I grew up in separate worlds— a Chinese one at home and a non-Chinese one elsewhere. My parents reinforced a Chinese mind-set of obedience, compliance, respect and manners. At one time, in a rare instance of rebelliousness and self-contempt, I rejected my Chineseness, wanting blue-eyed, blond-haired children when I became a mother in the future.

Years later, in an art history class, I viewed Ashile Gorky's portrait of himself with his mother. That pictorial manifestation tapped into my innate sense of family and reminded me of the Chinese women I knew who were courageous, strong, dominating, dynamic in their traditional roles as mothers but were also household and economic partners to their husbands. My mother was one of these women.

Societal guidelines in Confucius China dictated sexism which rigidly oppressed females. Uneducated and born into a subordinate life in China, Chinese women served their men and families (Yung, 1986). My mother—second wife to my father, Seow Hong Gee—was one of these compelling women who courageously emigrated to America after marrying as a "picture bride." As a young wife she became caretaker for my aged grandmother and my half-sister. She gave birth to two daughters, conceived when my father visited her in our family village of *Goon Do Haung* in Toishan. Like most Chinese who dreamed of a better life in the United States, she thought America was *Gim Sahn*, gold mountain. The truth of struggles, racism, sexism and plain hard work awaited her. While she adapted with bitterness and resentment she pulled energy out of those distorted dreams to become a resilient partner with my father in America.

Another piece of art, Edward Hopper's silent painting "Chop Suey," touched me in a way similar to Gorky's painting. It reached a truth within me with its flashing neon sign beaming into the dark restaurant interior capturing a musty feeling of the old-time Chinatown second floor restaurants with wooden tables where people dined on the bean sprouted, celeried Cantonese dishes (Goodrich, 1983). The environment he painted with dark colors revived for me the few second floor restaurants with their curtained booths which once operated in Oakland Chinatown. Hopper spoke of isolation/alienation, the universal feelings encapsulated in "Chop Suey" for customers and workers alike. He focused on non-Asian customers, not telling the story of the Chinese workers—people like my family—who, as a general rule, labored intensively for sixteen hours a day to earn a livelihood. Years later, in 1985, after embracing Hopper's "Chop Suey" to heart, I showed my mother in a piece entitled "Sitting-Thinking" which showed one of those weary Chinatown restaurant workers sitting on the family couch which did not seem to give her the rest she needed.

Hollywood's celluloid efforts portrayed Chinese and other Asian Americans as subservient stereotyped human beings. Chinese were depicted as evil villains, bowing, scraping servants and maids, or hatchet men involved in tong wars in an exotic ambiance. Many times Chinese men in films puffed addicting opium in smoke-filled dens as young temptresses massaged their spiritless bodies. The Chinese women represented in films such as *Suzy Wong, The Good Earth* and *Flower Drum Song* did not reflect any truth at all. Even when intelligent sympathetic Chinese females were shown, white actresses played the roles of these virtuous nurturing women. Hollywood's stereotyped characters such as Fu Manchu or Charlie Chan insulted us and denied us our dignity (Young Yu, 1979). In the movie depictions Chinese characters spoke in sing-song style, a patronizing judgement imposed on us as one dimensional characters. In reality when I and others spoke in *slee yip*, the fourth district dialect of Cantonese, we addressed one another by our names, giving dignity to ourselves and to those who named us. Our Chinese names were poetic, filled with hope and anticipation, and based on generational categories to indicate a family relationship: Mine is "Ling Oy" which means to solicit love.

When the Chinese settled in the United States they maintained the patriarchal family: authoritarian, hierarchical and sexist. The collective sense of family superseded any individual needs while obedience to parents was paramount. Gender value provided a sub-structure within the confines of family with emphasis put on males because they carried the family name in perpetuity. An inflexible support system for sexism was reinforced by formal titles for family members; the titles for elders were based on gender classification. A father's parents were the "inside" grandparents because males were treasured as they carried the family name, the family history.

Females were adjuncts of males. Undervalued, we could be mothers, daughters and sisters—temporary family members to be married into another family. The 1985 drawing, "Li Hong & Henry," showed my sister dressed in the traditional wedding *kwa* (bridal jacket) next to her Western-suited husband who selected her from photographs after one of his friends decided he did not want to marry her (Fig. 1). Li Hong, like my mother before her, had no choice of her husband. Her marriage was arranged as a negotiation between my parents and her future in-laws. When females gave birth to sons their merit in Chinese society rose (Yung, 1986). "On the Table," another drawing

completed in 1985 showed Li Hong and Henry's offsprings, Vicki and Melvin, sitting atop the table in the back booth which served as the family's headquarters in Great China Restaurant. When Melvin was born Li Hong then gained stature previously denied to her. She relived my mother's past history, my mother only receiving value when she gave birth to my brother Bill.

With its rigid family emphasis the traditional Chinese culture was one in which I felt a duality and tension. As a compliant daughter I sublimated all feelings of self towards the family and community, service to family and others I knew well. From the age of five, I worked daily in the restaurant, doing small chores until I graduated into waitressing. I drew myself in two works titled "Standing on Webster Street" and "Wiping the Table" as the teen-age waitress who worked after school and on weekends.

At the same time I responded to my American upbringing and yearned for self-development and recognition. Shapeless and formless, that self-need manifested itself when I took art classes, after first teaching, marrying and having children. I shared that need with an instructor who stated that since I was Chinese American whatever I created would be Chinese American art. Lacking courage, I listened to him and continued to create in the Eurocentric art school style. After much agony I met the challenge head-on, shedding previous inhibitions and deep-seated fears. I faced what I had to do, nourished by a Filipino art instructor who included sacks of rice in a sculpture exhibit based on his youth as a migrant worker in America. Eventually, I came to my artistic path.

Prior to my mother's arrival in the 1930s, America had passed many legislative restrictions including the Alien Land Law which prohibited aliens from owning land. These immigration restrictions led to the decline of the Chinese American population from 132,000 to 62,000 people in 1920 (Association, 1982). My father was already in America when his first wife died in China. Needing someone to care for his aged mother and his young daughter he married my mother through the traditional arranged marriage (Yung, 1986). As a "picture bride" she remained in China while he stayed in America. He, dutifully, sent money to support his family in China which enabled my mother to purchase her own servant girl, a *moy nuey*. That economic factor elevated my mother's prestige in our village as a wife supported by a husband who resided in America.

Racism, supported by anti-Asian/anti-Chinese laws, superimposed its precepts upon the traditional Chinese family structure which was the distinct social unit that allowed for the development and sustenance of Chinese culture in America. Fearing economic usurpation and an intrusion of the "yellow peril" the United States' passed the Chinese Exclusion Law in 1882 (Mau Dicker, 1979). It suspended immigration

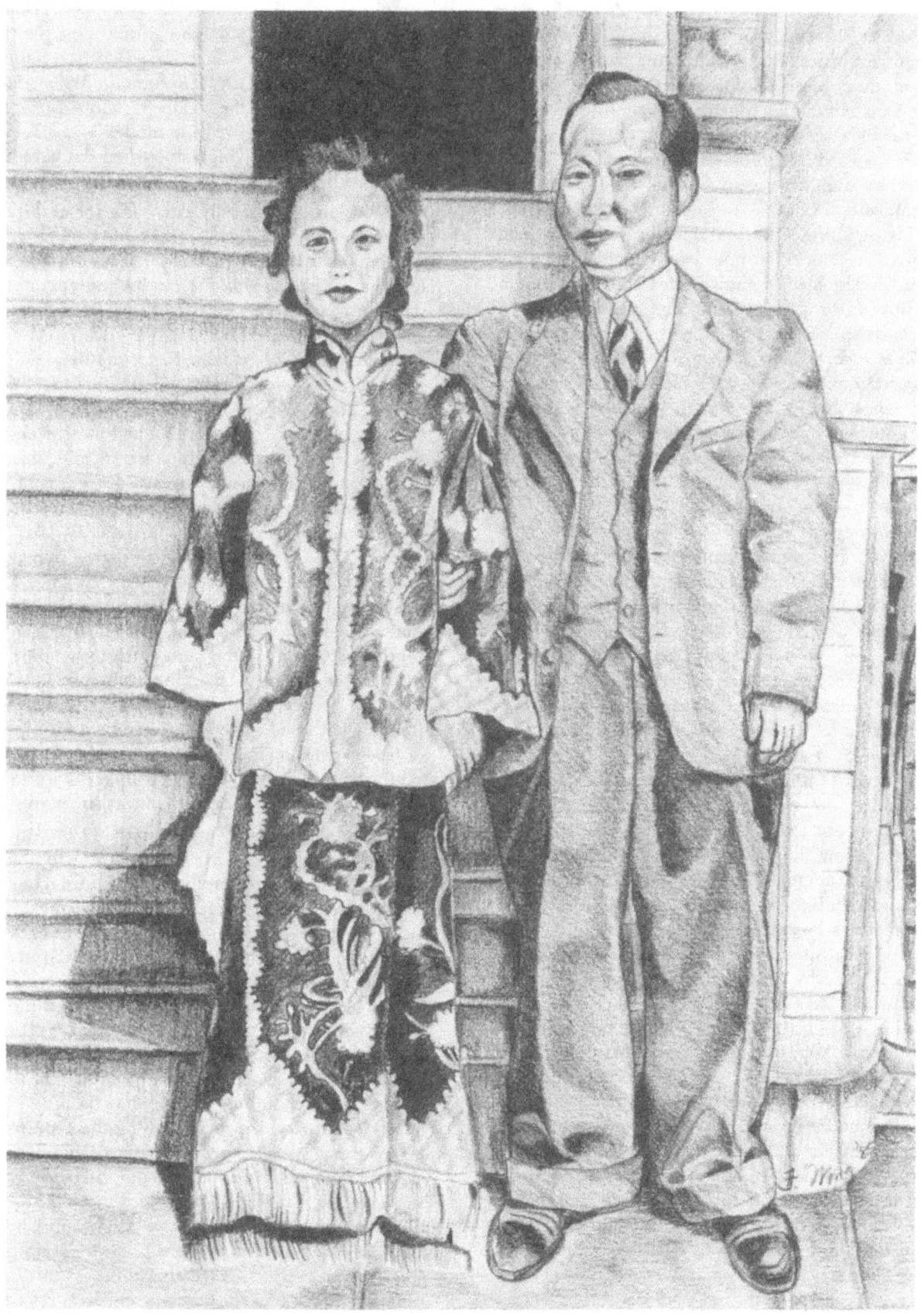

Fig. 1. *Li Hong and Henry*. 17 1/4'' x 14 1/4'' graphite drawing. (photograph courtesy of Florence Wong)

to the United States and formally prohibited naturalization of Chinese in America, stopping large scale Chinese immigration for 60 years (The Association of Chinese Teachers, 1982).

Forty two years later, in 1924, Congress passed a law which prevented Chinese women from entering the United States as wives of Chinese Americans, perpetuating and making possible the concept of a bachelor society (Association, 1985). The intent of these laws was to stop Chinese immigration and to prevent the growth of the Chinese family in the United States. Regardless of immigration restrictions, loopholes existed to allow Chinese women to enter the USA as sisters of men already working here or as prostitutes to service the needs of the lonely men (Yung, 1986). The bachelor society of single Chinese men provided a viable labor force in and out of Chinatown. In several drawings of the *Oakland Chinatown Series* I paid tribute to these members of the bachelor society, the *slan doy*. "Enriched Rice: Gnah Toy Lee and Yu Yoong Goong," a mixed media piece completed in 1989, shows one of our cooks and the Chinatown bean sprout merchant eating birthday cake at a family party in our home. Men like them became part of our extended families as they had no families of their own in America.

As a result of these restrictive entry laws, a clandestine network of illegal immigration, "paper people," flourished. Chinese, aided by lawyers and others involved with the immigration bureaucracy, could purchase "false papers" to allow Chinese to emigrate. A natural geological disaster unwittingly contributed to the increase of Chinese in America. During the 1906 San Francisco earthquake, many official Chinese records were lost, allowing a build-up of false documents when order was restored. To increase immigration, Chinese men reported additional children, especially sons, born in China. They filed this bogus information on new forms with the immigration authorities who were unable to check their authenticity; they also sold these new papers to desperate families who wanted to bring their members from China (Mau Dicker, 1979).

My mother arrived under those circumstances. Not only was her marriage to my father arranged in the traditional Chinese way she also became a *hoo gee*, a "false paper" woman of America. My father was able to purchase false immigration papers for her so she entered as my father's sister, marrying in name only a man called Sheng Wong. I, being one of her American born children, the sixth daughter, was known as a *hoo gee nuey*, a "false paper girl." My surname was that of the "paper father" I had never seen in my entire life. I grew up with the prevalent fear of disclosure and eventual deportation, afraid that my citizenship status would be rescinded. My siblings and I dared not to address our father as father. In public we called him "uncle."

In their new land my parents struggled, resettling in a hostile environment. The drawings of the *Oakland Chinatown Series* show them, years later, beyond the time of legislated anti-Asian exclusion and exploitation in the historical era of community development within Chinatowns (Shoichire Odo, 1977). I pictured them with the addition of their American born children who, as a unit, were hard working, overachieving, decent, law-abiding human beings. Because my father was an American citizen it was my mother who started her life deceptively in America because of anti-Asian legislation.

I drew the three of us in a composite drawing in 1983 titled "Mom, Pop, Me." My dad wore his Western suit while my mother, with short pulled hair, is shown in her passport image from China. When she first arrived, bearing that passport photo, to join my father as his sister she and my three China-born siblings stayed on Angel Island while they were queried about their entry into America. If they answered incorrectly or not to the satisfaction of the questioner, longer stays or return to China awaited them. Fearful and concerned, my father sought the help of sympathetic church missionaries. It was my sister who eventually expedited the release of my family when she flippantly retorted to a question of who she was when asked by an immigration official.

Once together, my parents emphasized the solidarity of the compliant family. We lived a duality of isolation/togetherness—isolation as Americans fostered by racism, togetherness as a tight family unit. Gathering together tenaciously, my parents provided warmth and intimacy within the infrastructure of the family unit. Milestone events—birthdays, weddings and holidays—played an important part in our Chinese American life. The family always gathered for major events. "Cutting the Birthday Cake," drawn in 1986, shows my father cutting into his cake while standing in front of the traditional scroll that regulated our activities as good Chinese people (Fig. 2). A 1988 drawing titled "Christmastime" showed my then young niece and nephew at our holiday celebration. At the same time, in keeping with a cultural humbleness/modesty, my parents were indirect in their praise of us as children. In a sincere attempt to be humble, my mother complimented her friends' offspring, lauding recognition upon their accomplishments. She hoped that her friends would praise her children in return. *Ay ge gall mall ai-ah* ("Let them wear the top hat") meant praise for others. It was a phrase we heard often and implemented patiently time and again. We were always expected to reflect positively on the family through hard work, good grades and eventually enter into the "monied" professions.

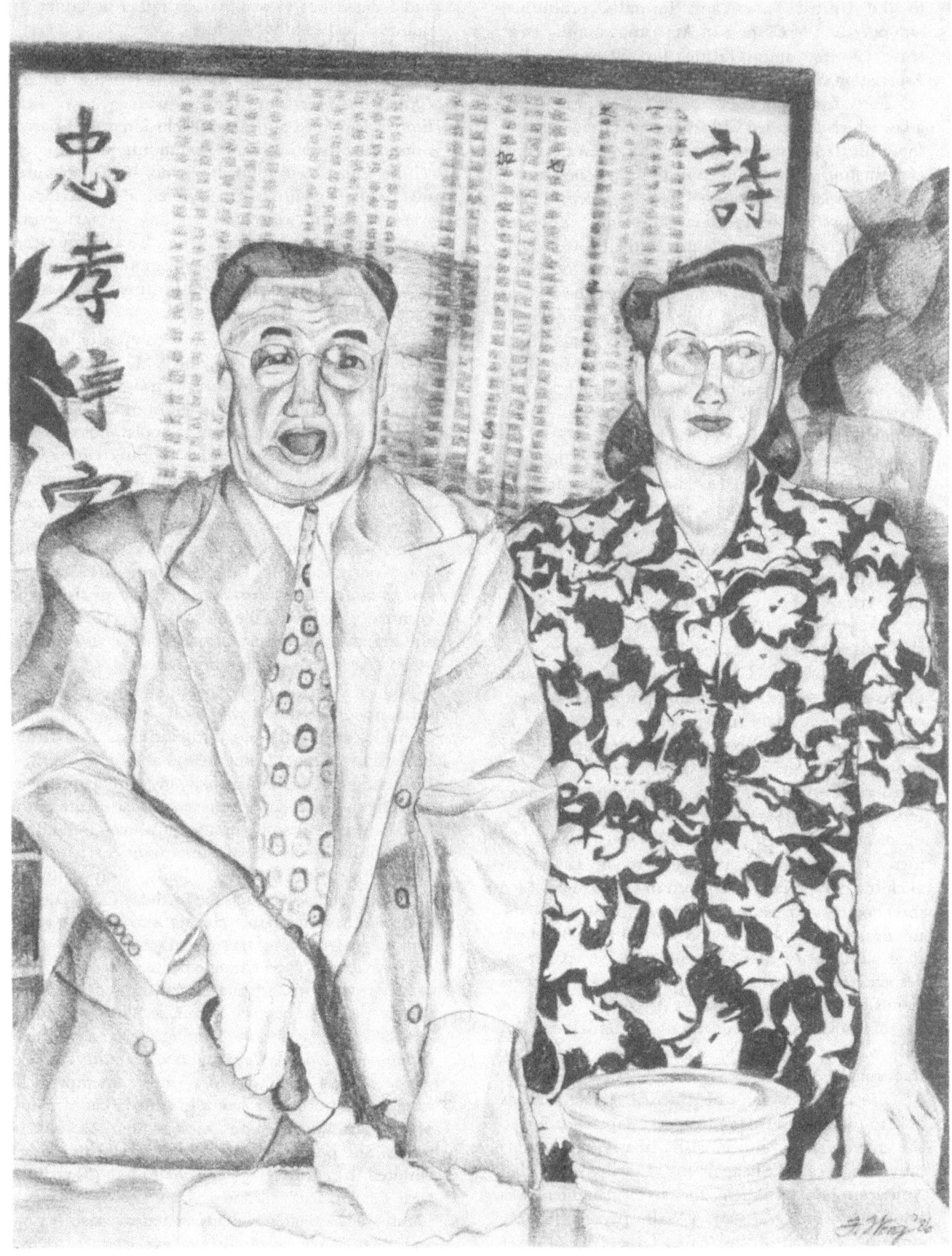

Fig. 2. *Cutting the Birthday Cake.* 20 3/8'' x 17 3/8'' graphite drawing. (photograph courtesy of Florence Wong)

That feigned humbleness impacted me deeply. It left me totally unprepared for outreach to the dominant American community and the directness I discovered in non-Asian communities. In my family, I did not learn to act for myself, acceding to others' demands and wishes. I transferred this passivity beyond my family into a wider societal context. As a result, I fell into the pre-conceived perceptions and stereotypes which severely limited humane interaction and dynamics out of the family infrastructure. I did not "make waves." My parents always made me aware that I was not white. Because of this fact they counseled me and my siblings to be cautious, to be careful. Therefore, I was safe to white America as a model minority. Chinese were accepted if we did not "rock the boat."

After searching for ways to support the seven of us, my parents opened the Great China Restaurant in the 1940s. From then on Great China became our window to the world. My earliest childhood activities focused on chores. For friendships I depended upon my siblings and our workers—the cooks and the dishwasher. The cooks humored me, allowing me to clang the metal cooking utensils in the huge wok atop a gas burner, letting me pretend that I was a great chef.

Because we were struggling to survive economically, leisure and recreation were luxuries within my family. Always under pressure to succeed, we worked and studied. When I could break away, it was to be with other children just like me. Then I hit milk carton baseballs with a broken tennis racket and rode a bicycle, renting it from a neighborhood "entrepreneur" for five cents an hour.

Living in Chinatown, I was family-based and community-focused. Upward mobility was attainable through education. My father, being in America, was open to the education of women. His vision resulted in the college education of an older sister, our only brother and myself.

Our family stayed cocooned within the confines of Chinatown and maintained a formal ethnocentrism which made me completely unaware of other cultures. The Chinese classified all non-Chinese into their separate "devil" groups, gwi (Mau Dicker, 1979). In the small town atmosphere of Chinatown we knew everyone, respectfully acknowledging the elders who were offended if they did not receive their formal recognition.

The approximately thirty-plus drawings of the Oakland Chinatown Series cover the time frame of the 1940s to the 1960s. In this on-going body of work I offer a visual microcosm of my subjective truth along with an investigation of order within a personal emotional chaos. Whenever I drew, as an adult supported by a husband and two children, I dealt with a lingering tension of family unity/individual freedom emanating from my siblings. At the same time I yearned to escape that sibling tension for individual freedom. Usually puzzled by the emotional stress of family dynamics I asked questions as I created. By the time I finished a piece I had an answer which sometimes was supported by fantasy of dreams of being in a timeless, whitewashed Chinatown.

The narrative drawings first started as accurate representations with a technical distortion because of my poor eyesight. The distortions were further heightened when I took my glasses off in order to see the minute details. That fastidious search for details triggered memories which blended with my technique, blurring while creating a newer clarity. Recently, I explored my self-image. Toward that end, I have created larger mixed media drawings with myself as an image. I have added the phoenix as my personal symbol to signify a rising from emotional ashes along with segments of Chinese rice sacks, some with the character, mai ("raw rice"). In the 1989 mixed media work "Phoenix Touches the Self," the feathers of the phoenix curve to touch the top of my head and the side of my body so that we rise from adversity together. "Phoenix Me," another 1989 mixed media work, showed me as a six-year-old, dressed in a starched pinafore, standing tall by my mother whose hand transparently reached into my body.

Historically, during that earlier time frame of the drawings, Chinese Americans expanded our sphere of activity within America by working in the war industries and joining the armed forces (Association, 1985). Because my sisters were the oldest, none of my family were directly involved in the American war efforts. My mother sewed parachutes for the soldiers. My father and oldest sister worked in a Naval shipyard before we opened our restaurant. At the same time our Japanese friends were taken away and interned in wartime relocation camps.

In 1943, the Chinese Exclusion Law was repealed and Chinese were given the right to become naturalized citizens (Association, 1985). As a child, ignorant of history, I ran around Oakland Chinatown absorbing what was to enter into my art.

Twenty years after I left Oakland for suburban life, I started the first drawing. I looked in retrospect at my family's struggles, viewing our adversities from a geographical and temporal distance. In 1983, I intended to draw people with a tool that would artistically say what I wanted to visually articulate. I was surprised that the people I could eventually draw with an authentic artistic voice were my parents, my siblings and myself. When I completed the first drawing, I framed it immediately. I then began another, searching hungrily for more family photographs which I took long ago with a camera someone had given me. Other photos my brother-in-law, Henry Lew, took with his camera.

The memories empowered me. When I drew "On Webster Street: In front of Great China Restaurant," the small rectangle on the restaurant window representing the daily menu took me back to the time when I typed and reproduced the menu on the yellowish gelatin pad. The tattered striped awning which framed the restaurant's exterior facade blew wistfully in the wind once again.

From the exterior scene of "On Webster Street," I moved to the interior. "In the Kitchen" and "Eating at Great China" record actual restaurant activities. "In the Kitchen" showed my mother chopping, prepping for the cooking time. A cousin leans against the room-size refrigerator case. (My family brought relatives from China and guaranteed them jobs as required by law. This cousin was one of those relatives we supported.)

Our nuclear family extended to include the workers—cooks, dishwasher and waiters. That sharing is revealed in "Eating at Great China" which shows my brother eating with the taciturn dishwasher, Lo Wong Bok, and the white capped cook, Chell Goong. A bottle of whiskey sits on the table. Chell Goong is shown in his draped cook's apron separated from my brother and Lo Wong Bok, eerily visible, is lightly drawn and distant to the right of the shiny table.

I drew another interior scene titled "Great China—The Front Counter" (Fig. 3). Three men inside the restaurant are separated from one another by the long counter. A quietness is present; two customers look downward. My brother-in-law, Henry, stood smiling inside the counter. The three are together, but there is no human interaction. Ironically, the customer seated way in the back of the drawing eventually married my husband's sister.

Since creating the *Oakland Chinatown Series* I have exhibited my drawings in many different spaces to a variety of audiences, both Chinese American and non-Chinese. I am always surprised at the impact these works have upon those who view my art because my story is intensely personal. To understand this impact one first must comprehend the lack of support for art in the traditional Chinese American culture.

In the history of the Chinese in America, little cultural appreciation developed in our community because of our struggles. While culture was supported in an elitist way in traditional China, a vast difference was noticeable in our parents' lives in America. As first generation Americans, we earned a living to get ahead, striving to improve our lives. Little time was set aside for cultural appreciation. Seldom did we deal with our emotions. We never learned to invest our feelings in art nor were we aware that art was an appropriate forum for us.

My parents were Cantonese peasants who looked towards American education as economic mobility, directing us towards acceptable occupations. An older

sister and I became teachers while another who showed artistic talent was not encouraged to attend art school.

I am unique as a Chinese American because I am a contemporary artist. I am also unique because I have probed my past so directly with the narrative drawings of the *Oakland Chinatown Series*. I, like so many other contemporary Chinese American artists, poets, writers and filmmakers, take responsibility for telling our stories. We recognized that outsiders have not been able to create what we wanted to have created about us. By expressing ourselves, we invent our visions and participate in our future, eliminating a past dependency on others to act for us. This self-actualization allows us to develop new models of institutional support and to be recorded within American art history.

My photo-realistic pencil drawings touch people in different ways, impacting Chinese and non-Chinese viewers. Two years after I started the series in 1983, I returned to Oakland Chinatown and showed in a one-woman exhibition at a gallery where my mother once sewed parachutes during World War II. At that premiere, I watched as Chinese Americans of my generation and older looked at the drawings, one of the first times they saw themselves reflected in the art world as real people.

Many people in the audience were viewing an art exhibit for the first time. It was also the first time for some to be acquainted with the artist or the people captured in the work. They discovered that it was appropriate to create art and to express the personal emotions they had learned to suppress within their traditional culture. They discovered that, in this case, art was not lofty or pretentious but rather that art came from themselves. They saw humane portrayals of familiar people and scenes. Their own Chinatown lives also flashed before them. Their long ago experiences, as children of Cantonese immigrants or as immigrants themselves, were finally mirrored.

In 1987, outside of the safety of the Chinese community, I showed several drawings at a contemporary Pan Asian American exhibit in an emerging suburban California museum, displaying to a heterogeneous audience. I was not sure of the audience and how they would reflect what the museum so courageously showed. There, at the opening, I heard a man, when he looked at my drawing titled "Wedding: Li Hong & Henry," say, "I know where that is. That's 34th and West Street in Oakland." I could not believe what I heard. Very few people would know that my sister and brother-in-law posed in that old West Oakland neighborhood so many years ago. I tapped him on the shoulder asking, "How do you know that?" He answered: "I haven't been in Oakland for thirty years, but I lived nearby that house. I recognized the stairs."

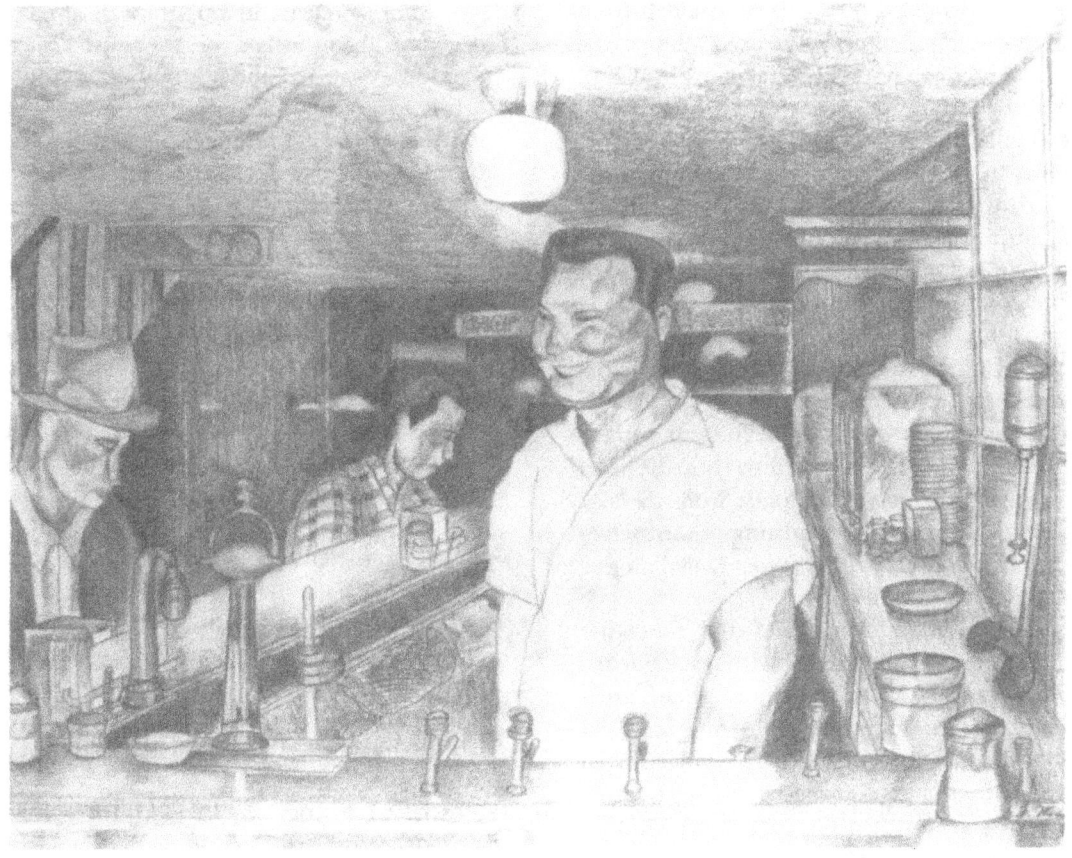

Fig. 3. *Great China: The Front Counter.* 17 1/2" x 20 3/8" graphite drawing. (photograph coutesy of Florence Wong)

He spoke of a small bit of background, a small section of a Victorian staircase. My sister and her husband in their wedding day finery was the important issue for me, not the stairs I had put in behind them. Yet, this particular viewer saw behind the newlyweds to elements that released a thirty-year memory buried within him. He related to my work outside of the realm of heritage identification. It was a personal recollection.

Others who viewed that same exhibit also related to my drawings in a similar way. In "Cutting the Birthday Cake," I revealed my father's happiness as he sliced into a decorated cake. Many people understood a celebration like that, a ritual which acknowledged our similarities as human beings. Because my images were of real people I captured a significant moment in time, first for me and then for them.

As a late-blooming artist, I now serve as a role model to the newer generations of Chinese Americans, speaking to them about my work. In many of these lectures I have seen and felt the impact of the *Oakland Chinatown Series* on college age students. I recently presented my work to an Asian American student organization at a local university. Although that audience was years younger than I, they identified with

my art because my drawings gave them a key to their parents and grandparents, many of whom originally lived in Chinatowns similar to Oakland's. A number of the students had been unable to articulate with their families their feelings of growing up Chinese in a contemporary America. A voiceless articulation about themselves was pervasive. Their ethnic identity was a silent part of them. When I finished that presentation, a student responded: "I have to say something. I was so homesick when you read your poems and showed your slides. My parents also owned a restaurant. It was also called 'Great China.' I too started working there when I was five or six. I can't believe this. Wait till I tell my parents."

Again, I was suspended into disbelief at this sensitive touching of one another as human beings. On a conscious level I would have been unable to knowingly produce that specific response. But, somehow, when I tapped into my personal visual energy and gave it life through my drawings, I converted that source into a truth for this young student separated from me by age, time and origin of geographical distance.

Recently, I shared my newer drawings with the fourth through sixth grade elementary school children in the art classes I teach. I showed my latest mixed media piece, "Phoenix Ed." Two of my students from the communicatively handicapped class studied the drawing with much interest. I had drawn my husband, Ed, sitting but without a chair to hold him. Julio, a student usually highly animated and full-of-energy, slowed down to observe the billowing shirt and the folds of Ed's trousers. He noticed something: "If you show him sitting, Mrs. Wong, why didn't you draw a chair?" "I don't know, Julio," I responded. "What a wonderful observation." His friend Alex studied the drawing intently. "I know why," he answered. "He's Chinese and Chinese are magical. That's why he doesn't need chair."

I wanted some school administrators to witness that exchange. These students went directly to the heart of my work which triggered dialogue from them. I was so proud of them and their trusting of themselves to reveal what was deep within them. Our dialogue confirmed the power of art.

My *Oakland Chinatown Series* and the other bodies of work I have created are my visual statements, my knowing myself. My directedness as an artist demystifies a segment of real people—my family—within an environment that has changed since I lived there. My drawings show a place—The Great China Restaurant—which nurtured the core of my family's existence within a miniscule Chinatown. My drawings present a non-stereotyped humane portrayal of a resilient Asian family in America, an authentic view rarely seen in contemporary visual arts.

Aesthetic and creative issues surround this body of art on which I have worked for seven continuous years. Why am I willing to invest such a block of time to develop this particular narrative story. Why would I, as a Chinese American contemporary artist, deal so directly and personally with my parents and siblings as my images? By confronting ethnicity so directly do I lose the simplicity, mystery and tension that is deemed necessary in high art? Why did I not try to disguise our non-white appearances? Why did I draw my parents/siblings as strong people in pencil? Would another media have produced the clarity and vision I wanted? What is the significance of the gradation of value in the countenances of the people, with some noticeably darker than others? A sense of light appears to come from the core of some of these drawings. What is the implication of this lightness/darkness? In twenty-eight of these drawings I drew females of all ages. Does the overabundance of female images convey feminist work? What does it mean for me to show a variety of ages? Why do I show quiet energy through these drawings? In many of the pieces the subjects are lying down or sitting. They never appear to be comfortable on the surfaces. Several are sitting without a structure. What message am I stating with these aesthetic nuances?

Another point in question is: am I really that different from artists of the past? Mary Cassatt, Toulouse Lautrec and Vincent Van Gogh are three artists who come to mind as painters of families, members of the working class and their communities. Cassatt painted women and children. Several of my works, "On the Table," "Shadows at 687" and "Sony & Boogie," showed my nieces and nephews. Lautrec depicted the Parisian bars, dance halls and restaurants. He and Alexander Calder were fascinated by the circus. Their bare back riders and horses gave energy from the working class arena. Did I give anyone energy from the drawings titled "Les" and "Bill in the Back Booth," which show my sister and brother at our family table at Great China? Do viewers understand the use of the cigarette with the curling smoke in Les' hand? Is the cigarette compatible with her glamorous image? Is there a connection between "Li Keng," my 1985 full face drawing of my sister, to Van Gogh's "Head of a Peasant Woman: Full Face"? In 1989, I drew "Phoenix Me" which includes an ancient Chinese plant form that bears uncanny resemblance to the cypress in Van Gogh's "Wheatfield With Cypresses" painted in 1889. Where did that resemblance come from? Is there a resemblance?

In art history the cross-cultural influences of artists around the world is acknowledged. The Japanese prints swayed the French. Diego Rivera painted his Hispanic murals throughout the world, having explored for some time Cubism in France. Picasso responded to the masks of Africa where undeniably the artists were people-of-color.

Am I also influenced by this cross-cultural connection? An arts writer once remarked that she saw a resemblance of my work to Egon Schiele's art. What made her say that? Until she mentioned Schiele to me I was not aware of him or his work. What did I put in my drawings that may have tapped into that creative energy from such a different time and space? Was she addressing my self-retreat, my self-encounter? Are my drawings highly subjective, emotional and visionary the way Schiele's art was interpreted to mean? Did she refer to the distortion I used as a parallel to Schiele?

My final questions are these. Is it not legitimate for me to create that which has not come forth from the mainstream art world? Is it not legitimate for me, an American artist of Chinese descent, to create a hybridized east/west bi-cultural art form? Is it not legitimate for me to acknowledge the art of root country artists of Asian countries who create traditional/contemporary works but at the same time invent an entirely new art space/form for me and others like me? Is it not legitimate for me, as an artist of emerging consciousness, to confront the empowerment of using symbols from an ethnic community-Chinese American-that has suffered from racism, invisibility and the patronizing "model minority" mentality that accompanies the *cultural apartheid* in America?

I do not know what the answers are to these questions. As an artist I do not try to answer them. I leave that to the art historians and those that are well-versed in classification and categorization, searching for themes that I and other artists may be pulling out unknowingly when we create.

All I know is that—

> I am sixth daughter
> daughter of Chinatown...
> linked to Great China Cafe
> establishment of life and all. (Wong, 1979)

All that I have addressed in this essay is directed toward adaptation to an environment. For myself and the Chinese in America this adaptation has been molded by the historical racism which forced the creation of Chinatowns, the wellspring of my art. In contemporary America these Chinatowns are currently incorporating the second wave of immigrants from Southeast Asia. What my parents and other early Cantonese immigrants have set in place hopefully will help the newer groups of Chinatown inhabitants. What I have drawn in the *Oakland Chinatown Series* unveils contemporary visual images, representing an illusionary reality of my truth of growing up non-white in America. My narrative efforts hopefully transcend that personal truth to take viewers to a newer artistic vision, both in and out of Chinatown.

> You don't get to know me
> by just watching
> the New Year's parade in Chinatown
> or by lighting a firecracker
> that explodes my spirit
> so that I don't count
> till the next New Year
> of the dog, the cat, the horse, the etc.
> For
> there's more to being Chinese in America
> than chop suey
> Not stoically,
> Not humbly
> and
> Not inscrutably. (Wong, 1979)

# Works Cited

Association of Chinese Teachers. *A brief chronology of Chinese American history*, San Francisco: Author. (1982).

Association of Chinese Teachers. *A brief chronology of Chinese American history*, San Francisco: Author. (1985).

Goodrich, L. *Edward Hopper*, New York: Abrams.

Lai, H.M., Lim, G. and Yung, J. *Island: Poetry and history of Chinese immigrants on Angel Island 1910-1940*, San Francisco: Chinese Culture Foundation of San Francisco. (1989).

Mau Dicker, L. *The Chinese in San Francisco*, New York: Dover. (1979).

Shoichire Odo, F. *In movement*, Los Angeles: Visual Communications. (1977).

Wong, F. I am sixth daughter. Unpublished poem. (1979).

Wong, F. You don't get to know me. Unpublished poem. (1979).

Young Yu, C. *Pearls: History of Asians in America*, Springfield, VA: Educational Film Center. (1979).

Yung, J. *Chinese Women of America: A pictorial history*, Seattle: U of Washington P. (1986).

# Author's Notes

The Chinese words/phrases which I have used in this essay are *slee yip*, the fourth dialect of Cantonese.

The *Oakland Chinatown Series* drawings are based on photographs from my personal collection and that of Henry Lew.

I gratefully acknowledge Steve Weber, Felicia and Edward Wong for their help in preparing this manuscript. I also acknowledge Connie Young Yu for help in the research of the Chinese American history information.

I thank the art curators and jurors who have selected the *Oakland Chinatown Series* for exhibition.

# Art Bridging Boundaries

## Shifra M. Goldman

The border is a laboratory in which we can experiment. We are focusing regionally, but our purpose is to break down the borders that exist between people of all cultures.

Guillermo Gómez-Peña

What is at stake is not only the hegemony of Western cultures, but also their identities as unified cultures; in other words, the realization that there is a Third World in every First World, and vice-versa. The Master is made to recognize that His culture is not as homogeneous as He once believed it to be.

Trinh T. Minh-ha

The signs have been there for over a decade; we just did not recognize their full significance. In the art world, it began in the late 1970s with the term "pluralism," a term and a concept which distressed mainstream critics who could no longer concentrate their energies on the four or five recognized artistic modes in fashion with an institutionalized modernism. Instead they found themselves confronted by a multiplicity not only of styles but of content which emerged out of the political and social ferment of the 1960s and 1970s. Women, Blacks, Chicanos, resident Latin Americans, Asians, Native Americans and non-mainstreamists of all descriptions were forging new artistic languages and, with them, new meanings.

Also coinciding with the end of the 1970s, a portion of the New York avant-garde, with eyes turned toward main chances and finding their justifications in the nihilist writings of Jean Baudrillard, produced a "New Wave art" which plundered the exhausted and abandoned modes of the past in order to create a simulacrum of a simulacrum: a neo-historicism in which the art market was cynically accepted as the determinant of artistic value. These were puzzle boxes to which the mainstream critics of the time had no keys unless they abandoned their formalist tropism and with it the now-eviscerated modernist paradigm which had precluded any analysis of emerging and non-utopian artistic productions within new social contexts. Postmodernism had been born, named and backdated to the 1960s—a period when Pop artists integrated the world of consumerism and mass media into the fine arts, some on a critical note, some not.

Significantly, the modernist/pluralist/postmodernist discourse coincided in the United States with the accession to power of the most naked ideological demagoguery of the century, figureheaded by Ronald Reagan. In the art world of the 1980s, resounding conclusions of powerlessness often found the most acceptance. The Reagan years proved fertile ground for a certain type of postmodernism that saw no possible position "outside" of the late capitalist "spectacle society" which has so successfully extended itself around the globe.[1] Nevertheless, within the paradigm of pessimistic postmodernist discourse is contained the germ of its antithesis: an updated and eclectic variety of oppositional art and activity that, borrowing freely from many of the poststructural concepts, selects those that are serviceable to the creation of a new and subversive culture within the very bowels of the thrashing shark. Given the fluidity of art-world interactions (even the occasional mainstream interaction with marginal artists), neither those who use postmodern strategies in an oppositional manner nor those outside the postmodern discourse altogether are necessarily precluded from participation in mainstream formats.

My intention in what follows is to track the trail of oppositional artists and art groups who are concerned with bridging boundaries (or borders)—whether those exist between nations, ethnic groups, races or genders—particularly of those addressing themselves to solidarity with the beleagured peoples of Mexico and Central America. Since what is described below occurred within the last ten years or less, it is too recent, in my opinion, to attempt any serious socioartistic theorizing. Beyond setting up a framework of events, most of the material is descriptive of activities and movements as they play themselves out under a set of existing circumstances. Granted that the circumstances themselves have a long history, the artistic responses are in a constant state of flux as the artists evolve new solutions by redirecting traditional aesthetic languages into new channels, or inventing new vocabularies to meet their needs.

### The United States-Mexico Border

Does art follow life or life follow art? Or are the two so intertwined that artistic inspiration, derived from lived reality and translated into the artificial but emotionally-heightened language of art that communicates in a more effective manner than unfocused

126

experience, can be turned back into the fabric of reality itself? Which is the mirror: art or life? A recent transposition of this sort occurred at the US-Mexico border, the scene for about five years of installations, performances and exhibitions of a binational group named the Border Art Workshop/Taller de Arte Fronterizo (BAW/TAF). Founded in 1984 by artists from cities on both sides of the international border— Mexicans, North Americans and Chicanos, men and women—undertook to define the myriad levels of a border consciousness.[2]

The occasion for the recent transposition was an assembly of vehicles at the San Ysidro (California)-Tijuana (Mexico) border on April 27, 1990 to protest the entry of what the vehicle owners called "illegal aliens" bringing drugs and diseases into the United States. This campaign, called "Light Up the Border," was promoted on the airwaves by the ultra-conservative former mayor of San Diego, now a radio talk-show host, from March 1990 up to this writing. After five previous gatherings, more than a thousand vehicles lined up facing a border area where the undocumented crossed the Río Grande river in the face of Immigration and Naturalization Service agents and helicopters with spotlights. The Anglo drivers, belligerent and racist, were urged to turn on their car lights as a sign of protest. A particularly creative counter-manifestation was planned by Mexican and Chicano community organizations from both sides of the border, with the input of BAW/TAF artists Robert Sánchez and Richard Lou, and an activist group of women artists from Tijuana called Las Comadres, among whom were Berta Jottar and Carmela Castrejón. Stationing themselves at dusk in front of the cars, several hundred counter-marchers held up mirrors or aluminum foil and mylar-wrapped cardboards which effectively reflected the car headlights back at their owners who were disconcerted at being seen and identified. The obvious symbolism of the mirrors and mirror surrogates constituted an artistic statement of signifying power, a potent real-life art performance in which art and life interfaced in a way impossible to (re)capture in a gallery or museum setting. The text for this performance was contained in the placards carried by the counter-demonstrators: "This is a nation of immigrants; no deportatión" (Este es un pueblo de inmigrantes, no a la deportación) and "Down with the Immigration Service, stop the militarization of the border" (Abajo la migra, alto a la militarización de la frontera).[3]

The Border Art Workshop/Taller de Arte Fronterizo began its series of "Border Realities" installations and performances in 1985 within the ample space of the Centro Cultural de la Raza, located in Balboa Park in San Diego. To detail one such event, the 1988 "La Casa de Cambio/House of Money Exchange" sets forth the richness of imagination and complex but understandable artistic language employed by the group as an example of art that bridges boundaries of many kinds.

In their fourth multimedia installation of "Border Realities" the artists of BAW/TAF evoked one of the oldest architectural constructions of ancient history— the labyrinth—as a metaphor for the social and political complexities and absurdities of the US-Mexico border.

According to a Greek myth older than Homer, the original labyrinth was built on the island of Crete by the magician-engineer-artist Daedalus, who later invented wings cemented with wax so he and his son Icarus could escape their imprisoning environment. The labyrinth hid at its heart the most fearsome symbol of human irrationality: the minotaur. Half-human, the bull-headed monster exacted terrible tribute from the bull-worshipping Greeks. Now the children of another miscegenation—the Olmec were-jaguar, half-human and half-tropical tiger—have built their own labyrinth at whose heart is the monster of "border relations," whose guardians are the officers of the Immigration and Naturalization Service (INS) and whose rituals are often as heartless and bloody as those of the minotaur. Invoking, exploring, revealing; through simile, metaphor, allegory and pun; playing with visual and verbal texts, with image and sound, with interface and juxtaposition; the BAW/TAF caused the House of Change (where pesos and dollars confront each other in daily and deadly equivalencies) to become the House of Changes where realities are deconstructed, stripped of their ideological clothing and legalistic accessories and made visible in new ways to their victims on both sides of the border. "Change" can be a noun or a verb, can be coins or reforms, can be superficial or structural.

To carry out this (re)formation of consciousness, the Mexican, Chicano and North American artists of the BAW/TAF (Victor Ochoa, Michael Schnorr, Emily Hicks, Berta Jottar, Guillermo Gómez-Peña, Robert Sánchez, Deborah Small and others) installed a huge tunnel made of wood draped with immense sheets of pliable black plastic in San Diego's Centro Cultural de la Raza. Navigating in almost claustrophobic darkness, various niches or room-size spaces opened in the wall to reveal the inner workings not only of "border relations" but to reveal the idea of the border "line" itself—that geopolitical line dividing two nations whose territories were reconstituted by virtue of a nineteenth century US conquest (the second in Mexico's history), whose apologia was "Manifest Destiny," and where today economic power is juxtaposed with and exploits economic necessity. In the hands of the BAW/TAF magician/artists, the line has been broken, an idea celebrated in a bilingual interdisciplinary magazine published by Guillermo Gómez Peña (and friends) titled *The Broken Line/*

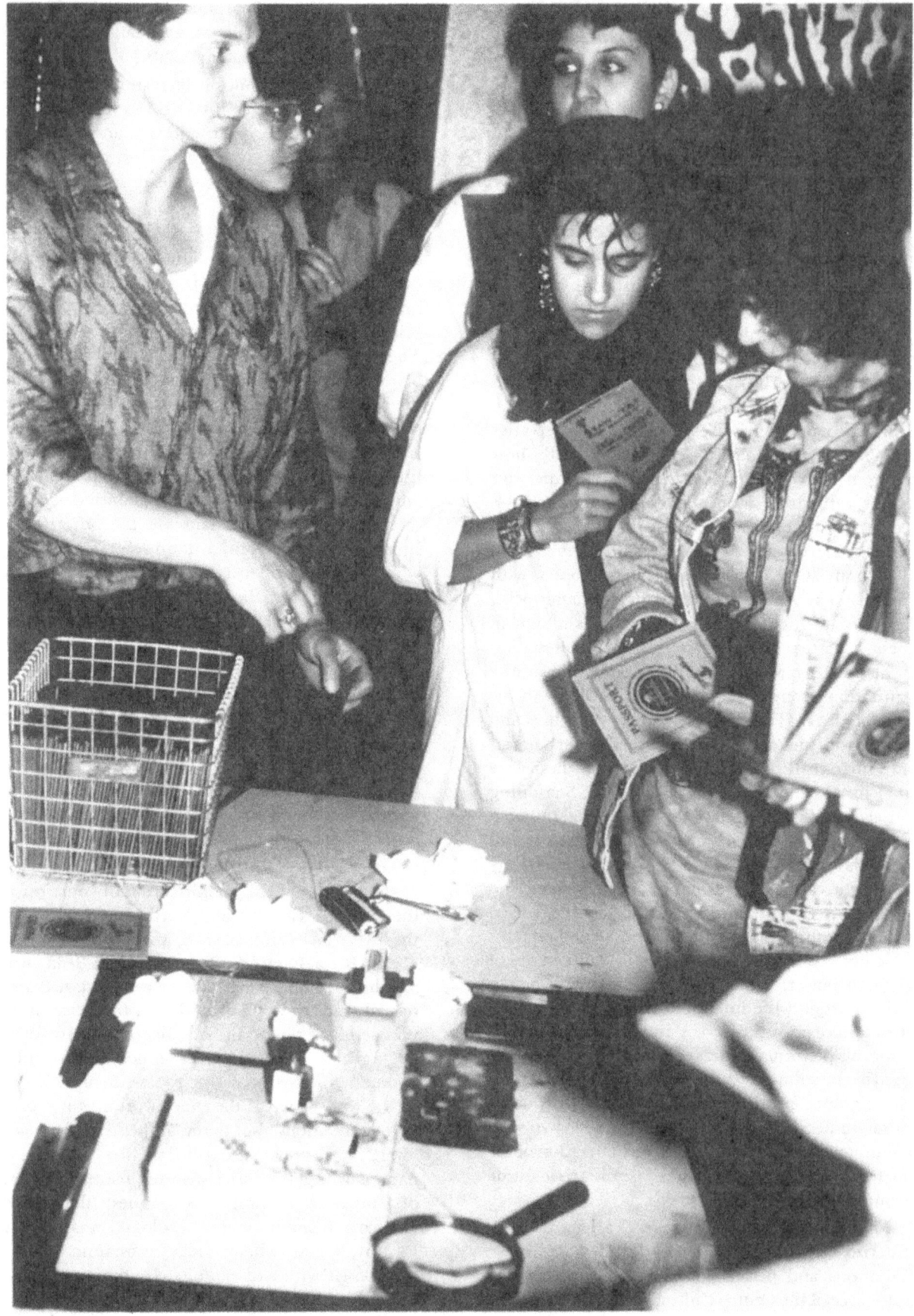

Border Art Workshop/Taller de Arte Fronterizo, *La Casa de Cambio* (House of Money Exchange), 1988. Centro Cultural de la Raza, San Diego, CA. (photograph by author)

*La linea quebrada,* excerpts from which occupied one of the "galleries" hollowed out within the winding tunnel for this exhibition.

Entering the labyrinth, the experience began with miniature dioramas scooped from the wall: palm trees in ghostly white, a money exchange booth, a performance-art installation. Suddenly there was a break into open space as the labyrinth ballooned out. This first "gallery" contained (among other things) two black velvet paintings (shades of Tijuana tourist art). One painting, *La frontera es de moda,* featured a Mexican revolutionary masked as the famous wrestler "Mil Mascaras." The other, *Souvenir de la frontera,* pictured John Wayne (with black eye patch) as an immigration officer. Thus immediately the two protagonists of the scenario are thematically confronted: the ultimate Mexican fighter with his opponent, the ultimate jingoistic Anglo. Both have been popular mythic heroes in their respective universes; now they have become Tijuana-style "souvenirs" of their confrontation. Beyond these two, the "gallery" was hung with visual and verbal documents from *La linea quebrada* by artists and intellectuals who undertook to redefine the geographic, economic, cultural and psychological spaces known as "borders."

Proceeding through a door marked by a large chained and handcuffed heart of leopard-skin fabric, the viewer entered the "passport room." On a table adjacent to a gigantic thumb print, visitors found green paper passports (green cards?) which they were invited to initial with their thumb print and signature and deposit in a wire basket. Displayed were a gardening tool, a kitchen utensil, a car washing tool, an ironing board with iron—all the implements necessary for the low-paid jobs on the US side of the border for which green cards can be issued.

Beyond was located a bridge which passed over a huge underground pipeline through which undocumented workers could (at the risk of their lives) cross the border surreptitiously, as shown in the film *El Norte.* The bridge straddled a "colonization" room. Here history started with a 1492 quotation from Columbus stating that "all the inhabitants could be taken away to Castile, or made slaves on the island. With fifty men we could subjugate them all and make them do whatever we want." A Spanish conquistador followed by a nude Indian were blown up on the wall from an old print. On another wall could be seen an historical drawing of the infamous slave ships showing how many Africans could efficiently be crammed into the hold of a ship; counterpoising this image the artists hung a reproduction of a 1939 mural by Black artist Hale Woodruff commemorating the centenary of a slave mutiny on the ship Amistad which resulted in the return of the Africans to their native lands. Resistance offsets conquest and enslavement. Facing

this image was a photo blow-up of contemporary "colonizers" behind a blue rowboat identified as the USS Amnesty, referring to the present law which pretends to solve the problem of undocumented workers in the United States.

Through another door, a life-size cartoon cutout (with movable armholes and faces through which visitors could substitute themselves for the painted areas) was fully equipped with the "blessings" the US could bestow upon the new immigrants: evangelical preachers, skate boards, blaster radios, cars, immigration officers and factory assembly lines.

The final major space might be dubbed the "ideal home" installation, complete with patio, umbrella, table and chairs, a television set on which is shown a specially prepared video, *Erasing the Line,* and white picket fences behind which photographs and statements taken from residents of San Diego and Tijuana give "testimony" of their viewpoints. The "ideal home" itself, equipped with a green lawn, a fence, a neatly coiled water hose and a trellis was startlingly framed by a tube of red flashing lights which provided the gate toward the exit.

When the exhibit opened, visitors were plentiful and could be seen at every stage slowly navigating the labyrinthian tunnel looking, reading, thinking and discussing. Humor and shock effects were not lacking and provided that element of entertainment so many demand from art. Nevertheless, the process of reframing conventional notions and stereotypes about the border and the relationships in which people living on both sides are entangled had obviously been set in motion through the experience.

If the artwork that comprised the *Casa de Cambio* installation was powerful and effective, it was, correspondingly, far from being polished. Eclectic postmodernist strategies were employed throughout, but the success of the work did not depend either upon their utilization or on the elitism of an audience prepared for avant-garde visual languages. Viewing the installation, one young Mexican woman living a green-card existence in the United States exclaimed: "This is just how I feel; this explains things I have experienced but didn't understand." "Border art," says professor Harry Polkinhorn who teaches on the Calexico (California) side of the border, "since it undoes power, extends the traditional function of avant-garde art...to include its own unmasking. This it does in a variety of ways. Imperfection, blurred edges, ugliness, incompletion, disharmony, mixed modes and registers, polyvalencies can all be discerned in the art object or event. The matrices for power's appearances then shift." In other words, the art is accessible not because of postmodern populist or "pop" strategies but because images and the relationships they represent are recognizable. Though raw in execution, though pushed to their extremes, though speaking a conceptual language, they are not foreign to the understanding, and this is the secret of their comprehensibility. They demystify, and therefore empower the viewer to analyze reality—if not all, at least portions of it.

This account of Border Realities IV would not be complete without mention of a performance-art piece, *Border brujo*, simultaneously presented by visual poet Guillermo Gómez-Peña, assisted by Tijuana artist Hugo Sánchez. Over the nude and motionless body of Sánchez lying on the ground (the assassinated, the destroyed, from Cuauhtémoc to the undocumented worker of today), Gómez-Peña, dressed in an incredibly bedecked military-style jacket and boots, circumnavigated the "victim" proclaiming his rich effusion of meditations on the border. Past history lived again, grafted to the most contemporary permutations of border punk, to the fusion of cultures and languages, to the inseparability of Latin American/North American experience, each feeding on and spewing out the other. This ritual, this incantation, depended heavily on the earthy yet incandescent use of words and was dazzling, energetic and visually evocative. The performance functioned as an integral part of the whole, setting forth whole constellations of ideas that underscored the structure of the labyrinth. Gómez-Peña became the Greek Daedalus to the imprisoned minotaur.

### Bridging Boundaries Between Central America and the United States

By 1981, it was clear that the Reagan administration not only stood for an aggressive resurrection of the Cold War with its nuclear arms buildup and the danger of global destruction, but a revival of Manifest Destiny policies in Latin America (to say nothing of interventions in other parts of the world). The US government supported (and supports) brutal military-backed regimes in El Salvador and Guatemala where the military (and its shadowy death squads) have been responsible for more than 170,000 deaths in little more than a decade and 30,000 *contra*-initiated deaths in Nicaragua. The *contra* mercenaries based in Honduras and Costa Rica conducted a not-so-secret low-intensity war aimed at the overthrow of the sovereign nation of Nicaragua which was combined with a policy of economic blockading aimed at destabilization through attrition—a ploy that lies behind the Sandinista electoral loss in 1990. Gunboat diplomacy, a relic of nineteenth century imperial tactics, has been employed in Grenada and, more recently, in Panama and threatens (as of this writing) the defiant existence of Cuba, weakened by a three-decades old US blockade and the astonishing upheavals and policy reversals of the Soviet bloc. The specter of another Vietnam (or as Che put it: one, two, many Vietnams) in Central America and the

Caribbean has been alarming artists and peoples of conscience since the early 1980s.

The paradox of United States foreign policy—and one would think the government would understand such dialectics by now, except that "understanding" is requesting more rationality than is inherent in the process—is that every excess, every injustice, every infringement of sovereignty has brought a corresponding response not only in the afflicted nation(s) but among US citizens and residents as well. Thus, the earliest depredations in Central America by the Reagan administration, a scant few years after the triumph of the Nicaraguan revolution against the US-installed Somoza regime, brought into being the largest and most enduring of artistic responses this country has seen in the second half of the 20th century.[4] As increasing numbers of North Americans visited Central America and brought back political, social and artistic evidence that contradicted US claims about the nature of the conflicts, there began to circulate in the artistic community films, photographic journals, poster exhibits, slide talks and illustrated articles. Artists were particularly incensed by the cultural destruction: the closing of universities; the imprisonment, torture and murder of teachers and artists; and the decimation and displacement of Indian populations resulting in the loss of their rich heritage.

By the summer of 1983, more than sixty North American and Latin American artists and art critics in New York formed the organization known as Artists Call Against US Intervention in Central America. The original plan was to present several exhibitions in homage to the people of Central America in conjunction with INALSE (Institute of the Arts and Letters of El Salvador in Exile). Such tremendous enthusiasm greeted the Call's effort that, in January and February 1984, New York City hosted more than sixty-seven exhibitions, film showings, poetry readings, street demonstrations with banners and performances involving hundreds of artists.[5] Pop artist Claes Oldenburg designed a three-color poster featuring a splintering phallic banana being pulled down by the people of the so-called banana republics. Its text opened with "If we can simply witness the destruction of another culture, we are sacrificing our own right to make culture" and went on to condemn US intervention in Central America and Grenada.

In 1984, twenty-seven cities in the United States (in addition to Paris and Mexico City) participated in a multiplicity of Artists Call activities in which the greatest number of activities took place in New York, Chicago, San Francisco, Philadelphia and Los Angeles. In January, Los Angeles put together a six-hour live radio broadcast of music and poetry readings and published full-page advertisements signed by 100 arts people in three periodicals. This was followed in October by a month of art shows, videos,

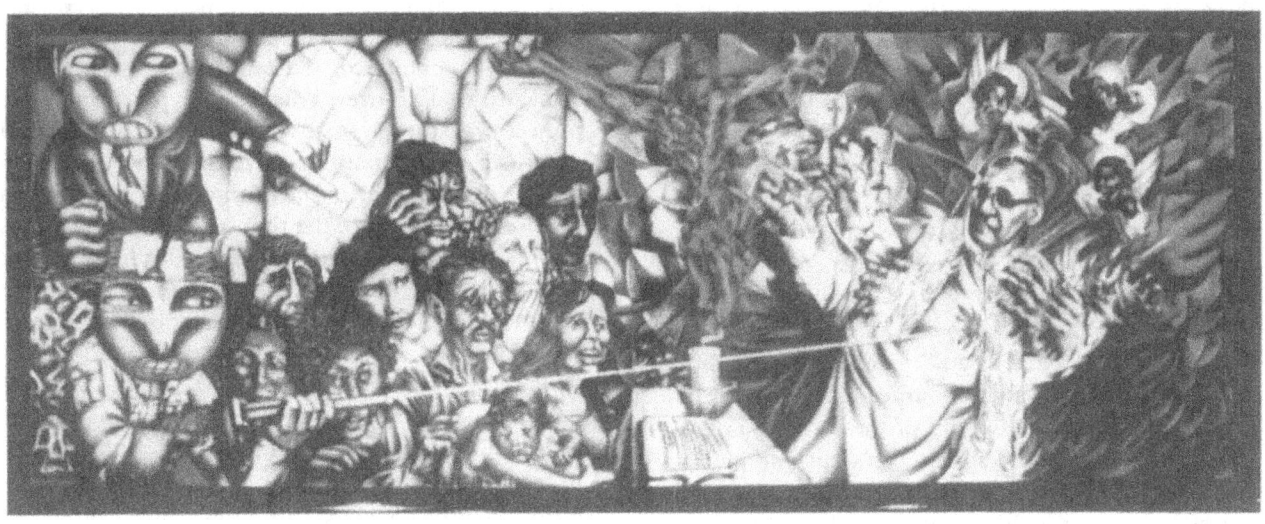

J. Michael Walker, *The Assassination of Archbishop Arnulfo Romero of El Salvador*, 1983-84, colored pencil, 30" x 84". (photograph by author)

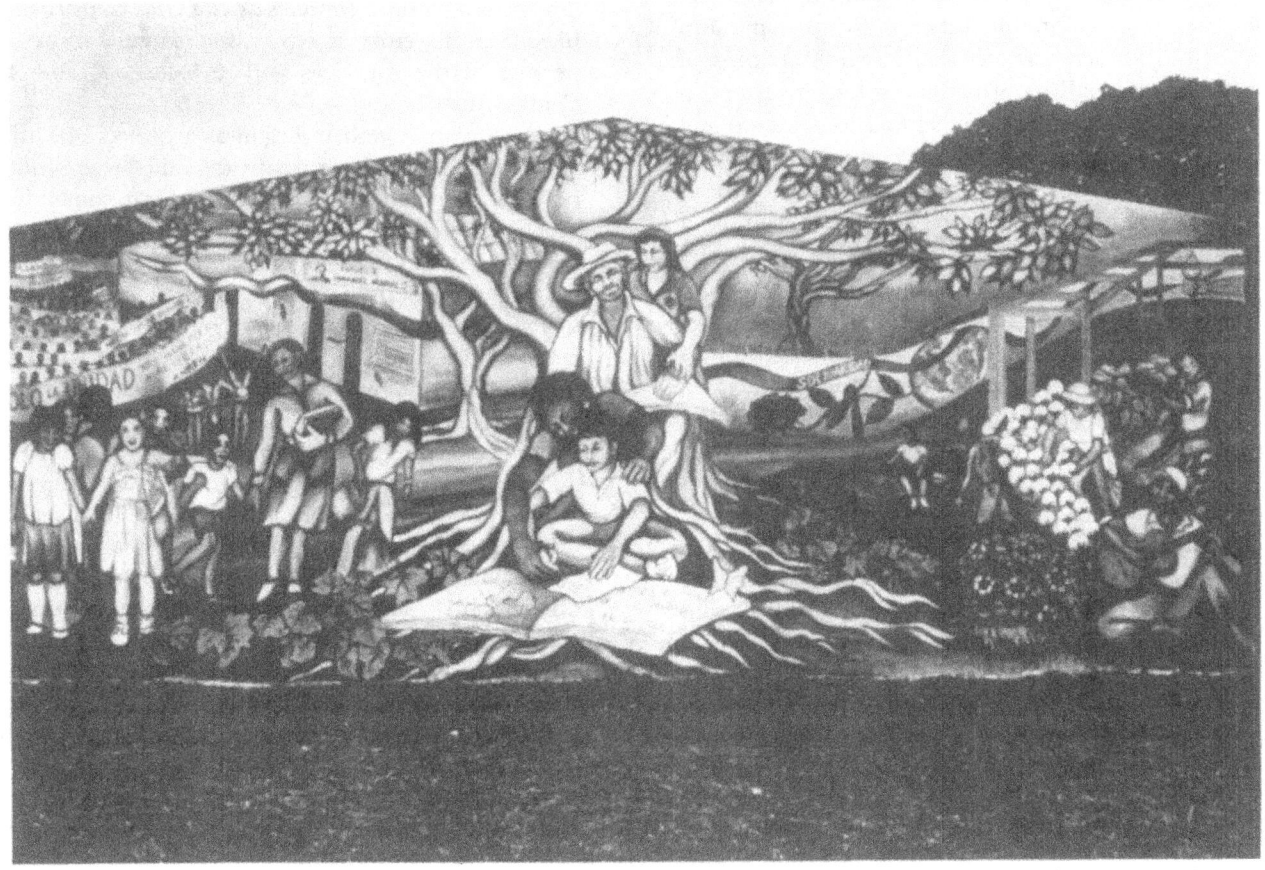

Miranda Bergman, Juana Alicia, Artella Seidenberg, Arch Williams, *El Amanecer* (The Dawn), 1986, mural in Nicaragua. (photograph courtesy of Miranda Bergman)

performances, literary readings, slide lectures and teach-ins titled "Flowers of Life for Central America" and publicized with a poster featuring a work by John Baldessari. In 1985, Los Angeles' Artists Call held an "Arms Out" Postcard Exhibition and Mail-in during the course of which 20,000 pre-printed postcards were distributed throughout California; recipients were invited to do their personal artwork on a tear-off portion and mail them either to Artists Call (which exhibited four hundred cards in a traveling show) or to President Reagan and their Congresspersons. In 1987, an "Artists Call: Recall" exhibit of Latin and North American artists was mounted. The most recent activity featured an exhibition of three young artists from Costa Rica whose testimony on Central America took the form of twenty-seven magnificent drawings that circulated throughout California for a full year (1988-89), with a catalogue dedicated to the Peace Plan proposed by Costa Rica's former president, Oscar Arias.

Felicitously, the initiative opened by Artists Call for artistic collaboration between North and Latin American artists—and between Latin Americans of different nationalities, which has a longer history in multinational cities like San Francisco, Chicago and New York—has expanded since the mid-1980s as multiculturalism (or cross-culturalism) evolved. Artists have made common cause on behalf of a cultural agenda. For example, Chicano artists who earlier drew their inspiration from Mexico and from Native Americans with whom they identify have focused on Central American issues. Yreina Cervántez's silkscreen of a woman combatant from Guatemala confronting the ubiquitous helicopter with the aid of a rifle and the ancient symbol of the tropical jaguar and Ester Hernández's silkscreen *The Disappeared*, in which a Guatemalan fabric is laced with helicopters, skulls, dead bodies and drops of blood, speak to this new commitment. North American Lisa Kokin has created incredible three-dimensional quilted and embroidered batiks on subjects taken from Central America while Michael Walker's large, complex and magical colored-pencil drawing, *The Assassination of Archbishop Oscar Arnulfo Romero of El Salvador*, has proved so popular that it was made into a poster in 1984. The original was donated to a sanctuary church in Los Angeles.

Both Kokin and Walker have co-exhibited with self-taught Salvadoran artist Edgar Aparicio who escaped to California in 1982 after six members of his family were assassinated. Finding catharsis in highly-original relief sculptures, he enriches these wall-hung works of carved wood with paint, photographs, fabrics and metals collaged on the surfaces. Aparicio, whose first exposure was with Artists Call, has since exhibited in several non-profit galleries but generally does not care to sell most of his work which he reserves for exhibition as political statements.

In San Francisco, the multiethnic group *Placa* dedicated itself to street muralism. Its most ambitious project was the close to thirty murals on Central American themes painted in 1984 on the fences and walls of Balmy Alley in the heart of the Latino/Asian Mission district. Since the thousands of street murals that pervaded most major US cities during the 1970s and 1980s have been a notable example for other countries, it should come as no surprise that murals were painted in solidarity with the Nicaraguan Revolution by mixed groups of artists. Miranda Bergman and a San Francisco team painted a Children's Library in Nicaragua in 1983 and returned in 1986 to paint *El Amanecer* for ANDEN, the teacher's association. In 1986, a group of Chicanos and Latinos from Los Angeles calling themselves Chica-Nica also painted a large mural in Nicaragua. Finally, Chicano artist Leo Tanguma of Denver, has been displaying around Colorado since 1986 his monumental three-dimensional mural, *Después de esta cruz*. Constructed like a flaming cross, it depicts the struggles of many peoples of the Americas with a focus on those of Central America.

If cross-nationalism began as a project of Latin and North American artists in the mid-80s around a political agenda, it has since flowered into something much more pervasive. Today there is an increasing US interest (and perhaps in France, too, if we are to judge by the controversial 1989 global art exhibition in Paris, *Les magiciens de la terre*) in the politics of cross or multiculturalism—a concept mandated by statistics and the pressures of changing domestic and global demographics and the political and economic potentials of those demographics.[6] If terms like cross- and multiculturalism signify the cutting edge of political and artistic alignment by those involved in bridging or breaking restrictive borders/boundaries, "multicultural diversity" (a diffuse label favored by officialdom) seems to suggest that the dominant culture is being prodded to abandon its monolithic grip without, ultimately, relinquishing its hegemony. It is simply recognizing that there are "others" out there, and that their existence (if not necessarily their validity) must finally be acknowledged.

# Notes

*Reprinted with the permission of the Binational Press/Editorial Binacional (Mexicali, Mexico and Calexico, California), and the author.

   [1]Jay Murphy. "Elizam Escobar's Art of Resistance, *New Art Examiner*, 17(8), (1990): 32.

   [2]See *The Border Art Workshop/Taller de Arte Fronterizo (BAW/TAF): 1984-1989* catalogue, San Diego (CA.), 1988.

[3]See "Manifestantes a favor y en contra del indocumentado se enfrentan en San Ysidro," *La Opinion*, April 29, 1990.

[4]In terms of artistic action on political issues, nothing since has matched the type of engagement seen during the 1930s and 1940s. In the post-World War II period, McCarthyism and Cold War ideology effectively separated artistic endeavor from political activity until the Vietnam War period. Unlike the Korean conflict, however, the undeclared Vietnam War paralleled the explosion of the civil rights, the free speech, and the counter-culture movements of the 1960s, all of which eventually realized the interconnectedness between US domestic and foreign policies. From that realization developed widescale artistic protests against the Vietnam War in both New York and Los Angeles—an issue that was revitalized in the 1980s for further examination by artists and filmmakers. See the catalogue *A Different War: Vietnam in Art*, text by curator Lucy R. Lippard, Seattle: Real Comet Press, 1990.

[5]See Jamey Gambrell, "Art Against Intervention," and Eva Cockcroft, "Heroes and Villains: The Latin American View," in *Art in America* 72, No. 5 (May 1984), 9-19; and Lucy R. Lippard, "Art and Politics: Questions on a Politicized Performance Art," *Art in America* 72, No. 9 (October 1984), 39-45.

[6]Two notable examples can be mentioned: 1) the 1989/1990 series of three symposia at the San Francisco Art Institute organized by Institute professor, Carlos Villa, as "Sources of a Distinct Majority"—a reference to the fact that, in California, Third World residents now form a majority and are no longer "minorities." Addressing and attending the symposia was a spectrum of Third and First World peoples seeking knowledge of each other's cultures without (necessarily) abandoning their differences. See *Artweek* 20, No. 37 (November 9, 1989), "Coming Together," and "Shifting the Mainstream;" Moira Roth, "The Art of Multicultural Weaving: Carlos Villa's *Ritual*," in *High Performance*, Fall 1989; and the Fall 1989 issue of *Visions Art Quarterly* dedicated to Acculturation vs. Assimilation; 2) an exhibition (with a catalogue) in March 1990 co-sponsored by the Guadalupe Cultural Arts Center and the Instituto Cultural Mexicano in San Antonio, Texas and called "Contemporary Art by Women of Color." The four jurors (as well as the artists) were Chicana, Black, Asian and Native American while the keynote address was delivered by white art critic and feminist Lucy Lippard, long known for her cross-cultural agenda.

# Contributors

**Mario Asaro** has been teaching art in New York for the past six years. He is presently co-chairing Artists/Teachers Concerned, a group dedicated to the implementation and sharing of socially relevant lessons in the art classroom. They sponsor exhibits, seminars and workshops in the New York City area. Mr. Asaro is also an active member of the National Art Education Association, the New York City and State Art Teachers Associations, the United Federation of Teachers, Educators for Social Responsibility, the Professional Disarmament Network, the Fellowship of Reconciliation and Central Committee For Conscientious Objectors. He would like to thank Kathleen Haspel and Doug Blandy for their assistance in assembling "Art Criticism as Social Change."

**Terry Barrett** is an Associate Professor of Art Education at The Ohio State University. He is the author of *Criticizing Photographs* (Mountain View, CA: Mayfield, 1990) the past editor of *Columbus Art*, a bimonthly regional tabloid of art criticism, and next editor of *Studies in Art Education*. He reviews exhibitions for *Dialogue*, *New Art Examiner* and *Image/Ink*, and his articles are published in the *Journal of Aesthetic Education*, *Studies in Art Education*, *Art Education*, *Exposure*, *Camera-Lucida* and *Afterimage*.

**Doug Blandy** is an Associate Professor of Art Education at the University of Oregon. He is co-editor, with Kristin G. Congdon, of *Art in a Democracy*, published by Teachers College Press in 1987. His research is published in *Studies in Art Education*, *The Journal of Multicultural and Cross-cultural Research in Art Education*, *Art Education* and the *Visual Sociology Review*. At the University of Oregon, he teaches courses and supervises student research that examines art and community service, art education and people experiencing disabilities, and the role of art in a democratic society.

**Kristin G. Congdon** holds The William and Alice Jenkins Endowed Chair in Community Arts at the University of Central Florida. She is co-editor, with Doug Blandy, of *Art in a Democracy* and has published articles in *The Journal of Aesthetic Education*, *Art Education*, *Studies in Art Education*, *Journal of Multicultural and Cross-cultural Research in Art Education*, *Visual Arts Research* and the *Journal of Social Theory and Art Education*, among others. In 1988, she received the Manuel Barken Memorial Award from the National Art Education Association and in 1989 the Mary J. Rouse Award from the Women's

Caucus of the National Art Education Association for outstanding teaching, leadership and scholarship. She has taught art in university settings, museums, treatment facilities and community centers.

**Howard Davis** is Associate Professor of Architecture at the University of Oregon. He studied physics at The Cooper Union and at Northwestern University, and architecture at the University of California, Berkeley. His professional work is in the area of housing and community design, and he is a co-author, with Christopher Alexander and others, of *The Production of Houses* (New York: Oxford University Press, 1985), the account of an experimental housing project that is a model for a new system of housing production. His current research is concerned with the history of vernacular architecture, concentrating on issues of the social relations surrounding the building process. He teaches studios in architectural design and lecture courses and seminars in architectural theory, housing and vernacular architecture.

**Linda F. Ettinger** is an Associate Professor of Art Education at the University of Oregon. Her academic interests include critical theory, multidisciplinary curriculum design and qualitative research methods. Dr. Ettinger served for four years (1983-1987) as the director of the Annual Pacific Northwest Computer Graphics Conference. Currently she is director of a multidisciplinary master of science degree program in information management, serving in-career management professionals in the Portland metropolitan area. She edited a journal titled *Controversies in Art & Culture*, investigating the topic of criticism in art and design.

**Paulette Spruill Fleming** is an Associate Professor of Art at California State University, Fresno, where she teaches in the art education program. She researches and lectures on the subject of African American aesthetics and art history. Her research interests involve African retentions at the Somerset Place Plantation on North Carolina's Eastern coastline.

**Shifra M. Goldman** has a Ph.D. in art history from the University of California at Los Angeles (UCLA), with a specialization in modern Latin America. She is Research Associate with the Latin America Center, UCLA; has taught art history at UCLA and California State University, Los Angeles; and presently is Professor of Art History and Department Chair at Rancho Santiago College, Santa Ana, California. Her first book, *Contemporary*

*Mexican Painting in a Time of Change*, appeared in 1981 (Spanish edition published in Mexico City, 1989), and she co-authored the bibliography and theoretical essay, *Arte Chicano: A Comprehensive Annotated Bibliography of Chicano Art: 1965-1981* (1985) with Tomás Ybarra-Frausto of Stanford University. Dr. Goldman has had major essays included in a number of anthologies and has published numerous essays and articles on art in Europe, Latin America and the United States. Her work can be found in newspapers and magazines like *La Opinion, Art Week, Aztlan, Arte en Colombia* (Bógota), *Art in America, Art Journal, Casa de las Americas* (Cuba), *Plastica* (Puerto Rico), *Plural* (Mexico), *Studies in Popular Latin American Culture, New Art Examiner, Tendenzen* (Munich), etc. She has lectured widely on many aspects on Latin American and Modern art and recently completed the manuscript for *Dimensions of the Americas: Art and Social Change in Latin America and the United States* (forthcoming).

**Karen A. Hamblen** is Professor of Art Education in the Department of Curriculum and Instruction at Louisiana State University. She has been the recipient of the Outstanding Higher Educator in California Award, the Mary Rouse Award, and Manuel Barken Award. She is currently the Director of the Southeast Regional Higher Education Division of the National Art Education Association and the Senior-Editor of *Studies in Art Education*. She has served as consultant, writer, and evaluator for art museums, teacher institutes, school districts, arts councils, state departments of education, and the U.S. Department of Education. She has publications in art education, arts policy, anthropology, and sociology research journals.

**jan jagodzinski** is an Associate Professor in the Department of Secondary Education, University of Alberta, where he teaches art education, gender issues and curriculum theory. His interests are in the areas of ecology, critical social thought, feminism and philosophical anthropology. He is past editor of *The Journal of Social Theory in Art Education*. A book entitled *The Proto-Cultural Evolution of Esthetic Consciousness* is pending publication.

**Betty LaDuke** is an artist and a Professor of Art at Southern Oregon State College. Her books include *Companeras: Women, Art, and Social Change in Latin America* published in 1985 by City Lights, and *Africa Through The Eyes of Women Artists* to be published by the Africa World Press in 1991. Betty LaDuke organizes exhibits of art by Third World women and has participated in numerous national and international one-person art exhibits.

**John Wilton** is a Visual Arts Professor in the Southeast Center for Photo/Graphic Studies at Daytona Beach Community College. He is currently serving as director of the DBCC Gallery of Fine Arts and president of The Volusia Cultural Affairs league. He has recently published a book of his paintings entitled *Down in F.L.A.*

**Kathryn Lee Seidel** is Associate Professor of English and Associate Dean of Arts and Sciences at the University of Central Florida. She has published essays on Kate Chopin, Ellen Glasgow, William Faulkner, Zora Neale Hurston, Toni Morrison and Alice Walker. She is the author of *The Southern Belle in the American Novel* (Tampa: University of South Florida Press, 1985), and co-editor of *Zora in Florida* (University Presses of Florida, 1991).

**Florence Wong**, co-founder of the Asian American Women Artists Association, is a contemporary Chinese American mixed media artist. She is also a poet, writer, elementary school visual arts specialist and a community arts advocate dedicated to cultural pluralism. As a visual artist, she has created and exhibited several bodies of work that speak of her Chinese American heritage in a contemporary way. A major body of work is the Oakland Chinatown Series. Another is the on-going 10'x20' textile hangings and installation which are hand-stitched from a ten year collection of Asian rice sacks. Recently, in response to the 1989 Tiananmen killings in the People's Republic of China she has painted, with a Chinese brush, her abstract, non-realistic statements to the call for freedom. She has also written bilingual English-Chinese poems inspired by the Tiananmen work. Recent essays on her work have appeared in M/E/A/N/I/N/G, A New York arts publication, and in *Gallerie*, a Canadian arts magazine. She is also featured in an upcoming book, *Silicon Valley: Inventing the Future*.